In memory of John Hyden,
my friend for 20 years,
shot dead by the 'Mafia' in
St Petersburg, 26 February 1996,
a victim of the peace he was
helping to build.

Contents

Maps, Diagrams and Tables

Acknowledgements

This book has a simple message: we are undergoing the most dramatic revolution in our thinking about war and peace for 200 years. After the Cold War, we have returned to a situation which in some ways resembles the later colonial era, and in others the eighteenth century, but the presence of an international authority to oversee the rule of law between states has made a difference. The clear distinction between 'war' and 'peace' has been blurred again, as we contemplate continuous engagement in other people's wars.

After two decades' study of the phenomenon of war, as an academic, a potential practitioner and a journalistic observer, it would be impossible for me to name all the people who have helped along the way, by accident or design. They know who they are: I thank them. Special thanks go to Dr Christopher Duffy at Sandhurst who, called in to Oxford to teach the Military History and Theory of War special subject twenty years ago, introduced me to Clausewitz, Corbett and Mahan. There is no substitute for fundamentals.

This book, however, is above all the product of a series of accidents, which took me out of the Army earlier than I would have wished, but which gave me access to the splendid Russian tuition at the Polytechnic of Central London (now less imposingly titled the University of Westminster). Accident took me on to work with my friend and mentor, John Erickson, Professor Emeritus of Defence Studies at the University of Edinburgh, whose encouragement, support and friendship have been cardinal. To John, Ljubica, and Kathie Brown, and to all my Edinburgh friends and colleagues, I owe a special debt.

By accident, I then found myself at the *Independent*, from where another accident – the RAF got me the right visa – propelled me to Saudi Arabia, to witness a historic, but I believe, untypical limited war in the gulf from January to March, 1991. And, rather by accident, there was Bosnia and Chechnya. I am grateful to the Editors, Deputy Editors, Foreign and Home Editors of the *Independent* and *Independent on Sunday* for entrusting important journalistic assignments to one who came late to the profession and who had no experience of journalism before 1990. Ian Hargreaves, Godfrey Hodgson, Harvey Morris, John Price, John Lichfield, Peter Walker and Andy Marshall – thank you.

The Gulf War united me with Heather, now my wife, whose support, encouragement and understanding were fundamental. I know every author says it, but I shall as well. Heather withstood the long months of separation – one in Chechnya and nine in Bosnia, in total – and the apprehension which those at home feel far more cruelly than those in the theatre of war itself, whose sights are focused only on the next meal, the successful accomplishment of a limited task, and getting that plane home. Then there were the long absences in the study at home, as the air turned blue with invective, and other interruptions to proper life. Finally, Heather acted as Josephine Public, reading the typescript with an eye to style and accessibility.

As the book was underway, Professor Richard Overy helped with his views on the evolution of total war. I received more specific help from General Jean Cot, whom I thank for inviting me to the splendid seminar on international peacekeeping at the Château de Montvillargenne, outside Chantilly, in June 1995, and Brigadier Andrew Ritchie, formerly General Cot's Chief of Staff in Zagreb, then military attaché in Paris. Colonel Richard Connaughton, formerly the Army's Director of Defence Studies, helped with his own studies of intervention. Colonel Alan Mallinson, who succeeded him at Upavon, was also very helpful, as was Colonel Jonathan Bailey at Camberley. I am indebted to Colonel Chris Holtom, the commandant of the Intelligence and Security School at Ashford, for inviting me to another seminar on the risk of conflict, which pointed me more precisely in certain directions, and to Bill Hopkinson, Assistant Under Secretary (Policy) at the Ministry of Defence, for his ideas and profound thoughts on these matters.

My thanks also go to Colonel Bob Stewart, formerly the commander of 22 the Cheshire Regiment, the first British battalion in Bosnia, for his help and ideas, three years on, and the commanding officers of the succeeding battalions, especially Alastair Duncan. Brigadier John Reith also advised me on the timing of crucial events. At the cutting edge of thinking about war and peace in the new world order, I thank Major General Mike Willcocks, formerly Director General, Land Warfare at the British Army's new 'think tank' at Upavon, Wiltshire – an organisation of which, sixty years on, Sir Basil Liddell Hart would have approved. On the specifics, I thank Lieutenant Colonel Charles Dobbie, who wrote the British Army manual *Wider Peacekeeping*, and who is now lost to the Army, pursuing doctrine in a different field, as a priest, and Colonel John Mackinlay PhD, joint author of *A Draft Concept of Second Generation Multinational Operations*. I want to thank all those in the Ministry of Defence and the Foreign and Commonwealth Office with whom I have had everyday dealings, but especially Brigadier Philip Trousdell, and his staff, for helping as we wrestled with the evolution of new doctrine and visions of future wars foretold.

In the field, I thank all my media colleagues whose attitude, without exception, was that we were all friends doing one job in our own, very different ways. In Bosnia Martin Bell, Alan Little, Malcolm Brabant and Mark Laity of the BBC, Geoffrey Archer and Colin Baker of ITN and Peter Sharpe and Dan Damon of Sky News and all their colleagues behind the cameras and the mikes, whom you never see, were all especially supportive. I must thank Paul Harris of *Scotland on Sunday*, a fellow oddball and kindred spirit, for pulling me out of a road accident and summoning the help of some shy soldiers from the West Midlands, who would not even let him take their photograph.

I am grateful to Michael Sissons, my agent, and Paul Sidey, of Hutchinson, for their understanding and sympathetic treatment of this book, and for nurturing it from the first, clumsy idea to something which, I hope, will be informative and thought-provoking.

Finally, I must thank Colonel Nayyar, of the Pakistan Army, and several British soldiers in Bosnia, whose names I do not know, who on several occasions probably saved my life – and certainly my liberty and health. The Pakistan Army rescued me from captivity; REME and the Royal Engineers pulled me out of a road accident and the Coldstream Guards even interposed their armoured vehicles between me and known sniper positions when crossing the icy front line through Gornji Vakuf. Thanks, guys. This book is named in your honour: knights in white armour.

Prologue: World Disorder

The Road to Mozdok, January 1995

Across the flat fields of snow, the dark shapes of the Russian convoy stretched from horizon to horizon: thirty-six armoured personnel carriers in ones and twos, interspersed with eighty trucks, usually in groups of four or eight, rolling down the greyish mud-and-ice road which runs through the flat country of the *Nadterech'ye*, on the southern edge of the Russian Empire. We were heading north, towards the river Terek, and on to Mozdok, the main headquarters for the Russian operation which had already reduced most of the Chechen capital, Grozny, to rubble. They were heading south, to join that battle. It was Saturday, 21 January 1995.

Occasionally, colour relieved the oppressive monochrome of the snow and steely sky. The vehicles all bore the red and yellow shield, the insignia of the Interior Ministry forces, not the Russian Army, and a badge indicating the division to which they belonged – a golden puma on a red circle. Some of the truck drivers had taken off their flak jackets and slung them over the doors of their cabs, below the window, so that snipers' bullets coming from the side – the most likely direction – would hit the front and back plates of the body armour, rather than the vulnerable side. Simple, but clever – a trick not, at that time, used by the UN drivers in Bosnia.

Scarcely had they passed, than another column loomed ahead. An officer in the leading armoured troop carrier waved us imperiously to one side, and we pulled up on the muddy edge of the road to give them a wide berth: another thirty-plus armoured vehicles, another eighty-plus trucks, but this time with no insignia. Many of the trucks carried ammunition, in slate-grey boxes. Some, under camouflage nets, carried what looked like big shells or rockets, without fuses in the nose, which must have been nearly a foot in diameter – maybe the 220 mm *uragan* (hurricane) or the 350 mm *smerch* (tornado). These were weapons designed for the Third World War, not for 'internal security' – but then, the Russians have never exactly been famous for 'minimum force'.

Other trucks, their fabric covers tightly laced shut, were marked *lyudi* (people). Some trucks carried firewood – a wise provision, as it was minus ten degrees Celsius that day, a real day for a Russian war. Some towed tanks of fuel on two wheels marked *ogneopasno* (fire hazard). And some towed small, two-door ovens – field bakeries. They were planning for a long stay.

Ammunition. Men. Firewood. Fuel. Bread.

Whether these men were on a delicate peacekeeping mission, or being thrown into a full-scale, vicious combat, they would need to be sustained – but these were Russian wartime logistics. I recalled the relatively sumptuous provisions of our own British troops in Bosnia. The more delicate the mission, it seemed, the more back-up you need – these Russians were not on a peacekeeping mission. They were the Russians we had come to know through years of study. The sleek, tracked BMP-2 infantry fighting vehicles – standing out as incongruously space-age among the rest of the force – had pine logs stowed at the back. The vehicles were very low, designed for concealment and protection on a nuclear battlefield. By backing on to the logs, the commanders could squeeze another couple of degrees' depression out of their vicious, long, thin 30 mm cannon – crucial in a close-quarter fight. The men were not eighteen-year-old conscripts. They looked in their thirties, maybe even forties, in fur collars and padded leather helmets, shielded against the cold. There were command vehicles bristling with aerials.

Further on, just south of the Terek, there was another force of about the same size, camped in a wild-west type circle, their guns facing outwards, with tents in the centre. The armoured vehicles in each of these groups made a battalion, and the eighty trucks in each could have carried another couple of battalions' worth of men. I might have seen the best part of three regiments – a division in all – on that frozen road that led from Mozdok, the main Russian base in North Ossetia, into Grozny.

The columns were part of a military machine that we had once admired for its grasp of the higher conduct of war, for its brilliant staff work, for its rigorous military doctrine that had influenced everything in the system, right down to the design of the vehicles, but everyone knew the command and control of the Russian forces was now a shambles. Units could not talk to each other. There were tales of Interior Ministry troops and the Army firing at each other – sometimes by accident in spite of known recognition signals, and sometimes deliberately. Visually, it was impressive, awesome. As a fighting force, so far, they had blundered, terribly.

Russian military doctrine had always said that 'internal' problems of this kind were for the Interior Ministry. Yet large numbers of Army units had been called in to support them. A single, strong-willed commander with the authority to grip the whole lot was vital. There was none. The Interior Ministry, Army and Air Force, and, even more disquieting, separate units within each service, seemed to operate almost independently. The indiscipline of the Russian forces was worrying.

The Russians had plenty of experience of street fighting in Stalingrad in 1942–43, in Berlin in 1945, in Budapest in 1956, and had evolved clever tactics for urban warfare. There was no evidence of them being used in Grozny.

They were ignoring their own doctrine, and their own history – surprising, for a nation that had, until five years before, routinely used military history as a tool for explaining and exploring issues of war and peace. But there is no magical, collective memory. Military careers are short. If lessons are not recorded, expertise practised, they will be forgotten. Real effort is needed to keep experience and knowledge alive – and in any case, much of the doctrine they had was now irrelevant. They had never thought or planned for a war within Russia against their own people. They fell back on every cliché in the book: on the utter contempt for human life which still seems to pervade Russian political and military thinking; on what Pasternak called the Russians' 'infinite capacity for suffering'; on their overwhelming strength in numbers and, even more, on their colossal firepower.

The inescapable impression was that this was a situation to which military power was not the best solution. Only the remoteness of the theatre – it was further east than Iraq, two hours' flight from Moscow and then six hours' drive to get near it – combined with the fact that it was within the legal boundaries of a great power whom no one wished to upset, made the brutal solution at all feasible. Strangely enough, the Russians had coined the best phrase to describe this problem: the *negodnost* – 'unusability' or 'inappropriateness' of military force for solving certain problems. Yet here they were, using it at its most 'inappropriate'.

A week later, I was returning from an expedition into the Caucasus mountains. Our car halted at the cleverly sited checkpoint which controlled all movement between Chechnya and the neighbouring republic of Ingushetia, to the west. A young Russian Interior Ministry soldier was practising firing his pistol, off to one side of the road, the spent cartridge cases bouncing off our windscreen. Satisfied that we were western journalists, and possibly under orders to be polite, he asked me if I wanted to try out his pistol. Wasting ammunition equals bad discipline. Bad discipline equals bad soldiers.

The ferocity of Chechen resistance owed as much to the indiscipline of the Russian troops as to the savagery of the Russian sledgehammer approach. Those sledgehammer tactics had defeated the Third Reich, but now they were inappropriate, politically unacceptable, maybe disastrous in the changed political and security climate, and under close media scrutiny. They served to unite the Chechens, few of whom, we discovered, had much love for the Chechen rebel leader Dzhokhar Dudayev, against the terrible Russian invader.

The presence of the media was another factor the Russians failed to grasp. The Chechen rebels were no angels – far from it – and they did not have the support of all the Chechen people. The Russians could have prevented any coverage of the events of that terrible January, or they could have tried to help the media – and, in so doing, given their side of the story. They did neither. Therefore, apart from clips from Russian television, which were widely used by western television stations, most of the reporting of the fighting came from the Chechen side. It was hardly surprising that the Russians, who were conducting what could have been presented as a justifiable military operation – though one abysmally handled – did not get their side of the story across.

In conventional military theory, selection and maintenance of the aim of the operation – what the US Army calls simply 'objective' – is the most important principle. Having given independence to former Soviet republics, like neighbouring Georgia, Russia was determined to hold on to the republics within the Russian federation. Also, Grozny is the meeting point of oil pipelines from central Asia and the Caspian Sea, so the Russians had to regain hold of the city.

The Russian treatment of Grozny may have ultimately achieved this objective, and any other republic which attempts to secede from the Russian Federation now knows it may suffer the same treatment, but it was a medieval solution: terror, accomplished with a mixture of medieval barbarity and some pretty up-to-date technology, and achieved at unnecessary cost.

Circling above Grozny, we saw Su-25 *Frogfoot* ground attack planes, which had caused great excitement when they first appeared in the early 1980s, screaming in to attack the city centre. Silvery apparitions, they seemed from a different world to the smashed apartment blocks below, where people carried water in buckets and clustered round fires in cellars to avoid the incoming ordnance as the Russian artillery tore the city apart, block by block.

Once, entering the city from the south, we came across a body, lying by the side of the road. The man had been dead some days, and a botched attempt appeared to have been made to scalp him, though some claimed he had been attacked by dogs – wild dogs roamed the countryside, and ate human remains. Whether human or canine was responsible, it was another lesson. However military technology advances, however precise the means of delivery or 'surgical' the aims, war remains bestial. There are no nice ways of killing people.

With a little tact and sensitivity, and above all with efficiency and discipline, the Russians could have achieved their aims, and more.

The Russian military system used in Chechnya was designed for major war against other nation states. It was manifestly unsuited to, and not practised in, civil war or 'operations short of war'. Nor did it have any military doctrine to deal with such circumstances. For an army so steeped in doctrine and so utterly dependent on it, that was even more of a disaster than for one like the British Army, which has tended to be more pragmatic.

Indiscipline, poor training and poor intelligence are not only wasteful: they are actually counter-productive.

The lack of discipline and control resulted, in part, from the violation of another key principle: unity of command. Three armed groups were involved on the Russian side: the armed forces proper – the Army and Air Force, plus marines from the Pacific and Black Sea Fleets; the Interior Ministry's own troops, who were supposed to be specialists in urban warfare; and the Security Ministry – the former KGB.

The Russians could and should have had a much more unified system of command. That, however, is not a luxury that western forces will enjoy in the kinds of conflict they are likely to be involved in. Those conflicts will be multinational, and with 'dual key' or 'treble key' systems of command – as in Bosnia. The UN, Nato and the individual nation states will all interfere and impose their own constraints. In classic military terms, it is not ideal, but it is the new reality.

In the new world disorder, therefore, a combination of political change and technological advance has changed or modified traditional military principles. Only one principle remains totally unaffected. War is hell.

The Russian forces sent into Grozny were not trained or psychologically equipped for an operation of this type. The only forces who proved competent were some elite paratroops and marines and, most notably, the real 'special forces', the *spetsnaz*. Not only were they more effective, but civilians felt safer when they encountered *spetsnaz* troops who knew what they were doing rather than ordinary troops who did not. The Russians, to their credit, took this lesson to heart. The 1600 strong brigade sent to northern Bosnia as part of the Nato-led peace operation in January 1996 was entirely drawn from the 50,000 strong airborne forces. And in February 1996 it became clear that the airborne troops were being used as the core of a quick-reaction force but reinforced with conventional tanks and heavy artillery, producing an interesting model. Special forces, traditionally used as ancillaries to heavy armoured units, became the main combat troops. And the heavy armoured forces, traditionally the main striking force, were placed in support. It was a 180-degree reversal of the traditional pattern, a formula which had emerged during the Grozny operation.

The number of troops and amount of equipment the Russians poured into Grozny was impressive: the performance of most of them at the 'sharp end' – the cutting edge in contact with the enemy – was not. In conventional operations, commanders try to have as many combat troops as possible relative to those dedicated to support. In operations like this there is a case for having massive back-up – supplies, accurate intelligence able to direct very precise weapons, communications and so on – but relatively few troops actually in contact with the opponent. It called for a variant of an emerging principle: maximum strength, minimum force.

The command and control of the Russian forces was unbelievably bad, partly, it must be said, because three organs of state – the interior ministry, the security ministry and the armed forces proper, were all involved. A really competent command authority could have pulled them together, but this appeared to be absent. The Russians fell down in many areas where one would have expected excellence. They did not even have the right maps. The Russians also failed to understand the impact of the news media. It was the first time they had carried out an operation in the glare of the international media coverage which has characterised all recent conflicts and will in future be unavoidable. But the Russians army only helped the Russian media, whose coverage was also bizarre: long, grisly shots of wounded Russian soldiers, which were presumably permitted because they might stir up hatred against the Chechen rebels. They probably had the opposite effect, reinforcing demands from a newly well-informed Russian public for the operation to be terminated. The western media, meanwhile, saw the war mainly from the Chechen side.

A year later, the war was still going on. The bludgeoning tactics that had worked in 1941–45 had not succeeded in annihilating the enemy this time, but merely strengthened his resolve. Once the Russians had embarked on their ill-advised course, they felt obliged to continue it. In this case, a military solution was not the best one. It led to a nightmare, in which they kept blowing the enemy to pieces, but he nevertheless refused to go away. If, as seems likely, the Russian objective was simply to secure Grozny and the oil pipelines running through it, they surely could have done that much more efficiently, and perhaps made some allies instead of enemies, while still sending a tough message to any other republics contemplating secession. Wherever possible, a military commander makes friends, not enemies. A point which the great Genghis Khan (1155–1227) knew well, and which the Russians should have understood, along with many other relevant points, if they had only re-read their history.

Rwanda, August 1994

'Dogs carry rabies. If one shows an interest in you, *shoot it*.'

Five British paratroopers – parachute-trained Royal Engineers – had been on the American C-5 Galaxy from Mombasa. It had taken 'Chalk 9' (the detachments are called 'chalks') a week to reach Kigali, the Rwandan capital, from Brize Norton, in Oxfordshire. We had been on the same plane. In a screened enclosure by the side of the tarmac, the men were getting their arrival briefing.

By 14 August 1994 most of the human bodies had been cleared from Kigali's streets, but dead dogs were everywhere.

'Someone's been slotting them' (Army slang for shooting). 'Why don't they bury them?' someone asked.

'Because they can't even bury their own people,' came the reply.

It is difficult to hide the remains of perhaps half a million dead, in a country which was densely populated with 7.3 million. Near the British UN camp, next to Kigali stadium, there were piles of human bones and skulls. By the side of the track, there was a boot, with two grisly bones – a fibula and tibia – sticking up from it. At first, I thought it was a joke in bad taste – someone had taken a couple of pig or sheep bones and arranged them neatly in the boot.

'No, they're human. There's still flesh inside the boot,' said a major. It looked as if the leg had been hacked off below the knee, and then gnawed by dogs.

The stadium itself, where up to 100,000 refugees, many suffering from dysentery and cholera, had been packed together, still stank.

'When we arrived it was awash with shit and piss,' said the major. 'The locals are cleaning it up, bit by bit.'

The British had chosen to camp, instead, in a neighbouring field. The neat olive-green tents, bounded by shiny new razor-wire, were a marked contrast to the stadium.

Driving north, to Ruhengeri, near the northern border with Zaire and Uganda, you would not guess what had happened here. The countryside – terraces on hillsides – looked fertile and well-cared for, although the Red Cross said some crops had not been harvested for three years. We were close to the equator, and it was August, but we were also higher than Ben Nevis. The crops were verdant, and the wind rushing past the open-topped Land-Rover was actually cold.

Ruhengeri even had running water, though it was not drinkable. The Engineers had fitted two water purification plants into the system, each able to purify 100,000 litres a day. One of the principles of wider peacekeeping – what some would call 'peace-building', in this case – is that you have to replace certain components of the state structure.

The British were not in the worst areas – the teeming refugee camps on the border with Zaire or across it. There the overall UN commander, Canadian General Romeo Dallaire, had a wider strategy. The following year he stressed the point at a French-speaking seminar on the use of military forces in peacekeeping operations. The aim, he said, was to get people to return to their homes, eventually, and everything had to be directed towards that end – the refugee camps in Zaire had been made too comfortable, compared with the appalling conditions the people had come from. It was a hard philosophy, but those putting it into practice in 1994 had clearly understood their commander's intent. As Oliver Cromwell had told Parliament in 1654, 'though peace be made, yet it is interest that keeps peace.'

'Where I'll be saving lives is not putting people's legs straight,' said Captain Paul Taylor, twenty-six, 'but in convincing people there's an infrastructure to come back to.' Here was a principle which I had seen in Bosnia. There has to be a rapid improvement in amenities if peace is to hold.

Captain Taylor had just straightened a woman's leg which had healed in a bent position after she had been shot in the back of the knee. 'I put her under heavy sedation,' he continued. 'The next best thing to a general anaesthetic. I cleaned out all the pus and rubbish, so it was bleeding cleanly.'

Captain Taylor was a reservist – a Territorial Army parachute-trained captain, who was studying to be a surgeon at the new National Trauma Centre at Stoke-on-Trent. He had been on exercise with 5th Airborne Brigade on Salisbury Plain when they got the message they were going to Rwanda. He decided to go with them but was uncertain whether the hard-pressed National Health Service would give him a job back when he returned. Here was a key problem with large-scale employment of armed forces when their country was not 'at war'. Reservists' civilian jobs were not protected if they chose to put their talents at the service of the military, even to gain experience which was surely beneficial to their civil careers in the long run. The British government was due to introduce new measures to enable reservists to join the forces, even in so-called 'peace time', without putting their jobs at risk. The traditional distinction between 'war' and 'peace', it was clear, was no longer adequate.

Captain Julian Woodhouse had been a regular army doctor for a year. He was treating a little two-year-old girl with malaria, feeding her with a mixture of glucose and quinine, intravenously. He had done his medical training at the Royal Free Hospital, in Hampstead, north London. Then, like all regular army doctors, he went to Sandhurst for a month's course to learn about the army, and did a four-month course in specialised military medicine. The army doctor's patients are not usually old or very young, as they are in civilian life: they are young and fit, but suddenly they have burns and bullet wounds, gangrene and tropical diseases.

Then he did the selection procedure for airborne forces – the pitiless process originally designed to ensure that men could cover the likely distance from the drop zone to the battle, carrying everything they needed to fight, and were still fit and ready for action when they got there.

He conferred with another doctor, and diagnosed amoebic dysentery.

Then he turned back to me. 'The training was hell,' he confessed. 'Worse than this.'

It seemed slightly odd that these military men were here to save lives: not so much the doctors, but the engineers, signallers, mechanics and infantrymen who made up this élite force. The paras' philosophy was always 'maximum violence' or, at the very least, 'controlled aggression'. If there was ever a moment that highlighted the profoundly changed nature of the new art of war and peace, it was this.

The Germans had called the British airborne troops the 'red devils'. Here, their special qualities were being used to save lives. The 'red devils' were now angels of mercy.

The forces which intervened in Rwanda were committed too late to prevent genocide and events of unimaginable horror. All they could do was to try to rebuild the shattered nation they found. Their objective – General Dallaire's *stratégie* – was a combination of stick and carrot. The stick was not to make the refugee camps to which people had fled too comfortable; the carrot was the attempt to rebuild something to which people might want to return. The intervention forces failed in that too. A year later, the Zairean authorities tried to push the refugees out of the camps on the other side of the border, with limited success. If there is one positive lesson from this appalling story, it was apparent from the events described. The success of the airborne troops in their limited task showed that, for a really professional army, it is possible to combine first-rate combat readiness with compassion. And even in a limited operation of this type, reservists were a valued addition to the regular troops, but it was not an operation which could be classified as 'war'. Therefore, when the reservists offered their services they often gambled with their careers – a result of an outmoded distinction between 'war' and 'peace'.

The Prisoners of Vares, Bosnia, 22–23 July 1995

'Fancy a ride in a helicopter?'

It seemed the ideal way to travel, but the cavalier nature of the invitation should have warned of trouble ahead. Nobody should take anything lightly in Bosnia. Before the day was out I, two other journalists and the British Army press officer who had been so flippant and so misjudged the situation, would have the key principles of peacekeeping operations engraved on our hearts.

The day before I had driven over a mountain track to Vitez, in central Bosnia, from Tuzla, about six hours' journey to the north, where thousands of Muslim refugees had arrived from the former Muslim enclave of Srebrenica, which had been overrun by the Serbs. More were now expected from Zepa, a smaller enclave to the south. It was uncertain where they would cross the 'confrontation line'. The commander of the 1,000-strong British battalion group based at Vitez, Lieutenant Colonel Jeff Cook, had headed for Vares, a town roughly equidistant from all the possible crossing points on the confrontation line (see figure 0.1).

Working in Bosnia was reminiscent of naval strategy in the days of sail, both for the UN peacekeepers and for the press corps. You knew roughly what speed a body of refugees might move at, but you had no idea in what direction, and how the winds and currents – in this case the Bosnian Serbs

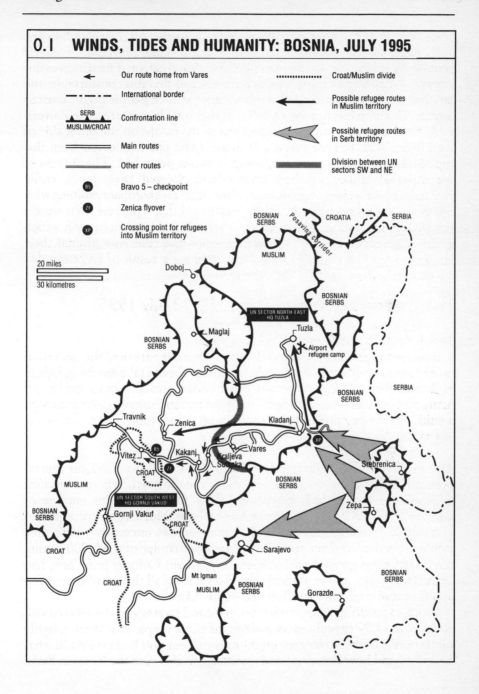

0.1   WINDS, TIDES AND HUMANITY: BOSNIA, JULY 1995

Our route home from Vares

International border

SERB / MUSLIM/CROAT — Confrontation line

Main routes

Other routes

B5 — Bravo 5 – checkpoint

ZF — Zenica flyover

XP — Crossing point for refugees into Muslim territory

Croat/Muslim divide

Possible refugee routes in Muslim territory

Possible refugee routes in Serb territory

Division between UN sectors SW and NE

20 miles
30 kilometres

Doboj

BOSNIAN SERBS

Posavina corridor

CROATIA   SERBIA

MUSLIM

BOSNIAN SERBS

UN SECTOR NORTH EAST HQ TUZLA

Maglaj   Tuzla

BOSNIAN SERBS   Airport refugee camp

BOSNIAN SERBS   SERBIA

Travnik   Zenica   Kladanj

Vitez   B5   Kakanj   Vares
CROAT   ZF   Kraljeva Sutjeska

MUSLIM   BOSNIAN SERBS   Srebrenica

UN SECTOR SOUTH WEST HQ GORNJI VAKUF   Zepa

BOSNIAN SERBS   Gornji Vakuf
CROAT

CROAT   Sarajevo

CROAT   Mt Igman   BOSNIAN SERBS
MUSLIM   BOSNIAN SERBS

Gorazde

and then the Bosnian government authorities – might affect their fate. You had to get yourself into the best position: if you advanced too far, you might miss them. Some of my press colleagues waited at one possible crossing point, at Kladanj, south of Tuzla. But there was no guarantee they would come through there, and there were no two-way communications, although I could send a story using my satellite telex transmitter.

The best guess was that the Zepa refugees would then be taken to Zenica, near Vitez. Vitez was relatively comfortable and had communications, so I had decided to wait for them there. If they went to Tuzla instead, then I could get back there in perhaps six hours. So that was my decision.

Lieutenant Colonel Cook had gone forward to Vares to reconnoitre it as a forward operating base, from which his soldiers could move to escort the refugees on to Zenica, wherever they crossed the confrontation line. The Bosnian government authorities were particularly annoyed with the UN at that time, blaming it for the loss of Srebrenica and Zepa. Colonel Cook arrived at the Pakistani UN battalion outside Vares to find it blockaded by unhelpful, even hostile troops from the 16th Division of the Bosnian government army, or BiH.

I should have known that to try to sneak into the Pakistani base in a helicopter, evading the BiH blockade, was a bad idea, but when the British Army offered such a facility, one naturally assumed they knew what they were doing. Half an hour by helicopter to Vares, ten minutes' chat with Colonel Cook, a few photographs, and I would have an exclusive interview and exclusive pictures. Then we would be back in time for lunch. Winston Churchill, a war correspondent for the *Morning Post*, probably thought much the same when he accepted an invitation to go on a reconnaissance into Boer territory in an armoured train in 1900. For him, as for me, Tom Carver of the BBC and his cameraman, Tony Fallshaw, things suddenly went wrong.

A UN helicopter – a British army Lynx – was obtained with surprising ease. In retrospect, it is clear that the UN's south-western sector, to which the British battalion belonged and which provided the helicopter, had no concept of the amount of tension there was in sector north-east, responsible for Vares and the Pakistani battalion.

When the helicopter reached the Pakistani base, it was obvious we were not expected. It tried to land on one of two circular heli-pads, outside the perimeter, and BiH soldiers pointed their rifles at it. It pulled away, and as it did so, one of them pointed a rocket-propelled grenade, with a big, bulbous silver bomb at one end, at the helicopter.

Then it tried to put down in the base itself, but clouds of dust came up and the crew thought they could see wires on the ground. At this point, if not before, the officer in charge should have known to abandon the mission.

Instead, incredibly, he ordered the helicopter to land on a road on the other side of the camp – once again, outside the perimeter. As it touched down, rotors whirling, it blew away most of a haystack in an adjacent farmyard. That probably upset the locals as well. Our intrepid UN officer climbed out and said, 'Follow me.'

I heard the crew say they would circle and come back for us. Meanwhile, we had no option but to follow our UN guardian towards the BiH soldiers maintaining the blockade of the Pakistani camp. The idea was to show the UN's moral authority: the combination of bravado and bluster that had worked when the UN had first arrived in Bosnia nearly three years before – but this time, the UN's moral authority counted for nothing. The soldiers, very jumpy, pointed their rifles and shouted something that could only mean: 'Hands up! Hands on your heads!'

We were spreadeagled against the wall of the shelter used by the BiH guards, and searched. The BBC's camera, mine, and all kinds of other equipment were thrown in a pile. The Bosnian soldiers were very, very nervous. They yanked the British officer's pistol out of his holster and started hacking away with a jack-knife at the lanyard which secured it to his person. Within a few minutes a Mercedes car arrived from Vares, and a BiH officer whom we later learned was 16th Division's security chief climbed out, brandishing a sawn-off shotgun, which he cocked, threateningly.

Rule number one. You can't peacekeep without the consent of the local parties. People who have never worked in situations like that often imagine that the UN could, if necessary, shoot its way through. Do that once, and the trust on which peacekeeping is based is destroyed – and anyway, it is only possible if prepared and equipped. It is, in practice, impossible to mix that kind of force with the day-to-day exercise of peacekeeping. Our UN escort had a pistol, but, in practice, it would have been very difficult to use it against the extremely frightened young military policemen who were only doing their job – and, it must be said, they did it very well. Had he tried to use it, we would all have been killed.

The helicopter did not return. We later heard the BiH had fired five rounds at it. It flew back to the south-west sector headquarters at Gornji Vakuf, and presumably reported that we had been captured.

Rule number two. Have respect for the local parties. The day before, following some other UN helicopter flights, the Bosnian forces had warned the UN they would regard as hostile any flights which they had not authorised. The Serbs had recently captured a number of UN white

vehicles around Sarajevo – twenty miles away – and might well have
captured helicopters as well. So when, in defiance of a clear warning by the
BiH, a white helicopter touched down, attempting to breach their
restrictions on the UN's freedom of movement, they were, quite rightly,
incensed. Either the UN was treating them with total disrespect, or this
helicopter contained Serb commandos. Either way, it did not bode well for
us.

'How dare you flout our airspace, flout our sovereignty!' We heard that
several times during the interrogation which followed. The four of us were
crammed in the back of the Mercedes and the security chief drove into
Vares at high speed, with another military police officer in the front
passenger seat, clutching a loaded pistol, looking at us jumpily. At 16th
Division headquarters, we were spreadeagled, searched again, and marched
upstairs. Then we were shown into the reassuring comfort of a boss's office.
Normally, when westerners are arrested in Bosnia, coffee with slivovic is
produced after a while. But this was to be an interview without slivovic.

We were captured at about noon. It took hours to find an interpreter, but
when one arrived, the interrogation began. The Bosnian officers could not
understand how anyone could authorise a helicopter flight without a sheaf
of written orders – our escort had none. And they could not understand why
the British Army would cart journalists around with it. They said UN
helicopters had no authorisation to fly into their territory without prior and
specific permission. 'The helicopter was authorised from Gornji Vakuf,'
our escort explained. 'I assumed . . .'

'You *assumed*? Call yourself a lieutenant colonel? *Are* you a lieutenant
colonel?'

Meanwhile, the Pakistani battalion, Lieutenant Colonel Cook and some
of his officers had witnessed what had happened outside the Pakistani base.
At about five in the afternoon the door of the room where we were being
interrogated was thrown open. In stepped the tall, very military figure of
Colonel Nayyar, the Pakistani UN commander. He sported a splendid
handlebar moustache and wore two rows of medal ribbons, from big wars
with India in 1965 and 1971, in which he had commanded tanks.

'You gentleman have caused me a great deal of trouble,' Colonel Nayyar
said in immaculate English. He spoke with a formidable combination of
authority and diplomacy. He berated our press officer – the lieutenant
colonel – for risking all our lives.

'What did you think you were doing, colonel? Did you have no idea how
sensitive matters are in this area?' He turned to the Bosnian officers. 'I think

it would be in *everybody's* interest that these gentlemen leave as soon as possible.'

Colonel Nayyar's own freedom of movement was restricted, but when he realised a UN officer and British journalists had been seized, he had headed straight for Vares.

'We have brought you some lunch,' he said. After a while we were ushered down to the canteen where lunch – the best takeaway in Bosnia – was unpacked. Fish curry and dal, bread and fruit squash. Things began to look better.

However, with a curfew in force after dark, it was already looking unlikely we would get away that night. We were informed we would each have to make a 'statement', and were taken to another site – the military police headquarters. We were told we should no longer converse with each other.

The Bosnian military police spent hours looking through the BBC's film. They had filmed the entire flight – Bosnian checkpoints we had flown over, even Bosnian government positions. The film had been running when we were told to put our hands up.

The relationship between captor and captive is a delicate one.

'What did you think of the film?' asked Tony, the BBC cameraman.

'Not bad. We especially liked the bit in the helicopter with the sun glinting off the helmets of the crew. Very artistic,' came the reply.

More waiting. Then one of the Bosnian military police stormed in with a notebook they had taken from the pile of captured equipment, which I recognised as mine.

'Whose is this?'

'Mine.'

'Can you read this?'

It was an old notebook. Before this latest trip to Bosnia, I had been working on a story about Chechnya. I had written some notes in Russian, in cyrillic script. As used by the Serbs. Oh dear.

I was the first journalist to be interrogated, at about midnight. I was told to empty my pockets, but there was no strip-search, mercifully. They asked me if I was a spy, and suggested I might be working for the Russians. Then there was a long statement, made longer by the need for everything to pass through an interpreter, and hammered out on a manual typewriter. They wanted to know how many times I had been in Bosnia, and every detail about the helicopter flight. Then they moved on to my views on the situation in Bosnia. Their behaviour throughout was very correct, and I was careful to compliment them on that. Finally they returned to the notebook.

'It's an old notebook. These notes refer to Chechnya. From before I came to Bosnia, this time.'

'But why do you write about this *in Bosnia*?'

The whole process took about two hours. When they had finished with me, I was sent to wait in another room, where I found the Dutch UN Military Observer in Vares, Captain Tom van Meer, whom they had arrested on suspicion of being linked with us. Eventually the British press officer emerged in turn from his interrogation session.

'Colonel, you have cost me six months' work,' said the Dutchman. All that work, trying to gain the trust of the Bosnian government forces, had been thrown away by a single, rash act.

At about three am they let the press officer go. They took him to Zenica, whence he was able to get to Vitez by dawn. The Bosnians had given him a hard time, he said. But now he was up against the British Army, which would give him a harder one. At eight am he was on the Brigadier's carpet.

Meanwhile, the rest of us – myself, the two other journalists and the Dutchman – were shown to a bunk room. 'Don't try to escape. There are plenty of guards outside.' Incredibly, we slept very well – we were so tired.

'I wonder if they'll bring us a cup of tea?' someone said the next morning.

'Oh shit, I forgot to fill in the card you stick on the door,' joked Tony.

A few minutes later a guard appeared with four big mugs of herbal tea.

It took all the next day to get us released. Tom van Meer was allowed to leave at about ten am. But they still held on to the three journalists. Our guards were now friendly. 'It's not up to us. It's orders. You know, the boss classes . . .'

Throughout the Bosnian war, I got the impression that most people just wanted to get on with their normal lives. A small number benefitted from keeping the war going. And they, unfortunately, were those in positions of power. In a normal society they would have moderately tedious jobs running the bus station, I thought. Now they command brigades and divisions.

One of the BiH guards was an ethnic Serb. He asked if I was related to the botanist, David Bellamy.

'Maybe,' I said. 'Not closely.'

'It's just that I watched all his TV programmes. I'm very interested in botany.'

He showed me a bunch of yellow flowers, collected from the mountains. He said they were called *kantarion*.

'These stop blood, you know.'

'Bleeding. A styptic, yes, I understand.'

The Bosnian government army might have been deprived of conventional medicine, but it was clearly aware of the uses of herbal medicines.

The decision to let the press officer go and keep us in jail was worrying. Tom Carver was very concerned about his father, who was ill, and we informed our captors of this. But as foreigners who had landed in the middle of somebody else's war, we had no right to ask for anything. Only the UN's 'moral authority' – what was left of it – and the compassion of our captors, plus the extraordinary correctness of the Bosnian military police, stood between us and being turned into kebabs.

I was particularly concerned that, following the discovery of the Russian notes, they would let the BBC men go but keep me. However, at about four pm, the botanist said he would have news for us shortly.

'Christopher, we have some good news and some bad news. Which do you want first?'

'The bad news.'

'We are keeping your cameras and film, under Bosnian Army regulation 211, ZKP-a.'

'And the good news?'

'You will shortly be free to go. The Pakistani battalion have been authorised to take you to Vitez.'

There followed hours of form-filling and issuing of receipts – for the camera, and even for the notebook – but it was all very reassuring. Suppose there had been a civil war in Britain or the US for three years. Would a sense of order and propriety have been maintained with people who fell into the hands of the warring factions, who had no right to be there? I doubted it. And at least we were to be taken directly to the edge of Bosnian government held territory, close to Vitez. At around five o'clock I went to look out of the window. White vehicles were drawing into the courtyard.

'It's Pakbat' – the Pakistani battalion, to take us home.

Because they were denied freedom of movement, and there had been no time to issue special orders, a yellow Bosnian Army Mercedes led the convoy, to explain our passage to the roadblocks. The Pakistanis were in small, four-wheel-drive Volkswagen jeeps: the Mercedes handled the rutted mountain roads equally well. On one occasion the Mercedes stopped, to pick up a couple of hitchhikers – young women, in short skirts. But then it picked up another two – older women in long skirts and headscarves. They were decent guys.

The road from Vares heads through empty, mountainous country as far as a little town called Kraljeva Suteska, where there is a splendid, Spanish-looking monastery. Then we were on the main road, to the 'Zenica flyover'.

Another checkpoint, and then to 'Bravo 5' – the checkpoint manned jointly by the Bosnian government army, the Bosnian Croat militia – the HVO – and the UN. These checkpoints had been established to police the February 1994 ceasefire between the Bosnian government forces and the HVO, on the former confrontation line between them. Bravo 5 was on the edge of the Croatian pocket around Vitez. Croats, surrounded by Muslims, nearly surrounded by Serbs – it was a measure of the complexity of the war.

On the other side of the checkpoint there was a BBC Land-Rover waiting. The Pakistanis had forewarned the British Army, who had told the BBC. We said goodbye to the Pakistanis and the Bosnian escort.

'Don't come flying in a helicopter again without our permission. It's very dangerous. You could have been shot down and killed. It's our country. OK?'

We stepped over the line. The BBC had a plastic bag full of cold beers waiting, and we sipped them as the Land-Rover sped on its way. There was to be a welcoming party at the BBC house in Vitez. Our absence had caused great concern.

As the Rover sped on through darkening lanes, not unlike parts of Britain, we pondered on what the Bosnian soldiers had said.

They were right. It was their country. It was their war.

In such an operation, therefore, you cannot operate without the consent of the local parties and you must treat them with respect. You are their guests: otherwise you have no right to be there, as they made very clear. You must understand their concerns (born of three years of civil war and atrocity, concerns which breed paranoia), and make allowances.

Whereas the Russians in Chechnya did not pay enough attention to media coverage, maybe the British in Bosnia were paying too much to coverage of the wrong type. In this case, a clear desire to get *something* positive on the television had led to a reckless expedition. It exacerbated an already high level of tension between the UN and the Bosnian government forces and nearly led to seven people being killed (the four prisoners and the crew of three) and a helicopter lost. No news story is worth that. But the incident underlined other things too. The sympathy which our guards showed, once they realised that we were not Serb commandos and that we were sorry for our stupidity, was remarkable. We could easily identify with the Bosnian troops' cynical disregard for their bosses. 'It's a job. We have our orders. Sorry.' And there was the common humanity which comes through when a shared interest or a shared experience emerges. In this case, it was something as unlikely and tenuous as botany. And that showed the value and growing power of the international media – particularly television

– in forging that bond. A bond of mutual experience and respect which, in most cases, makes killing or hurting one's fellow man more difficult.

CHAPTER ONE
THINKING ABOUT 'WAR' AND 'PEACE'

'The legitimate object of war,' said General William T. Sherman, 'is a more perfect peace.'[1] Sherman (1820–91) had practised war in one of its more absolute forms. He was responsible for the American Civil War march through the state of Georgia from Atlanta to the sea in 1864 which had cut the Confederacy in two. His march was part of an emerging strategy of 'total war'. The era of war decided by big battles fought by professional armies alone was ending: a move towards total destruction of the adversary's economy and infrastructure, which would last until the end of the 1980s, had begun.

But Sherman's view on the relationship between war and peace was shared by commentators throughout the ages. The aim of war is a better peace, and, in some cases, the horrors of war are preferable to an unjust peace, or to slavery. Throughout history, war and peace have alternated, like sickness and health in the life of an individual. A clear distinction between the two conditions was familiar to the ancients: as Tacitus, the Roman historian, said, 'a bad peace is even worse than war'.[2] The famous words of Isaiah, II, 4, also reveal a clear sense of war as a political act deliberately undertaken by nations: 'Nation shall not lift up sword against nation: neither shall they learn war any more.'

There was a clear sense that undertaking military campaigns was an expensive, unpleasant and risky business, and that 'war' was something different from normal daily life, risky, violent and uncomfortable though the latter could also be. But for millennia – since the first evidence of organised warfare around 3,500 BC – the economic and political life of states changed little in time of war. Even during the Napoleonic Wars, widely considered to be the first example of a more 'total' form of war, the writer Jane Austen could recount the preoccupations of her characters in southern England, apparently oblivious to the titanic struggle with

Napoleon, which preoccupied the government and the authorities at the Channel ports barely a few dozen miles away.

The distinction between war and peace became sharper with the demographic and industrial developments of the nineteenth century, and the idea of a 'nation in arms'. War was not just a different activity: it now required society to switch on to a different and alien footing as well. Nations were increasingly reluctant to engage in war, since to do so entailed mobilising large sections of the populace and industry: normal life and liberties were suspended; normal business took second place. Conversely, sections of the armed forces were not able to operate without mobilisation and reinforcement. The idea of 'wartime' and 'peacetime' took hold. Since the end of the Cold War, however, that distinction has outlived its usefulness.

By 1995, one third of the 120,000-strong, professional army of the United Kingdom was engaged, either on active service (real military business, as opposed to exercises), or preparing to take over from those who were, or recovering after a six-month tour in a real war zone. Among those 40,000 troops were 17,000 troops in Northern Ireland, and 8,000 in Bosnia, with another 7,000 on seven days' stand-by to join them. In December the Bosnian force was increased to 13,000. The United States had 9,000 servicemen and women involved in air and sea operations around and over Bosnia, 26,000 in the Middle East, mainly keeping an eye on Iraq, and 37,000 in South Korea. The US general Chuck Horner, who commanded allied air forces in the 1991 Gulf War, said that parts of the US Air Force were hard pressed to meet these real, operational commitments, in addition to training requirements.

The pressure of these 'peacetime' engagements led the US to reappraise the strategy it had enunciated in 1993, after a post-Cold War review, which said it should, if necessary, be able to wage two 'Major Regional Conflicts' simultaneously. If it was hard pressed to cope with limited 'peacetime engagement', that certainly cast doubt on its ability to cope with two big regional wars, even with massive mobilisation.

Neither Britain nor the United States considered itself to be 'at war'. But this clearly was not peace, either. 'I don't know what you call Bosnia and what's going on in north and south Iraq,' said Lieutenant General George Muellner of the US Air Force. 'But the operations' tempo associated with that may tend to be much more of a driver [for determining the future structure of armed forces] than dealing with major regional conflicts.'[3] Nearly two years before, Britain's Director General of Land Warfare, Major General Mike Willcocks, had said something similar.

> I do not think that anyone would consider themselves at war now and yet we have 20,000 soldiers employed on operations, and there have been sustained some 2,700 casualties in Northern Ireland (The Department of Peace and Conflict Research's definition of a major armed conflict is 1,000 battle-related deaths). I hope, therefore, that it will be accepted that we need a wider spectrum than simply peace or war.[4]

By 1995, it was not so much a distinction between 'war' and 'peace' as a distinction between a conflict in which one's own national interest was directly threatened, which was still called 'war', and involvement in 'somebody else's wars', which happened in 'peacetime'. The British Ministry of Defence's guidance on the subject was suitably vague. The regulations for handling the media in situations where British forces were fighting, issued in 1995, no longer referred, as they had during the stable, Cold War period, to 'War' and 'Transition To War', but to proposed working arrangements 'in times of emergency, tension, conflict or war' – a fairly catholic concoction.

The term 'war' had already dropped out of favour among purists, though it continues to be useful to describe major armed conflicts. A state of war has a precise legal definition, requiring an ultimatum and then a declaration of war. Not since World War II have all those conditions been fulfilled, yet it would surely be pedantic to challenge the common usage: America's 1965–75 Vietnam War, the 1982 Falklands War, the 1991 Gulf War. The British government resisted using the term 'war' in 1982, referring to a 'conflict' in the south Atlantic, on the grounds that it was a localised dispute in which the British were trying to implement United Nations resolutions. In the sense that Britain was fighting to get back what it regarded as its territory, it was a war. But 'war' immediately invokes all kinds of extraordinary powers, laws – and obligations – which the government sought to avoid.

The first attempt to define laws of war in the modern world also introduced the idea of a system of law to which all nation states were subject – and therefore the first hint that an international authority, like the United Nations, might one day be responsible for enforcing it. The author of De Iure Belli ac Pacis (On the Law of War and Peace), first published in 1625, was a Dutchman, Huig de Groot, better known as Hugo Grotius (1583–1645), a lawyer, scholar and diplomat. The basic idea also appears in his earlier work on the Law of Prize – the laws relating to seizure of shipping during conflict at sea – of 1606. Grotius's fundamental theme in both treatises is that nations have legal rights and duties and that war is a law enforcement procedure, akin to judicial remedies, to be employed to punish and redress infringements on those rights.[5]

At the time, it was not feasible for the family of states as a whole to come together to enforce justice. Therefore, Grotius wrote, let the defendant state first be called upon to judge – send it an ultimatum, in other words – and, if it denies justice, let the plaintiff act as judge. Let there be war.

In the *Law of War and Peace*, Grotius recognised that confederacies, or groups of states, could act as an intermediate authority, above individual states. The community of Christian states might be one, for example. But he was cautious of this because, extraordinarily for someone of his time, he was against any form of racial or religious discrimination. He was against any form of racial or religious discrimination. He disapproved of making a distinction between 'civilised' and 'barbarian' nations, between white and non-white, between Christian and non-Christian. 'The right to enter into treaties is so common to all men that it does not admit to a distinction arising from religion,' he wrote. And, aware of the colonial empires of the time – the century-old Spanish Empire, the burgeoning British and French Empires – he said it was 'equally shameless to claim for oneself by right of discovery what is held by another, even though the occupant may hold wrong views about God.'[6]

Such views anticipated the values underpinning the United Nations today, and in holding them, Grotius was well ahead of most of his contemporaries. Europe was undergoing a terrible war at the time – the Thirty Years' War of 1618–48 – the consequences of which probably affected central Europe for another century after it ended. The 'religious' war in Bosnia from 1992 was to recall that earlier long drawn-out conflict on several levels: the indiscipline and unpredictability of the armies, the atrocities, the slaughtered farm animals, the intermixing of small-scale war and large-scale banditry, the armies' penchant for siege tactics, the cold, central European colours and steep roofs, the burnt out villages, the unmade roads, and even the armour: heavy, bullet-resistant helmets and flak jackets, just like seventeenth-century cuirasses and back-plates, covering the most vulnerable parts of the body.

The peace which ended the Thirty Years' War, signed in the two Westphalian towns of Münster and Osnabrück in 1648, was the result of immensely complex negotiations and a remarkable achievement which marked the beginning of modern diplomacy. The treaty signed in Münster on 30 January 1648 ended the eight year war between Spain and the United Provinces of the Netherlands, while that signed in Osnabrück on 24 October ended the war between France, Sweden and the German protestants on the one side and the catholic Holy Roman Empire and German princes on the other. The tortuous and complex road to the Peace of Westphalia presents many parallels with the Bosnian peace of December 1995, although major nation states were participants in the Thirty Years' war, not merely observers. However, without the accelerated shuttle diplomacy made possible by aircraft, telephone and fax machine, the end of the Thirty Years' War took a lot longer to organise. There had been an abortive peace signed in Prague in 1635, thirteen years before, and the main parties to the war – Sweden, France and Spain – began preparing for a peace congress in 1640. Invitations to the congress went out in 1643–44, and negotiations then continued for another four years, as the 150 delegates, mostly from German principalities but also from the Empire, France, Sweden and Spain, argued about protocol and procedure, and in so doing stumbled on many of the methods of modern diplomacy. Inevitably, over such a long period of time, and without modern communications, the delegates started to find more in common with each other than with the distant rulers they represented, which contributed to a realistic settlement. The independence of Switzerland and the Netherlands was recognised, while territories remaining within the Holy Roman Empire were recognised as catholic or protestant, according to the situation which had obtained in 1624. Except in the Habsburg dominions, members of minority faiths within each territory were allowed freedom of worship and the right to emigrate.

Most importantly, the Peace of Westphalia enunciated the principle of 'cuius regio, eius religio' – 'to each his own area, to each his own religion' – in other words, the principle of non-interference in the internal affairs of other states.[7] That principle, though not universally respected, remained dominant for 350 years – until the Berlin Wall came down in 1989. You didn't attack somebody just because they did things differently from you. What they did inside their own borders was their business. If they attacked you, on the other hand, you could defend yourself.

The United Nations Charter, signed in June 1945, and little amended since, still concentrates on preventing conflict between nation states, and places the onus of deciding what constitutes self-defence on them. Article 2(7) of the Charter says:

Nothing ... shall authorise the United Nations to intervene in matters which are essentially within the domestic jurisdiction of any state or shall require the Members to submit such matters to settlement under the present Charter; but this principle shall not prejudice the application of enforcement measures under Chapter VII.

Chapter VII – 'Action with Respect to Threats to the Peace, Breaches of the Peace and Acts of Aggression' – sanctions 'such action by air, sea or land forces as may be necessary to maintain or restore *international* peace and security.'[8] There is no stated right to intervene in a state's internal affairs on moral or humanitarian grounds. The 1648 Peace of Westphalia still held sway three centuries later.

Since the end of the Cold War, however, there have been demands for the UN or other, UN-authorised groups of states to intervene in internal conflicts, reversing the long-standing principle enshrined in the Peace of Westphalia. In order to understand this major charge of outlook, we need to examine the shifts in thinking on war and politics that have evolved during the intervening 350 years.

Absolute and Limited War

More than two hundred years have passed since Karl von Clausewitz (1780–1831) first encountered war, as a boy ensign in the Prussian Army, in 1793. He is often mentioned, occasionally quoted, but little read. His name has come to be associated with Prussian militarism, and with the prosecution of war for its own sake – something he would have abhorred, and in fact the very opposite of what he was saying.

Clausewitz's portrait is not what you expect. You imagine a craggy, rugged Prussian militarist. Instead, in the surviving portrait of a brilliant man who shunned publicity and wrapped his writings in packets to be opened only after his death, there is a sensitive, youthful face beneath a slightly eccentric explosion of curly hair.[9]

Clausewitz did not mess about with a legalistic definition of war, but offered instead the image of a pair of wrestlers, each trying to use physical strength to compel the other to submit. 'War is thus an act of force to compel our enemy to do our will'.[10] No better definition has been devised. In the first chapter, which he said was 'the only thing I regard as being in final form', he continues,

Force, to counter opposing force, equips itself with the inventions of art and

science. Attached to force are certain, self-imposed, imperceptible limitations, hardly worth mentioning, known as international law and custom, but
they scarcely weaken it. Force ... is thus the means of war; to impose our
will on the enemy is the object. To secure that object we must render the
enemy powerless; and that, in theory, is the true aim of warfare.[11]

The rules attending this wrestling match may vary, from a very closely
refereed contest to an uncontrolled brawl in which one party or the other
ends up dead. The Bosnian conflict might be likened to a three-way fight,
in which the referee, the UN, tries to intervene, and becomes part of it.
But the use of force with the immediate aim of rendering the opponent
powerless remains crucial. Clearly, if we cannot identify an opponent,
then whatever we are engaged in is not war.

Aside from defining war, Clausewitz's most important insight was that
war was always a continuation of policy and politics, and that political
considerations had to be part of the commander's decision-making
process. While the nature of warfare itself naturally strove to an extreme,
it was always limited to a greater and lesser extent by politics, by
geography, by the 'friction' of its component parts, by human frailty and
human will.[12]

He did not finish what he intended to write, especially the crucial bit
on limited war, defined as war limited either by the resources devoted to
it, by the objectives expected of it, or both. That is a pity. For that is the
kind of 'war' that interests us most.

If Clausewitz had finished what he planned to write, he would probably
have highlighted two pairs of opposites, which mirror each other but are
not the same: the philosophical distinction between absolute violence,
and the way it is modified in practice; and the real distinction between
two kinds of war, unlimited and limited. He defines the latter, provision-
ally, as 'those in which the object is the overthrow of the enemy – to
render him politically helpless or militarily impotent, thus forcing him to
sign whatever peace we please' and those 'merely to occupy some of his
frontier-districts so we can annex them or use them for bargaining at the
peace negotiations.'[13] The prime example of the first kind is the Allies'
policy of imposing 'unconditional surrender' on the Axis powers in
World War II. The second is exemplified by the cessation of hostilities
against Iraq once Iraqi forces had vacated Kuwait in March, 1991.

Clausewitz approached his subject from a continental, land-bound
viewpoint, and this may have prevented him from seeing the full
significance of his theory. He had in mind two countries abutting on each
other. In such a case, the 'limited' capture of a piece of territory could

swiftly be reversed by the defeated side upping the ante to 'unlimited' war, seizing it back, and possibly destroying the initiator in the process. The line between limited and unlimited war was extremely fuzzy. It took two naval strategists, Julian Corbett (1854–1922) and Alfred Thayer Mahan (1840–1914), to see that the conditions for true limited war existed outside Europe, or at 'the extremities of vast areas of imperfectly settled territory'.[14]

Corbett believed that such theatres of operations 'can never have the political importance of objects which are organically part of the European system' – a statement probably no longer valid – but, equally important, 'that they can be isolated by naval action sufficiently to set up the conditions of true limited war.'[15] Corbett and Mahan had in mind the conditions of, for example, the Seven Years' War of 1756–63, in which Canada was isolated by sea-power, and within which a true 'limited' war could be waged, without threatening the home territory and national existence of either protagonist – France or Britain. In fact, France was a stronger land power than Britain, but by employing the limited form of war Britain was able to isolate a fraction of the French forces and impose its will by using its navy to guarantee home defence and secure the objective.

If such an example seems historically distant, consider the involvement of the western powers in the Gulf War of 1991, or present operations in Bosnia. Since the end of the Cold War, south-eastern Europe has reverted to the strategic situation to which Mahan referred at the end of the nineteenth century:

> South-eastern Europe, owing to the weakness of Turkey, brings to the back door of Europe just that sort of condition which, for the most part, is to be found only in the remoter regions which navies reach.[16]

The concept of limited war, sometimes more clearly focused through the prism of naval strategy, is cardinal to the present book. So is Clausewitz's insistence that warfare – or military operations, of whatever type – is the continuation of policy by other means and therefore, in practice, always limited.

Clausewitz would never have agreed that commanders should be given a 'blank cheque': peace ends, war begins, here you are, get on with it. Even today, there are some senior officers in the British and US armies who would like a blank cheque, and who believe that the military should be a caste apart from the rest of society. That is as impossible as it is undesirable. The 'wars' we are involved in now are, as Clausewitz put it, 'more political' than ever.

The less intense the motives, the less will the military element's natural tendency to violence coincide with political directives. As a result, war will be driven further from its natural course, the political object will be more and more at variance with the aim of ideal war, and the conflict will seem increasingly *political* in character.[17]

Clausewitz could have been describing the UN intervention in Bosnia exactly, with its timorous resort to pinprick air-strikes. He would have understood the UN's reservations about using greater force – force which was available to it – instantly and intuitively.

It was in part a historical accident that the Prussian philosopher-general lived at the beginning of an age which saw the power of the state increase. Its ability to channel more and more of its resources and the energies of its people into organised conflict grew, and so did the power of the means of destruction – though in many cases they became less discriminating. Clausewitz could not have foreseen the social and industrial changes which would involve more and more of the state and its resources in war. When he talked about absolute war he was not thinking about a conflict like World Wars I and II. He was using the idea of the absolute as a philosophical tool. He has been profoundly misunderstood.

Clausewitz has been vilified by people horrified at the slaughter of the two World Wars, for which his writings were blamed. Most influential was the military writer and journalist, Sir Basil Liddell Hart (1895–1970), who called him 'the Mahdi of mass and mutual massacre'. The most fervent advocates of 'total war' attacked him as well. General Erich von Ludendorff, the World War I German Field Marshal, and author of a tract on *Total War*, for example, remarked that even during the wars against Austria in 1866 and 1870–71, Germany 'had not yet set itself free from the doctrines of Clausewitz with regard to the nature and essence of warfare' – in other words, from the use of war as a tool of policy.[18] He was right. The relatively swift campaigns against Austria in 1866 and France in 1870 were probably the closest thing to Clausewitz's image of 'absolute' or 'unlimited' war. They were professional campaigns, fought, by and large, by soldiers, with big battles and clear results. Clausewitz would have been appalled by what happened in 1914, when entire nations were sucked into war, which became an end rather than a means.

Clausewitz's contemporary, Baron Antoine Henri Jomini (1779–1869), also approached the issue of limited war. Jomini, like Clausewitz, often expressed himself in geometrical and mechanical terms, though as a professional soldier he understood the human and emotional aspects of war instinctively. Jomini undoubtedly knew that war was, as he said, 'a great drama ... which cannot be reduced to mathematical calculations', although the way he expressed himself suggests the opposite.[19] He had a journalistic talent for reducing complex issues to simple statements, expressed in geometrical and spatial terms and simple diagrams, of which his most famous was his stress on the value of 'interior lines'. The side operating on interior lines – from the inside out – could move more quickly and easily from place to place than one closing from the outside. His work appealed to a generation unnerved by the apparent chaos unleashed by the French Revolution, and his geometrical style fitted the strategic pattern which unfolded with the development of railways.

For Jomini, limited war was primarily about gaining territory while absolute war was about destroying enemy forces regardless of where they were. In his chapter 'On Great Invasions and Distant Expeditions', he pointed out the dangers of taking the conditions of war between contiguous states and applying them to those separated by large areas of land or sea. But he did not explore the significance of being able to isolate a theatre of war and control the flow of reinforcements and supplies to it. The 1991 Gulf War land campaign showed classic Jominian geometry, but had Saddam Hussein had just a few submarines, the flow of Allied, particularly US, troops and matériel into the theatre would have been profoundly impeded. Freedom of Movement is an important consideration in the conduct of peacekeeping operations. In a vastly wider sense, it is a key component of twenty-first century strategy.

The changes in methods of transportation in the modern world have not made the views of naval strategists less relevant: on the contrary, they are more so. The instinctive approach of the maritime strategist – that large tracts of the planet are available for free movement unless specifically opposed – applies with even greater force to the air and to space.

Corbett lighted on the words of the Elizabethan statesman Francis Bacon: 'He that commands the sea is at liberty to take as much or as little of the war as he will, whereas those that be strongest by land are nevertheless many times in great straits [that is, their freedom of movement and action is impeded].'[20] In other words, the outcome of limited wars is not decided by the armed strength of the belligerents but on the amount they are able or willing to bring to bear. To take the two pairs of opposites identified by Clausewitz and bring them together again, a war – or military action short of war – may be limited physically, by the strategic isolation of the object, as well as psychologically or morally by its comparative importance.

Wars of Necessity, Wars of Choice, Wars of Conscience

Since the Peace of Westphalia, the principal European nations and, later, those of North America, have generally refrained from intervening in each others' internal affairs. They only fought when vital national interests were at stake. These were wars of necessity. Since the end of the Cold War, however, there has been increasing pressure to intervene in other people's wars, leading to wars of choice. Sometimes, national interests are involved here, too. But sometimes they may not be the principal cause of intervention. The parties intervening may not even regard them as wars – but they are wars for the people intervened against. They are wars of choice and wars of conscience, where outsiders intervene out of what Michael Ignatieff has called 'moral disgust'.[21] This phenomenon is not totally new. The temptation to play the role of *deus ex machina* ('we, the "civilised world", decree') and to dictate to those we regard as culturally inferior played a part in European colonial expansion in the nineteenth and twentieth centuries, although greed, and the search for natural resources were probably more important.

As this book is written, the legality of intervention in a state's internal affairs is one of the most important issues of international security. The supra-national organisation of the UN, it appears, may intervene in the internal affairs of a weak or disintegrating nation state – like Bosnia, Rwanda or Somalia. Yet it would never dare interfere in the internal affairs of a strong one – like Russia, in its internal operation against Chechnya in 1994–95, however appalling the abuses of human rights and however well publicised.

Since 1989, the UN has been under pressure to redefine the limits of legitimate involvement in the internal affairs of member states. An important factor is that even the most 'internal' crisis tends to have international consequences because refugees tend to flood across international borders – as happened in Kurdistan (April 1991) and Rwanda (June 1994). At the time of writing there is no consensus as to whether a right to intervene in a sovereign state to prevent 'human rights abuses' – starvation, rape, massacre and torture – exists.[22]

Before 1945, *cuius regio, eius religio* – and its secular implications – held sway. In the nineteenth century the great powers threatened and in some cases carried out a number of interventions; for example, the deployment of 6,000 French troops to Syria in 1860 to protect Christians there after thousands had been massacred. In the same year, the Taiping rebellion in China threatened the great foreign trade emporium at Shanghai, and the British and French resolved to defend it, and to intervene in operations in an area within 30 miles of the city – an early 'safe area'.[23] Such western intervention operations were mainly to rescue foreign expatriates, or based on self-interest. The League of Nations, the inter-war precursor of the UN, did not provide a right to intervene, and neither did the 1928 Convention on Duties and Rights in the Event of Civil Strife and the 1933 Montevideo Convention on the Rights and Duties of States.[24]

Ironically, one of the first decisions of the UN was to agree a Genocide Convention, in 1948. The Convention authorised any member state to call on the UN to 'take such action as they consider appropriate for the prevention and suppression of acts of genocide'. In practice, the Convention stressed subsequent punishment, rather than prevention. Until very recently, no one intervened: Rwanda, Bosnia and Cambodia spring to mind.[25] In 1994 US officials were instructed to avoid use of the word genocide when referring to the slaughter of half a million Tutsis in Rwanda in case that triggered calls for intervention.

With one exception – UN intervention in the Congo in 1961 – the UN remained unwilling to do anything before fighting actually erupted and was equally reluctant to deal with internal or civil wars. The watershed came in 1991, when UN Security Council Resolution 688 authorised the operation to alleviate the plight of the Kurds in northern Iraq. The UN determined that the suffering of the Kurds, and their northward flight into Turkey, threatened international peace and security. As one authority has commented, 'The phrase "threat to the peace" is the magic formula that allows the UN Security Council to overcome the restriction of Article 2(7).'[26] Resolutions 770, authorising UN military protection for humanitarian convoys in Bosnia, and 794, authorising similar action in Somalia, followed.

In the case of the Congo, the first three Security Council resolutions stopped short of finding any 'threat to peace', even though they formed the basis for deploying troops. The Congolese government's invitation was enough. Only in the fourth resolution, following the murder of the Prime Minister and losses among the UN force, did the UN consider the danger of widespread civil war and bloodshed a threat to international peace and security and authorise the UN command to use force to prevent civil war.[27]

With that single exception, it was not until 1991 that the paradigm began to change, permitting intervention in the domestic affairs of a state which would have been unthinkable five years earlier. The UN took action where there was no existing government, in Somalia; where the 'legitimate' government was too weak to be effective, in Bosnia; or where the existing, still strong government refused to recognise the scale of the emergency which was spilling over its borders, in Iraq.

Yet it is more complicated than that. Michael Ignatieff has pointed out the similarity between intervention, under the UN umbrella, to influence events in somewhere like Bosnia, and the 'white man's burden' of the colonial era. Joseph Conrad's 1898 novella *Heart of Darkness*, reveals the same sense of 'moral outrage' at other people's 'savage customs' that arguably led to the UN intervention in Bosnia. In the book, Kurtz, who set off into the African jungle in search of ivory, is entrusted with making a report to the Society for the Suppression of Savage Customs. He believes that the 'civilised' races must 'necessarily appear to them [savages] in the nature of supernatural beings'. He continues: 'By the simple exercise of our will we can exert a power for good practically unbounded.'[28]

There is a terrifying similarity with the motivation felt by many of us who were involved in the Bosnian operation from 1992. At first, it seemed to work. The white knights of the UN were the only guarantee of law and order in a lawless land. They prevented several massacres, and maintained a kind of moral authority through impartiality and superior technology. But they could not fool all of the people forever, and it soon became obvious they were not invulnerable. The locals started taking pot shots. Peacekeepers started dying. When the first British armour headed up the road into central Bosnia in autumn, 1992, the local Croats cheered, because they thought they were going to fight the Serbs. When it became clear they were not, they started throwing stones.

And when it went wrong, when it became obvious there were no 'good guys' and 'bad guys', the sentiment, in Conrad's words, 'blazed at you, luminous and terrifying, like a flash of lightning in a serene sky. "Exterminate all the brutes!"' Or, in Bosnia, perhaps, 'Let the brutes exterminate each other.'

The question of motivation remains: had this intervention been purely selfless, or had some national interest – the desire for international prestige, to 'punch above our weight' – not played a part?

The world post-1989 is coping with the breakdown of two groups of empires; namely, the European empires in Asia and Africa, and the Soviet empire – including other Communist states. The breakdown of the

Soviet or Communist empire in turn raises the ghosts of earlier imperial entities – the Habsburg, Ottoman and Russian empires. Western intervention in the post-1989 period has striven, consciously or otherwise, to eschew imperial undertones. The interventions in the 'New World Order' in Bosnia, Somalia, Kurdistan and Rwanda were all motivated by the need *to do something*, as an act not of self-interest but of conscience.

To be fair, the first of these new-world-order interventions, in Kurdistan, attempted to avoid seizing territory on the ground and limited itself to providing air cover and aid to the Kurds, to enable them to help themselves. In Somalia the need to ensure a quick exit precluded the establishment of control over the country. In Bosnia, the UN constantly resisted the temptation to move in seriously, to secure aid routes and defend 'safe areas'. The military insisted that much larger forces would be required to perform these tasks: the political will to provide them was not there.

Ignatieff sums up the dilemma:

> What else but imperial arrogance could have led anyone to assume that any outside power – even one mandated by the international community – could have gone into Somalia, put an end to factional fighting and then exited, all within months? Who but a European or an American could have believed that the simple 'exercise of our will' could have stopped the Yugoslav catastrophe? Was our intervention there not coloured by an imperial hubris which believes we have the right to spread civility and civilisation among the sub-rational zones of the world?[29]

The idea of using force to spread 'civility and civilisation' to people who, by definition, were outside the inner circle of global power politics would have been anathema to Clausewitz. He did not live in the era of global telecommunications, when news reports could influence public opinion and, both in parallel and in turn, government policy. Dag Hammarskjöld, the second UN Secretary-General, recognised this change, welcoming what he called 'the final, least tangible but perhaps most important new factor in diplomacy: mass public opinion as a living force in international affairs.'[30]

Mass public opinion needs the media to fan it. The extent to which media coverage has stimulated intervention in other people's wars has been a subject for considerable study and debate. Although others may disagree, the intervention of western forces in Kurdistan, Bosnia and Somalia was probably driven to a considerable extent by press coverage, leading to public outrage and demands that 'something must be done'. The circumstances in which the media operate in crisis areas reinforce this tendency. The Bosnian Muslims and the Chechens tolerated the intrusive presence of the media because they believed that coverage would bring their plight to the world's notice and thus bring assistance. In contrast, the twenty-year conflict in East Timor, which began in 1975, and the long-running war in Sri Lanka since the Tamil revolt of 1982, which have both accounted for a massive number of deaths, have not been subject to the same demands. That is partly due to their remoteness and the comparative lack of news coverage. In the case of East Timor, the Indonesians actually killed five reporters to stop them getting their film out and thus alerting the world to the Indonesian invasion.[31]

At the time of writing this book, there is no clear consensus about whether we are entitled to intervene, when it is appropriate to do so, and what form our intervention should take. We are on the fault line between a world populated by nation states, each of which ultimately pursues its own interest, and a global society in which power is dispersed between multinational authorities like the European Union, embracing nation states and subjugating them, and multinational corporations, which undermine them from within.

The time may have come for the imposition of internationally agreed norms of behaviour by the UN or some similar body. But such a body cannot intervene on a subjective basis, driven solely by the amount of news coverage a particular crisis or atrocity has generated. Like the law which imposes certain commonly accepted standards in society – which tries to prevent people abusing their children or relatives, for example, even within the privacy of their own home – international law needs to be clear on what is and is not acceptable, and to set out criteria for intervention. But, as with law in the community, prescriptive international law is to a large extent dependent on the ability to enforce it. The Victorians had far fewer policemen and no social workers. Therefore, the authorities waited until people screamed for help, created a public affray, or someone was killed before intervening.

Internal and External Wars, and 'Failed' or 'Weak States'

The UN's historic preoccupation with international conflict stands in stark contrast to the reality of the modern world in which most conflicts are 'primarily internal' or 'internal with external intervention'. In the 265 years between 1720 and 1985, 230 of 654 recorded conflicts worldwide

were primarily internal and 164 'conventional interstate'. Since the end of
World War II internal conflicts – either those which stay internal or
those in which people intervene from outside – have killed most people.
However, World Wars I and II together account for an estimated 55 per
cent of all deaths attributable to war in the quarter millennium since
1720, suggesting that, for all its faults, the UN is right to attach top
priority to avoiding World War III, whether or not it has a nuclear
component.

Whereas a Third World War is looking increasingly unlikely, population growth and global warming – both of which will push more people
across international boundaries – are definitely happening.

Since World War II, wars have become increasingly ill-defined,
particularly internal conflicts where there is usually no formal notice of
the start or end. A thorough survey of conflicts in progress carried out by
the Canadian Department of Defense in 1985 showed that there was a
marked decline in the length of conflicts from 1800 to 1950, followed by
a reversal of the trend since. The Canadian team believed this was due to
the onset of a number of 'apparently endless' internal conflicts concerned
with the devolution of power in the post-colonial period, a trend which
has undoubtedly been enhanced by the break-up of the Soviet and
Communist empire after 1989.[32]

During the Cold War the main issue in preserving peace was the
maintenance of stability between states. Indeed, the same could be said of
the preceding 170 years, back to the end of the Napoleonic Wars. The
end of the Cold War saw the break-up of the alliances and partnerships
which had held the international system together, bringing new and often
weak states into the arena. The recognition of Bosnia as a nation state
before the Sarajevo government's authority over its diverse population
was established compounded the dilemma. 'Weak' or 'failed' states are
susceptible to ethnic and religious tension, secession and straightforward
banditry.[33] It is such failed states, including Somalia and Bosnia, and
attempts at secession – as in Chechnya – which are likely to be the main
areas of conflict for many decades to come. There will be even more
internal wars than there have been.

Revolutions in Warfare – and Peacemaking

'Revolutions in warfare' fascinate military historians. Clausewitz and
Jomini codified the change brought about by Napoleon, involving the
mobilisation of larger numbers of troops, changed tactics, and the

prosecution of war with greater determination and more uncompromising objectives. Yet all these changes were more complex and less
instantaneous than they seem at first. A popular image of the changes
associated with Napoleon includes the replacement of long thin lines of
troops with dense columns. Lines meant that more of the available
firepower could be brought to bear on the enemy, but required long
service soldiers to be immaculately drilled and disciplined so they could
maintain them on a battlefield. Columns were suitable for less well-
trained troops. Yet the French Royal Army had experimented with such a
change in the 1770s. The use of 'light infantry' – skirmishers – deployed
in loose formations ahead of the main body of troops to soften up the
enemy battle line was also an eighteenth-century innovation. And the
armies which, in the end, defeated Napoleon used old-fashioned tactics –
notably the British.

New ideas whizz around for a long time before somebody pulls them
all together. And things overlap. The development of an efficient tactical
system based on the English longbow in the early fourteenth century, for
example, drew on earlier campaigns against the Welsh and Scots, and
reached its full deployment on the battlefield at the same time as the first
guns, which were around from 1326. It was another two hundred years
before firearms usurped the position of the bow on the battlefield. The
consummate sailing ships, the tea clippers, reached perfection in the
1860s, well after the appearance of steam, and so on.

Revolutions in warfare therefore have much in common with revolutions in science, the subject of Thomas Kuhn's famous work on *The
Structure of Scientific Revolutions*.[34] The history of science, like that of war
and peace, is permeated by a number of apparent leaps or revolutions.
Kuhn argued that these were not usually the exclusive work of the person
whose name is associated with them: Copernicus in astronomy, Einstein
or Newton in physics, for example. Nor do they take place instantane-
ously. Rather, they are what Kuhn calls paradigms. A paradigm is a state
of mind – a 'mind-set', if you will – that embodies a whole package of
theories, practices, procedures and laws. It is the dominant theory and
institutionalised practice within the relevant scientific and professional
community.

Even then, the old paradigm may still be more useful as a 'rule of
thumb' in certain conditions. Kuhn uses the example of the change from
Newtonian to Einsteinian theory. As long as bodies concerned are
moving fairly slowly – compared with the velocity of light, that is – then
Newtonian physics still provides a useful approximation. Only when they

start whizzing around at great speed does Einstein's theory, with its emphasis on the velocity of light, start making a great difference.[35]

We have already touched on one new paradigm: the change of attitude towards intervention in states' internal affairs, after the 343 years between the Peace of Westphalia and UN Resolution 688. Like all paradigms, it is complex: a mixture of changed views on the meaning of international law and more emotive feelings of 'moral disgust'. The emergence of a supra-national authority which may intervene in states' internal affairs, combined with the decline of the nation state as the only political authority and the one most associated with recourse to war, is a paradigm change which clearly dwarfs the revolutions in warfare of preceding centuries.

A brief summary of those earlier revolutions may be helpful at this point. The Napoleonic 'revolution in warfare' had most to do with the *levée en masse* – the idea of making more of the population liable for military service. It had little to do with technology – unless the earlier, modest improvements in artillery associated with the eighteenth-century French designer Gribeauval are counted. Subsequent revolutions in warfare – new paradigms – are invariably associated with technology, and the way political and military thinkers and society responded to them. The next was the 'mid-nineteenth century revolution', which led to World War I. The advent of steam power on land and sea was central, leading to the kind of land strategy exploited by Helmuth von Moltke (1800–1891) and Alfred von Schlieffen (1833–1913), and by Mahan at sea. But communications – the telegraph and then the telephone – and a range of improvements to weapons were also contributary factors in a dramatic change of paradigm. Hard on its heels came the next revolution, which centred on the petrol engine, on land and in the air, and the wireless, which led to the form of war commonly called blitzkrieg. Then came the nuclear weapon: an exponential increase in firepower. All these paradigm changes overlapped. It is often argued, for example, that nuclear weapons made effective the kind of air strategy that earlier thinkers had dreamed of. Finally came the 'rotary wing' revolution – the helicopter; the introduction of precision-guided weapons and extremely accurate means of navigation; and modern information technology. The last four – helicopters, precision-guided weapons, knowing where you are, and information technology – have all overlapped with our new and greater paradigm change: the disappearance of a single, identifiable 'threat' and the emergence of a supra-national authority potentially able to promote or enforce peace.

The successive revolutions in military affairs, up to and including the appearance of nuclear weapons, while interesting, all ran in the same direction. They focused attention more and more on absolute or total war, making wars bigger, bloodier, more expensive and more destructive. There is one arguable exception to this: the development of aircraft.

The conquest of the air was initially hijacked in the service of total war, but it had greater potential than that. In the inter-war period, air power was used for imperial policing, demonstrating how aircraft could monitor and possibly control vast areas far more economically than would otherwise have been possible. The 1948 Berlin airlift showed the capacity of air transport to keep people supplied in ways and over territory that would have been impossible before. Recent military and aid operations have been heavily – sometimes almost exclusively – dependent on the delivery of supplies by air.

There was another significant adjunct to the development of air transport: it meant that negotiators – soldiers, diplomats and politicians – could move about far more rapidly than previously. Neville Chamberlain's infamous return flight from Munich in 1938 was an early and perhaps inglorious example. But US envoy Richard Holbrooke's negotiations with representatives of three sides in the Bosnian Civil War in 1995 would have been unthinkable without a worldwide network of airlines and airports. Shuttle diplomacy had arrived.

Theory and Practice

The first known attempt to formulate a theory of war – a rational basis for the planning and conduct of operations, but distinct from transitory changes in technique – was *The Art of War* by Sun Tzu, believed to date from the period 400 to 320 BC. It is also probably the most timeless. It is possible the thirteen chapters of *The Art of War* were a collection of aphorisms from a number of adepts, but Samuel B. Griffith, the distinguished US Marine officer and Chinese scholar, believed that 'the originality, the consistent style, and the thematic development suggest that "The Thirteen Chapters" is not a compilation, but was written by a singularly imaginative individual who had considerable practical experience in war.'[36]

Sun Tzu believed that the acme of 'war' was to win without fighting, 'to subdue the enemy's army without engaging it, to take his cities without laying siege to them, and to overthrow his state without bloodying swords.' To take everything intact, or as near as possible, was the proper objective of strategy. Such a goal required sound planning based on the best possible intelligence. Sun Tzu was also the first authority to appreciate the effect of war on the economy, notably the way prices increased whenever military operations commenced.

Sun Tzu's aphorisms have been widely followed and adapted. His principles surface in Russian military doctrine, and with great frequency in the thoughts of Mao Tse-tung (1893–1976). In his first chapter, 'Estimates', he enunciates five principles: moral influence, weather, terrain, command and doctrine. The first is usually translated as 'The Way' or 'The Right Way', and in Sun Tzu it refers to the morality of government, specifically that of the sovereign. In international operations in our own time, it might refer to the 'moral authority' conferred on the UN. Weather includes the influence of the seasons, to which the Bosnian conflict, for example, has been particularly susceptible. Terrain means not just the sinuosities of the ground, but distance, and 'whether the ground is traversed with ease or difficulty, whether it is open or constricted, and the chances of life or death.'[37] Command, says Sun Tzu, refers to the general's qualities of wisdom, sincerity, humanity, courage and strictness. Doctrine embraces all aspects of organisation, administration, supply and what we call 'logistics'.

Because Sun Tzu laid special stress on achieving one's aim, if possible, without fighting, he is of particular relevance to us today. So, in the context of wider peacekeeping, are his comments on how an 'army'

> may be likened to water, for just as flowing water avoids the heights and hastens to the lowlands, so an army avoids strength and strikes weakness. And as water shapes its flow in accordance with the ground, so an army manages its victory in accordance with the situation of the enemy. And as water has no constant form, there are in war no constant conditions.[38]

This principle – 'going with the flow' – is especially relevant today in the context of wider peacekeeping and peacemaking, and anticipating demographic, geographical and climatic trends. Unless you are planning total war, it makes sense to follow the flow, rather than erect flimsy barriers against it.

Turning to the great military thinkers of modern times who thought in terms of strategy on land, Clausewitz remains the most universal. Jomini, who was considered far more important shortly afterwards, has far less to tell us now. Jomini lived longer, into the age when warfare was affected by the Industrial Revolution. Aware of a vast increase in firepower, he even anticipated the reappearance of armour protection on the battlefield.[39] Whereas Clausewitz believed that 'civilised' armies tended to develop technologically at the same rate, Jomini survived into an era when it started to become clear that technological advantage could be decisive. But Clausewitz's philosophical approach has given his work longevity. He did not go in for prescriptive writing, for concise aphorisms to be followed as rules. Nor was he as elliptical and rarefied as Sun Tzu. He followed a process enshrined in the German educational system: examine every highway and by-way of the argument. He furnishes questions, rather than answers. Enigmatic, brilliant, incomplete, essential – that is Clausewitz.

Until the end of the nineteenth century, there was no naval strategy comparable with the works of land strategists. That is probably because the art of navigation at sea in the age of sail was so complex in itself, and so uncertain. 'It was not possible for the admiral to convert his distances into days,' wrote Mahan, 'as the general did into so many marches. Nelson, in pursuit, beat furiously against a west wind, while 200 miles away, the fleeing Villeneuve [the French admiral whom Nelson defeated at Trafalgar in 1805] sped by Gibraltar before an easterly gale. Land warfare knew vicissitudes enough, but there was no such perpetual disconcerting uncertainty as this.'[40]

The introduction of steam and other forms of artificial power made possible the evolution of naval strategy and principles of sea war. It rapidly became clear that naval operations unfolded on a vastly greater canvas than those of armies. And whereas armies seized their key positions as part of their wartime operations, naval bases were generally acquired in peacetime. Naval strategy, as Mahan wrote,

> differs from military strategy, in that it is as necessary in peace as in war. Indeed, in peace it may gain its most decisive victories by occupying in a country, either by purchase or treaty, excellent positions which would perhaps hardly be got in war. It learns to profit by all opportunities of settling on some chosen point of a coast . . .[41]

The possibility of concentrating fleets before the outbreak of hostilities, and the fact that their concentration, unlike that of armies, did not of itself initiate hostilities, gave naval warfare a subtlety and flexibility unknown on shore. Naval strategy bridged the gap between war and peace, partly because of its interrelationship with trade and commerce. Generals were worried about their own supplies, but not usually anyone else's. The use of troops to escort 'humanitarian aid' nowadays is another example of how operations on land may be approaching the traditional paradigms of naval warfare more closely.

Ships were also inherently more mobile than men and horses on land, able to carry several months' provisions, and weapons and ammunition which would have been relatively immobile, if not unthinkable on shore. Naval war also had an unforgiving totality. A duel between capital ships was 'kill or be killed' writ large. Navies' principal units – ships, nuclear submarines, or whatever – were always the peak of technological achievement of the time, and represented a concentration of national power unparalleled in any other medium. Admiral Sir John Fisher's famous comment that he, as commander-in-chief of the British fleet at the start of World War I, was the only man who 'could lose the war in an afternoon' summarises it perfectly. Naval strategy was the nearest the pre-nuclear age knew to nuclear strategy.

Unlike an army unit in barracks, a warship at sea is ready for war. The combination of perpetual readiness for war, even in time of 'peace', the enormous value of naval units and their prominence as highly visible chunks of sovereign territory, gave naval commanders a peculiar authority. As Nelson said, 'a naval officer must have *political* courage'.[42]

We have already seen the similarity between the changes and quantum leaps in the science of war and peace and those in natural science. The first military theorists of the modern, western world, Clausewitz and Jomini, expressed themselves in terms of the science of their day – Newtonian science. They talked of 'mass' and 'momentum', of 'force'. A scan of Clausewitz's chapter headings reveals titles like 'the maximum exertion of strength'. Jomini, more than Clausewitz, was highly geometrical, with his emphasis on 'lines of operations'. Their military science, like Newtonian science, was linear, though it was not purely mechanical. The psychological and moral factor was always there, but it was expressed in terms of the physics of the time.

Just compare Clausewitz's mechanical, Enlightenment terminology with the ancient writing of Sun Tzu, whose work, as one might expect from a more distant time, is filled with similes from nature:

> When campaigning, be swift as the wind; in leisurely march, majestic as the forest; in raiding and plundering, like fire; in standing, firm as the mountains. As unfathomable as the clouds. Move like a thunderbolt.[43]

The linear quality of scientific thought and expression remained appropriate right up to the Cold War, for which it proved particularly well suited, as there was only one 'threat'. The equation was almost one-dimensional. The 'threat' was this strong – therefore we needed that amount of strength to meet it.

However, the equation was not always that simple, and the linear approach had its limitations. Without an 'enemy', it was difficult to plan. Even in the inter-war period (1918–39), British military planning had to cope with the prospect of unforeseen problems developing around the world, which for much of the period was more of a risk than a resurgent Germany. In 1932, the Kirke Report, into the lessons of World War I, was candid. 'At present the enemy cannot be defined and this absence of a basis to the problem adds enormously to the difficulties of its solution.'[44]

If the potential 'enemy' could not be defined then, it is utterly impossible today. It is now commonly accepted that the world is a chaotic place. The new sciences of chaos and complexity accept that complex systems have their own, self-determining evolution, and interact as well. Ecological systems – including the weather, anthills, beehives, the human brain and nervous system, and increasingly complex man-made systems like computer networks – are obvious examples.[45]

A modern science of war and peace needs to be modelled on chaos and complexity. The world is a messy place, and is not susceptible to a few self-evident simple laws. Computers can model chaos and complexity in a way that mathematical calculations cannot. It was the development of computers, and computer graphics, that permitted images and predictions of chaos to be made. Computers have been used to model the flow of forces on a battlefield for years, and the evolving digital battlefield – where information passes up and down the chain of command and from side to side – will also permit more accurate models of the dynamics of a military clash to be made. But that is the simple part: a refinement of the mechanical clash of armies, with their mass, momentum and centres of gravity. Sophisticated computers take us much further, permitting us to model the complex interaction of parties in a many-sided conflict, where force is not used with freedom.

Actors and Factors

Clausewitz and Jomini lived in an age when natural resources were perceived to be infinite. Clausewitz probably did not have much of an idea of a 'future' which was technologically different. Jomini lived long enough to begin wrestling with the idea. But neither of them expected factors outside their familiar, civilised world of strong nation states to impose themselves on human societies. Military theory could afford the luxury of office politics. The bitter winds, floods and earthquakes of new factors – environmental change, population growth – and perhaps new actors – states able to rival the established European powers – were not expected to impinge on the deliberate use of military power as a tool of state policy. The rise of Japan in the nineteenth century, and the way its military power was grossly underestimated, first by the Russians before 1904 and then by the British between the World Wars, is a clear example of how contemporary strategists were not fully prepared for the appearance of a new actor.

Clausewitz and Jomini, like all those who wrote about war and politics until recently, were dealing only with human actors: 'war is an act of policy to compel our enemy to do our will . . .' But as the twentieth century nears its end, the actors are complicated by new factors, possibly beyond the immediate control of nation states. Clausewitz and Jomini, Corbett and Mahan, Moltke and Schlieffen; the theorists of the petrol revolution, Major General John Fuller (1878–1966) and Basil Liddell Hart; and even the theorists of guerrilla and nuclear warfare, could all confine security problems to those arising from more or less deliberate decisions by people.

In the 1990s refugee movements have become a key security issue, to a greater extent than at any time, perhaps, since the waves of 'invasions' (in fact, prolonged migrations) of Huns, Avars, Magyars, Angles, Saxons and Danes of the first millennium. Population growth, pressure on resources and the loss of large, densely populated coastal areas to a rising ocean will produce external pressures on human society, unknown to the minds of the Enlightenment and the nineteenth-century Industrial Revolution, and will create new security problems, regardless of political will. Few of these new problems require a response that is predominantly military, in the traditional sense. And yet they have military connotations, and the military is well attuned to dealing with large-scale problems in the open air. The more delicate and finely tuned world of the present Industrial Revolution – the Information Revolution – will have to cope with these challenges to security, which are profoundly greater and more complex than anything faced by military strategists before.

CHAPTER TWO
TO THE EDGE OF
ARMAGEDDON

Every summer, a military display is held in London, called the Royal Tournament. Each year, there is an underlying theme, as well as acts by units of the various British services and guests from foreign armed forces – motorcycle stunt teams, RAF police dogs, displays and music evoking foreign military traditions, and so on. A couple of years before this book was completed, I was invited to the headquarters of the Household Cavalry Regiment in Knightsbridge barracks for a preview of the Tournament for that year. The star attraction was the Four Horsemen of the Apocalypse, described in the Book of Revelation and brought to life that year by a renowned theatrical designer. The four horses – the white horse of conquest, the red horse of war, the black horse of famine, which follows war, and the pale horse of pestilence and death – were ridden by cavalrymen concealed in spectacular costumes.

'The new world order, I suppose?'

But that was not the idea. The four horsemen, the Tournament's patron explained, appeared as harbingers of Armageddon. The idea was that we had been on the edge of Armageddon, as the Cold War had reached its most active phase, but that the lessening of east-west tension, the collapse of Communism, and the conclusion of nuclear and conventional arms treaties, had drawn us back from the brink.

The four horsemen then trotted out into Hyde Park, causing motorists to screech to a halt in astonishment. So, we had come that close to Armageddon. But they were not a bad image for the new world order, either.

The ride to Armageddon had begun 180 years before. Waterloo was not the culminating land battle of the Napoleonic Wars. That battle had taken place nearly two years before, from 16 to 19 October, 1813, at Leipzig. In the 'Battle of the Nations', half a million men – 300,000

Russians, Austrians, Prussians and Swedes on one side and 200,000 on the other, led by Napoleon, converged in a battle on a scale not to be repeated for a hundred years. Napoleon was nearly surrounded and crushed in a trap, but slipped out to the west, having lost 80,000 men to the Allies' 50,000. The very scale of the engagement prevented one side gaining a decisive grip on the other, to use Clausewitz's analogy of two wrestlers, and in that sense also Leipzig was a vision of the future. It was probably Leipzig that Clausewitz had most in mind when he imagined the phenomenon of absolute war. He was there as a staff officer and observer, thereby gaining the necessary experience and knowledge to write the crucial chapters of *On War*. In the interim, he had recalled how that summer a decisive clash between nations-in-arms had threatened to engulf Europe:

> By revolutionary methods the French had burned away the old concept of war as if with acid. They unleashed the terrible power of war from its former confines. Now it moved in its naked form, dragging massive force with it . . . However, a new system of war was yet to be clearly perceived. War was handed back to the people, from whom it had been taken away in part, by the use of select, standing armies . . . Now war had thrown off its shackles. That was all that could be understood of this new development. What would be built upon this broader and firmer basis would only become apparent little by little.[1]

The age of 'Cabinet wars', waged by governments and armies, in which nations took part only insofar as they were directly affected by the presence of troops nearby, had passed. The Napoleonic Wars put quite different national forces into the field, but although an expert like Clausewitz could see the way things were going, warfare had not yet assumed an 'abstract' or 'absolute' character. Most of the subsequent wars of the nineteenth century actually reverted to an earlier type. The Franco-British expedition to the Crimea was more like an eighteenth-century excursion. The great battles of Magenta and Solferino between the French and Austrians in 1859 were Napoleonic battles fought with rifled ordnance, and in the American Civil War of 1861–65, as Engels noted, men resigned 'themselves to the fate of the big battles'.[2] But the American Civil War became a total war, and the first great industrial war, to boot. Europe saw nothing like it until 1914. As Field Marshal Ludendorff later wrote in his book on total war,

> the wars of 1866 and 1870 had not yet brought any real knowledge

concerning the nature of warfare, although in France the war under Gambetta [1838–82, who continued the struggle after the French armies were defeated in the field in 1870], had assumed forms which showed that the nation itself was being involved in the struggle, and an energy was displayed which we had not previously been accustomed.[3]

In Germany, warfare remained an Army affair: as Ludendorff said, Germany 'had not yet set itself free from the doctrines of Clausewitz with regard to the nature and essence of warfare.' Such tendencies had been apparent in 1814, as the Prussian and Russian generals pressed towards Paris, bent on revenge, and keen to take political and diplomatic decisions. Gneisenau said he would blow up the Arc de Triomphe if he reached Paris first. Clausewitz felt much the same, but later came to believe they were wrong and criticised military leaders who overstepped the proper boundaries of their role.[4]

Meanwhile, something else was happening. In 1830, the London and Manchester railway carried a regiment of soldiers 34 miles in two hours. It would have taken soldiers of the time two days to march that distance. Two years later, General Lamarque told the French chamber of deputies that the strategic use of railways would lead to 'a revolution in military science as great as that which had been brought about by the invention of gunpowder'.[5] In the same year the wireless telegraph was invented. Armies could move up to twenty times as fast as they had been able to and communicate almost instantly.

The first use of railways to move troops operationally was in 1849, when a Russian corps was moved from Warsaw to Vienna, which was being threatened by Hungarian rebels. The first large-scale use of railways in concert with military operations occurred in 1859, when both the French and Austrians moved forces into northern Italy by rail and, fully aware of their strategic importance, attacked each other's railway lines and bridges.[6] The railway, and then other forms of mechanical transport, would affect strategy profoundly.

Quality versus Quantity

During the nineteenth century a system of universal military service – 'conscription' – was introduced in all the major developed countries except Britain and the United States. All the young manpower of the nation, apart from those with obvious medical conditions, was liable for military service. With some exceptions – university students, for example – men were called up for a period with the regular forces and then remained liable for recall as a member of the reserve for a further period. The last great power – apart from Britain and the United States – to adopt such a system was Russia, in 1874. Once one nation, France, had adopted conscription, everyone else (apart from the British, who retained an abhorrence of the idea of compulsory service) had to follow suit or be colossally outnumbered. The aim was a straightforward military one: in war, numbers matter. The only way of getting numbers at reasonable cost was to force people to become soldiers at miserable rates of pay. But the system also blended well with the increased power of the nation state and its increased interference in the lives of its people. National service was also seen as a 'school for the nation', and an extension of the education system, which also became compulsory during this period. A further period of harsh discipline, mixed with occasional first forays into the pleasures of adult life, was an ideal way of producing a compliant populace. Such a system still exists in many European countries today, although the recent decisions by France – where conscription originated – to end it is a further indication of the fundamental changes we are witnessing.

Conscription was, and is, primarily a means of getting armed forces at reasonable cost. But many people believed – and still believe – it had other benefits for the state. Teenagers are not fully developed physically. People over the age of about twenty are more robust, and some countries did not conscript people until they reached that age. Young people between eighteen and their early twenties can learn quickly, are physically active, rebellious, but not particularly productive in real jobs. Conversely, you do not want to take older people, who are becoming expert in their occupations, and starting families, to be soldiers, except to recall them in time of dire national emergency. Before population growth became the security issue it is now, lack of population growth was seen as more of a military problem. Nations wanted people to breed – but not to start too soon. If you want cannon fodder, school leavers are the people you can most easily afford to lose.

These armies were led by short-service officers, selected on the basis of educational attainment, or from 'white collar' or professional jobs. The higher command and general staff was, generally speaking, the preserve of professional soldiers, who opted for a military career at an early age. The divide between conscript and regular further influenced the development of a distinct and élite general staff corps in certain countries – notably Germany.

The combination of big, short-service conscript armies and lines of movement anchored to railways created a dilemma for military strategists. Surely, some reasoned, this would bring about a decline in the art of war. Armies would not be able to manoeuvre as artfully as they had: they would be like 'rams', colliding on utterly predictable courses down the railway lines. The movement and concentration of future armies, wrote one Russian officer, 'will require more time. Every wrong direction, every mistake, will take longer to correct. In a word, there will be a definite slowing down in the development of all strategic operations.'[7]

Such a view had been widespread since the 1850s. Karl Marx wrote that the siege of Sevastopol in 1854 had been

> striking proof of the fact that, in the same proportion as the *matériel* of warfare has, by industrial processes, advanced during the long peace, in the same proportion has the art of war degenerated. A Napoleon, on seeing the batteries before Sevastopol, bristling with eight- and ten-inch guns, would burst out in a fit of irresistible laughter.[8]

By the 1890s, some professional soldiers were arguing that the size of armies would have to be capped, along the lines of civilian industry where fewer but more highly skilled workers were being employed. Otherwise, the 'art of war' would decline and it would be impossible to attain the previous 'artistry' in operations.[9] Others, like the Russian Captain Martynov, said that was nonsense. Mass armies existed and – like nuclear weapons today – could not be disinvented. Nations were not interested 'in the purity of strategic art, but in military *success*', said Martynov. A return to small, highly professional armies was 'completely impossible'.[10] Nations wanted to win and if that meant driving million-strong armies down fixed railway lines then so be it. Others were more optimistic: the technological changes that had produced these massive military instruments could also improve their control. 'New, powerful factors – electricity and steam, which have increased the contemporary army to colossal dimensions' wrote the Russian Chief of the General Staff, 'can increase the power of the commander correspondingly.'[11]

The renowned futurist H. G. Wells wrote about the same issue before the First World War. He contrasted the 'enormous defensive power of small, scientifically, handled bodies of men' with the huge conscript armies which were 'made up not of masses of military muscle but of a huge proportion of military fat ... Modern weapons and modern contrivances are continually decreasing the number of men who can be employed efficiently on a length of front.'[12] He believed modern war had created a need for men who were 'animated and individualised' and the 'intelligent handling of weapons so elaborate and destructive that great masses of men in the field are an encumbrance rather than a power.'[13]

Britain was in a profoundly different position to other European countries. National security rested primarily on the Navy: continental land expeditions were in the nature of the 'wars of choice' of today. Between 1800 and 1812 expenditure on the Royal Navy consumed between a quarter and a fifth of the nation's entire annual budget. In 1800 it also represented one third of Britain's entire war expenditure, including subsidies to allies.[14]

By the mid-nineteenth century a historic distrust of standing armies in Britain had been reinforced by a laissez-faire ideology which rendered the idea of compulsory service unacceptable. However, Britain's decision not to adopt conscription also rested partly on the peculiar requirements of British imperial defence. Maintaining overseas garrisons called for a steady flow of long-term volunteers, since it would be inefficient to send conscripts because by the time they had been trained and shipped out to distant parts their short period of service would be about to expire. The French had conscription to provide for European wars but, in an interesting variant of the British system, relied on the Foreign Legion – foreign volunteers with French officers – to provide for some overseas garrisons.

Defending the British Empire was therefore mainly the Navy's responsibility, with the Army weighing in at a quarter of a million men at the end of the nineteenth century, equivalent to a small Balkan state. Of these, 75,000 were in India. When an emergency erupted in South Africa in 1899, Britain was hard pressed to cope. A system which had been stretched to maintain peacetime garrisons in the colonies was brought to breaking point by the demands of what was, by the standards of the time, a 'major regional conflict'. Volunteer, militia and yeomanry units were all mobilised to back up the regular army, relying on a combination of patriotic fervour and poverty to attract middle-class volunteers and regular recruits from the slums. Of the potential recruits, half did not meet the medical and physical standards required – the same proportion as today, for different reasons. The cost of the war came as a profound shock to the Conservative government. In 1898–99 total defence spending was £44 million: in 1900–01 it was £95 million.[15]

The years between the Boer War and 1914 saw Haldane's army reforms, which created a superbly efficient British regular army but did not solve the problem of providing enough reserves – territorials and volunteers – to back it up in the event of a first-division continental war or to defend Britain against invasion when most of the regular army had been sent to the continent. There were a number of serious proposals to bring in compulsory service. In 1912, for example, it was reported that the general staff wanted a two-year period of compulsory service and an army of half a million to fight in Europe.[16] Nevertheless, the voluntary principle remained dominant through the first two years of the Great War until 1916.

Many British politicians had believed Britain's role in the next continental war would be primarily naval and financial, with the decision on land secured by the French and Russian armies, although there was general support for the deployment of the British Expeditionary Force as a small but significant reinforcement on the left of the French armies.

The collision between the advancing German conscript columns and the highly professional British regular infantry at Mons in 1914 is part of the folklore of military history. The unwieldy, conscript 'ram' rolled towards the small, professional force, described as a 'contemptible' little army. The British force, whose eyesight must have been better than that of modern soldiers, opened fire over iron sights at 900 yards – though the targets were columns, not individuals. Corpses in field-grey uniforms piled up on the canal bank. The British had exacted a grievous toll on the Germans. But eventually, as the 'quantity versus quality' theorists of the 1890s had predicated, the heavier combatant prevailed, and the British began to withdraw.

What happened next is less well known. The phrase 'contemptible' referred to the small size of the British force, but some German officers took it another way. The British Army were professionals. Therefore, as Kaiser Wilhelm decided, they were 'mercenaries from the slums'. British prisoners were to be treated 'with the utmost severity'. After Mons, a German officer reported his men as beating British prisoners to death.[17] British prisoners were singled out from the more numerous French and Russians, who, like the Germans, were mainly conscripts.

Exceptional brutality towards the 'mercenaries' continued through the first battle of Ypres, when captured British troops fully expected to be shot. The antipathy towards a professional army lasted throughout the war, and was reinforced by the British approach to total war: a naval blockade to starve Germany into submission. The British prisoners were worked particularly hard, and after the war, out of an estimated 140,000 British prisoners taken by the Germans, 22,000 – one sixth – did not return, having died in German custody from disease and ill-treatment.

Eighty years on, in 1995, the same thing happened in Chechnya, when a disparate new Russian Army took on the rebels. The Chechens seemed to treat the conscript prisoners well, but shot the 'professional' soldiers they captured – marines and airborne troops – out of hand.

The outbreak of the First World War led to a surge of volunteers, who formed the new 'Kitchener armies' of 1915. Social pressure on young men to enlist exercised a form of compulsion – men not in the forces for perceived 'legitimate reasons' wore a special armband with a crown to denote the fact. But reliance on volunteers could not survive the increased demands of what became, from 1916 to 1918, a true, total war. In 1916, compulsory service was introduced. Even then, there were anomalies. Some youngsters had lied about their age to enlist early, often at sixteen. Conversely, as men of forty with families died at the front, sixteen-year-old youths played uselessly on motorcycles at the seaside, to the annoyance of H. G. Wells.

The British Army's transition from a small, regular force to a formidable continental army (which, following the Russian revolutions and the French mutinies in 1917, and before the arrival of the Americans, took the major part in defeating Germany on land), is one of the most remarkable stories of military adaptation. It reflects the truth that the First World War, rather than the Second, was the defining watershed separating 'modern times' from what went before. Licensing laws, changing the clocks every spring and autumn, the emancipation of women, the right of the state to intervene and direct every aspect of people's lives, were all a function of the First World War. And the First World War, unlike anything known or imagined by Napoleon or Clausewitz, was 'total war'. Two of the empires which had started it – Russia and Austria-Hungary – destroyed themselves as a result.

'What made this war different from all others', wrote Field Marshal Ludendorff in 1935,

> was the manner in which the home populations supported and reinforced the Armed Forces. In this war it was impossible to distinguish where the sphere of the Army and Navy began and that of the people ended. Army and people were one. The world witnessed a war of Nations in the most literal sense of the word. In this mighty concentration of effort the great powers of Earth faced each other. And not only between the Armed Forces did the combat rage along those huge fronts and distant oceans. The moral and vital forces of the hostile populations were assailed for the purpose of corrupting and paralysing them.[18]

Ludendorff recognised how distinct this new and absolute form of war was. Clausewitz, he said, had 'touched neither on the necessity of the psychical solidarity of the nation nor on the importance of economic conditions for warfare.' Nor, he added, had Count von Schlieffen, author of the famous plan for Germany to outflank French forces at the opening of World War I, and a noted military theorist of the time. The Schlieffen Plan was compromised by reducing the strength of the right, attacking wing. What Ludendorff neglected to mention was that Schlieffen had demanded that if the quick-kill plan fail, Germany should at once seek a negotiated peace, and avoid the descent into total war.

Ludendorff recognised that colonial wars might also be total, for third-world peoples, if not for the colonial or colonising powers, for whom they were limited. In his view, the brief American intervention at the end of World War I was, for the United States, a 'colonial' expedition. That would not be true of the next war.

Ivan Bloch and Norman Angell – The Effect of War on the National and International Economy

Around the turn of the nineteenth century, two outstanding personalities addressed the possibility of a great war between the developed powers. Ivan Bloch (1836–1901) was a distinguished Warsaw economist, financier and statistician. At that time, Warsaw was part of the Russian Empire – indeed, as Karl Marx described it, the Empire's 'sword arm', sticking out between Austrian and Prussian territory.[19] The possible effect of a major war stimulated Bloch's interest in military questions, and he began to publish articles on the nature and consequences of a future great war in the early 1890s. The findings of the team which he directed (he certainly did not do all the work himself) were finally published in 1898.

Bloch's titanic, six-volume work, *Future War in its Technical, Economic and Political Relations*, has been widely taken out of context by people who have read the English translation of the final volume, *General Conclusions*, presciently titled *Is War Now Impossible?*[20] A common view is that Bloch, the civilian, predicted the character of the next war accurately while all the military got it wrong. That is quite untrue. In fact, Bloch's descriptions of the future battlefield are almost all drawn from contemporary military literature, and the references include numerous citations from French, German and Russian officers. These include eighteen German works on a possible German-Austrian-Russian war and eight by the most eminent Russian 'establishment' figures of the time, Generals Nikolay Mikhnevich and Henrikh Leyer. The Bloch study predicted a great, long war of entrenchments, prolonged battles, and appalling casualties.[21]

Bloch's well-researched views on technical matters and the nature of the future battlefield were not widely challenged by professional soldiers, although there is evidence of professional jealousy fuelled by anti-Semitism (Bloch was a Jew). Where Bloch got it really wrong was in his own area of economics. He assessed that in a protracted war, Russia, as an agricultural nation, less dependent on foreign trade and with a tougher, less 'excitable' population, would withstand the strain of war better than the more industrialised, urbanised nations. In fact Russia cracked first. Again, the erroneous idea that Russia (as the regime that entered the Great War) would last longest, rather than break first, was not peculiar to Bloch's team, but was proposed in another Russian book, *War and the Economy*, published in the same year, 1898.[22]

The Bloch study also noted the complex structure of international credit and trade, which made nations interdependent and therefore, it concluded, ensured that a prolonged war was unthinkable. If the developed nations fought each other for very long, they would all become bankrupt.[23] The same view was expounded by the noted British pacifist writer Sir Norman Angell (1872–1967), in his book *The Great Illusion*, first published in 1909.[24] Both Bloch and Angell were a little ahead of their time. Although the cost and destruction of the Great War and Second World War were incalculable, the combatant nations managed to survive for up to four years. This was partly because they drew on their own resources to an extent unthinkable before the First World War – which supports the argument that 'total war' really began in 1914–18. The fact that the United States was not involved in the Great War until 1917 also undoubtedly helped it consolidate its already vast economic strength and gain a dramatic advantage over Europe. In the Second World War, US war production, still safe from attack, created an industrial machine which guaranteed it economic hegemony for the best part of forty years after the war.

Yet now, nearly one hundred years on, Bloch and Angell's views have probably come to be true. Although there was much trading in stocks and shares during the early part of this century, the economies of the time did not depend, as ours does, on 'people opening doors for each other'. Making or growing things was still the main source of wealth. If anything, war stimulated that process. Furthermore, in both the First and Second World Wars, the United States formed a vast and unassailed reserve of wealth, to which the devastated nations could turn once peace was restored. That would not be the case in any future major war, while the computer systems on which the prosperity and day-to-day functioning of a modern nation depends are a soft target. Moreover, the international markets in 1914 or 1939 were primitive in the extreme compared with today. The fact that the American Stock Exchange crash of 1929 took so long to affect Europe illustrates the difference. Nowadays, international computer links and the internet ensure that the fates of Tokyo, Hong Kong, London and New York are intertwined – in a way that Ivan Bloch and Norman Angell could prophesy but not imagine. As with so many paradigms in the history of war and peace, the reality follows decades after the first theory.

Between Tactics and Strategy – the New Operational Level of War

For Clausewitz, armies moved strategically to a tactical fight. '*Tactics* teaches the use of armed forces in an engagement; *strategy*, the use of engagements for the object of the war.'[25] For thousands of years, this simple division of military art – or science – into two levels was fair enough. It was fine as long as armies or fleets spent most of their time in barracks, or port, or manoeuvring to meet each other under the most favourable circumstances. The way you fought a battle when you met the enemy was tactics. However, by the beginning of the twentieth century – most notably in the 1904–05 Russo-Japanese War – armies found themselves engaged for long periods, over long frontages. At Mukden, from 19 February to 10 March, 1905, for example, the battle extended over a 120 kilometre front and to a depth of 80 kilometres, over a period of twenty days. Inevitably, the battle broke up into a series of smaller engagements. Yet they were all linked by a common purpose and design, and aimed at the defeat of a single enemy army. They were not separate 'strategic' manoeuvres. The need for a new level between tactics and what had been called strategy became most obvious in World War I. Sir Douglas Haig, the British Commander-in-Chief in France, likened the entire western front experience to one gigantic, protracted four-year battle. Nonetheless, it would be absurd to call the conduct of this battle, tactics. It was aimed at the defeat of a single, large enemy force, and part of much wider strategic considerations, yet it united numerous, individual battles in one concept. It was something else. It was as a result of their experience in World War I that German military thinkers coined the term *operativ* – operational. The term 'strategy', they decided, should be limited to the most important measures of the High Command.[26]

However, it would be misleading to define the operational level purely in terms of increases in time and space, though those brought it into clearer focus. The operational level, freed from the most direct constraints and aims of the battlefield, was about concentrating on the will of the opponent, as Helmuth von Moltke the Elder (1800–91) recognised. The eminent British theorist, Major General John Fuller, defined it as 'grand tactics'. Minor tactics, he wrote, involved maximum physical destruction of the enemy at minimum cost. Grand tactics was about *mental* destruction: 'the battle between two plans, energised by two wills.'[27] Sun Tzu probably meant something similar when he said that 'what is of supreme importance in war is to attack the enemy's strategy.'[28]

There was another way of looking at the changed strata of conflict, however. Not only had battle itself changed, leading to the coordination of several tactical engagements, but strategy had also taken on a new meaning. The involvement of more and more of society – Ludendorff's 'total war' – and the involvement of coalitions of states had created a 'super strategy' or 'grand strategy'. Its aims could be couched primarily in economic or political terms. Mikhail Tukhachevskiy (1893–1937), one of the first five Marshals of the Soviet Union, proposed a different demarcation. Tukhacherskiy was a curious mixture: a former subaltern in the Imperial Guard, an aristocrat who made violins but planned to use chemical weapons against 'bandits' and had been converted to Communism, apparently, while in a German prison camp during the Great War. He was eventually executed, in Stalin's great purge. His proposal was for tactics, strategy (in its older sense) and 'polemostrategy' – war strategy or grand strategy – from the Greek *polemos*, a war.[29] The French strategist André Beaufre later proposed something similar – 'total strategy' – to cover a government's total approach to war in all its aspects.[30]

Tukhachevskiy's proposal did not find favour and from the late 1920s the then Soviet Union adopted the German terminology.[31] It was not until the early-to-mid 1980s that the Americans, and then the British, who were preoccupied with the Soviet Union as their most likely and formidable opponent, followed suit.

The last great military thinker of the era before the present revolution, and one whose ideas overlap with it, was Richard Simpkin (1921–86). He recognised that although the emergence of the operational level was intimately connected with the rise of twentieth-century large-scale and total war, it was not only relevant to that. He defined the operational level as the military operations having, as their aim, objectives lying 'at one remove only from an objective which could be couched in political or economic terms (in other words, from a strategic aim).'[32] In the context of modern operations, including 'wider peacekeeping', that is a good definition. And it is useful in helping to define where wider peacekeeping breaks down. In limited war, strategic aims might be achieved by small groups of special forces soldiers, hunting down some warlord, or by high precision weapons. Operational aims lie at one remove from that: in a struggle with the other party's will. As experience in Bosnia and Somalia shows, it is possible to use military force on a limited, local, *tactical* scale, without destroying overall consent at the higher level. That makes the dividing line between the two very important. The question is whether, in operations short of war, the higher level is operational – as in modern, conventional war – or strategic.

Planning for Protracted War

After the Armistice on 11 November 1918 and the botched intervention in Russia against the Bolshevik government, most of the great powers were happy to go along with the commonplace view that the 1914–18 conflict had been 'the war to end war'. Only in Soviet Russia was a combined military, industrial and economic plan put in place, from 1925, aimed at fighting and winning another great and protracted war. Tsarist Russia's collapse in 1917 was believed to have resulted from industrial and economic backwardness, as well as the corrupt aspects of the former regime. It would not happen again.[33]

Alexander Svechin (1878–1938), who had been a Major General in the Tsarist Army, emerged as one of the most important thinkers who would shape the conduct of total war. Abrasive and 'politically incorrect', he despised fashionable dogma and soon fell foul of the elfin and youthful Mikhail Tukhachevskiy.

Svechin's *Strategy*, first published in 1926, forged a vision of total war and the mobilisation of society, grimly presaging George Orwell's *Nineteen Eighty-Four*. War was not, as some liked to think (and the danger was never greater than in our own time, when people have grown used to surgical strikes and swift victories) a 'medicine for the State's internal illness'. It was 'a serious examination of the health of its internal politics'. Wars would be long.

The Interior Ministry must have its own mobilisation plan, which must take the steps necessary to maintain firm order in national territory during the time when huge masses are torn away from their work in the country to proceed to collection points to flesh out the armies, and the population of the towns doubles, to meet the needs of war industry. The crisis created by these population movements will be compounded by enemy propaganda, sharpened by the activities of enemies of the current regime, by the hopes which individual ethnic groups and classes will entertain as the ruling classes grow weary under the impositions of war. Order must be maintained along lines of communications, account taken of all dubious elements of society . . . special, ultra-reliable internal security units must be brought in or else the police must be strengthened . . . Aviation, radio, the need for an unbroken flow of masses of troops to the front, supplying them with munitions – all these factors now merge the battlefront and the home front . . . Now, the Armed Forces, like a sensitive seismograph, reacts to the slightest economic, social or political movements at home.[34]

In the West, the reaction against the 1914–18 war model led to a strong belief that there would be a return to the era of 'small wars', fought by élite, small armies of 'armoured knights' – another of those military-theoretical views which appeared decades (in this case sixty to seventy years) before its time.[35] Tukhachevskiy, having thrown Svechin into prison and stolen many of his ideas, railed against the 'massophobia' of western thinkers. 'In a future war,' one of his colleagues told the Communist Academy in 1930, 'the side which will come out on top will be the side with masses. Masses at the battlefront and masses on the home front [literally, "in the rear"].'[36]

The Soviet ideal (which, judging by their successors' performance in Chechnya, they never really achieved), was a high-technology mass army. Its most eloquent advocate was Corps Commander (Lieutenant General) Vladimir Triandafillov (1894–1931), whose talents were lost to Russia in an air accident leaving Moscow.

The best conditions for a return to free manoeuvre, for tactics and operations of great scope, will be attained not by going back to the small armies of 'cabinet' wars, but by *raising the mobility of modern, million-strong armies to the same degree.*[37]

Triandafillov was right, but these mass armies were blunt instruments. Everything had to be devised with the lowest common denominator in mind: the most stupid and the slowest, normal people whose reactions incline towards laziness and cowardice, and the profoundly unwilling.

Only now, as battlefields have got bigger and the range of weapons incomparably greater, is the return to small, highly motivated, highly competent armed forces able to deliver results with precision both plausible and essential.

Total War – 1939–45

The Second World War marked the high point of 'total' war, in terms of the number of states and people involved, the number of directly attributable deaths, and the extent to which the participants mobilised their full human and economic potential. The dead have been estimated at about 40 million, although that figure was arrived at before estimates of Soviet deaths were increased from the oft-quoted 20 million to 27 million. The countries which mobilised their potential to the maximum were Britain and the Soviet Union. Everything, down to ornamental iron railings, went to the war effort. It took Britain ten years to shake off food rationing, and the model of ever-increasing state control, as if the war had gone on, formed the basis for Orwell's *Nineteen Eighty-Four*, written in 1948.

As warfare became more total, it also became more imprecise, as we have already seen. That tendency affected even the most technologically advanced area, which creamed off some of the best people – the air forces. And air power played a crucial part in the growth of total war. Although the early air power theorists imagined aircraft could bomb precisely, it was not possible except where there was no opposition. Against defended targets, which had to be attacked at night, and from a relatively safe height, aircraft in the early part of the Second World War were unlikely to strike anything smaller than a town. Certainly, in the words of Air Chief Marshal Sir Arthur ('Bomber') Harris, they should go for 'large industrial areas', rather than 'individual factories and plants'.[38] Even under those conditions, the aircraft losses were very heavy.

The ability of air forces to reach deep into an enemy heartland, the even more uncompromising nature of war aims, the greater ideological extremism and increased technological and organisational efficiency of the governments involved made the Second World War even more 'total' than the First. In the First, killing civilians – for example, in air raids – had been an accidental by-product of what were still conceived as military operations. The Germans did mount some raids against London with incendiary bombs which were attacks on the civilian infrastructure and morale. Yet in so doing, they were tying down vast resources, in terms of men, guns and aircraft – far more than the tiny attacking forces – which otherwise would have been available for the battlefronts in France.

The Allied bombing of Germany in the Second World War had a similar, double effect. In 1914–18, the British confined themselves to military objectives, and even after the creation of an air force independent of the army and navy, stuck to targets that were 'strategic' but not 'psychological'. The first Chief of Air Staff was told to aim at 'demobilisation of the German Armies-in-the-Field by attacking the root industries which supply them with ammunition.' The distinction between 'terror' or 'psychological' bombing and military objectives was grasped very early. At the start of the 1914–18 war, Grand Admiral Tirpitz said he was resolutely opposed to 'frightfulness' and to killing civilians just for the sake of it.[39]

In the Second World War, terror bombing became an end in itself. The British Air Ministry directive of 14 February 1942 recognised the fact:

> The ultimate aim of the attack on a town area is to break the morale of the population which occupies it. To ensure this we must achieve two things; first, we must make the town physically uninhabitable and, secondly, we must make the people conscious of constant personal danger. The ultimate aim is, therefore, twofold, namely, to produce (i) destruction and (ii) the fear of death.[40]

If the Germans had won, Harris, who implemented this policy, would have been at the top of their list of war criminals, and some members of the post-war Labour government wanted to try him as one anyway. But Harris was simply in tune with what war had become. Absolute.

Nevertheless, the industrial cities of the time took a lot of punishment to knock them out. The attack on Hamburg with 2,355 bomber sorties over six days (24–30 July 1943), which included the first 'firestorm', had a physical and psychological effect comparable with the bombing of Dresden on 13–14 February 1945. A captured German report described

> a bombardment of unimaginable density and almost complete annihilation of those town districts [on the left of the Alster river] was achieved by the enemy in a very short time. Extensive parts of that area were enveloped in a sea of fire within half an hour. Tens of thousands of small fires united within a short period of time to conflagrations of typhoon-like intensity as a consequence of which trees 3 feet in diameter were pulled out of the ground.[41]

Yet although 970,000 people – half the city's population – were killed, evacuated or fled, and 74 per cent of its built-up area was destroyed, Hamburg's main armaments factories were producing 80 per cent of their previous output within five months of the raid. And in spite of Armaments Minister Albert Speer's assertion that another six such attacks would have finished the Third Reich, it was impossible for Harris to reproduce the combination of circumstances which had caused such awesome destruction in any city of his choosing.

Defeated in the air, the Germans responded in 1944 with two new types of weapons: VI cruise missiles and, later, V2 ballistic missiles. The Germans fired 9,000 V1s and 1,115 V2s at targets in Britain – mainly London – and also fired 1,341 V2 rockets at Antwerp, inflicting a staggering 30,000 casualties. Because of the relative inaccuracy of the weapons, the offensive was designed purely to disrupt and terrorise and also, once again, to divert people and equipment which otherwise could have been used in the war on the European mainland. Against the V1s – small unmanned jet aircraft – defence was possible, using fighters and a massive belt of anti-aircraft guns. Against the V2, which screamed in from a maximum height of 60 miles at 2,000 miles an hour, there was no defence. Like the Allied bomber offensive, the German missile offensive drew on the most advanced technology and scientific know-how available, although slave-labour played an important part.

Coming after an interlude when the British population had become unused to regular German air attacks, the effect of the V1s and V2s on morale was very marked – especially the V2s. Only when the launching sites 200 miles from their targets, in the Netherlands, were overrun by the advancing Allied armies did the missile offensive cease.

Yet even Britain was distanced from the horrors of invasion and occupation. The Russian war effort was the most total of all. The Red Army was actively involved in combat operations for 90 per cent of the 1,418 days of the war in the east, and by the end numbered 11,365,000 men. The cost of this 'total war' for Russia was even more staggering than Khrushchev's often quoted '20 million dead' – military and civilian. The 'global loss', which includes indirect losses through hunger, disease and the low birth-rate during the war years, is agreed to have been around 48 million – 23 per cent of the population. Battlefield dead accounted for 8.5 million, to which 18 million wounded, shell-shocked and frost-bitten must be added. Millions of civilians had died – nearly a million in the siege of Leningrad alone. Five million prisoners of war fell into Axis hands; only two million came back – most to fall into another category of casualties: the victims of internal repression, Stalin's own war against his people, which resumed in earnest after the victory over Germany, although it had continued throughout.[42]

There is only one example of deliberate restraint in the conduct of the Second World War: the use of chemical weapons. Chemical weapons had first been used in the Great War, in 1915, as a scientific panacea to try to break the trench stalemate. Armies gained a great deal of operational experience of chemical warfare – first with chlorine, then phosgene, then mustard gas, but, given that both sides had similar chemical weapons and means of defence against them, the overall effect was that it slowed operations down. Troops in protective masks and clothing rapidly lose efficiency, and the procedures for decontaminating people and equipment are time-consuming. The balance of advantage weighed against using chemical warfare, except in special circumstances.

That, and the fear of retaliation in kind, was the main reason chemical weapons were not used on any scale in the Second World War. In the meantime, the Germans had also developed nerve gas. The Allied landings in Normandy, with troops and vehicles crowded into the small landing areas, were the most tempting target, and Allied troops came ashore fully prepared to face chemical attack. But the Germans refrained from using chemicals, probably because they knew the Allies could – and would – throw far more back at them.[43] It was the first example of 'deterrence'. Saddam Hussein seems to have made minimal use of his chemical arsenal in the Gulf War.

The principles of restraint and deterrence transferred easily to nuclear weapons, which were used at the very end of the war. But paradoxically, because the nuclear weapon was so efficient and so devastating, it reduced the extent to which nations needed to mobilise their resources in wartime – or could usefully do so. And like naval strategy, as shown in Chapter One, it was a strategy that needed to be perfected in peacetime.

Absolute but not Total: Nuclear War

When the US aircraft Enola Gay dropped its atomic bomb on Hiroshima at 08.16 on 6 August 1945, it was clearly a new weapon of immense power, but neither western observers nor the Russians were immediately convinced of the overwhelming decisiveness of nuclear weapons. The prevailing view was that both parties exaggerated the effect of the bomb: the Japanese to excuse their surrender; the Americans to overawe the Russians. One remarkably consistent view, expressed by Field Marshal Sir

Alan Brooke and by the Russians as well, was that because of their construction Japanese cities were far more susceptible to the hot wind from a nuclear explosion than cities with brick and concrete structures would be. The great conventional fire raid on Tokyo, which killed 84,000 and wounded 40,000, was more destructive than either the bomb dropped on Hiroshima or that dropped on Nagasaki on 9 August. Many of the Japanese casualties from the nuclear strikes, it was believed, could have been saved with prompt medical attention, and many were due to secondary effects on a population which was quite unprepared for a surprise attack by a single, high-altitude aircraft – houses collapsed with gas stoves still burning.[44]

Nuclear strategy grew directly out of the strategy of strategic bombing which the western Allies had been pursuing. As the revision of Sir Henry Tizard's British report of 30 January 1946 noted, 'the most obvious result is that the bombing of towns and industry now give a far greater return for war effort expended and may therefore become the most profitable type of war.'[45] By contrast, the effect of a Hiroshima or Nagasaki type bomb on army targets appeared to offer little return on the investment. Dispersed and well-dug-in fighting troops might be disabled out to 1,200 yards; columns of vehicles on roads might be destroyed over a length of four miles – 120 vehicles, if they were 50 metres apart. Atomic bombs, it must be remembered, were very rare: by June 1946 the United States had nine, a year later, thirteen.[46]

The Russians, who had used air power overwhelmingly in support of ground troops, had no tradition of strategic bombing to destroy the enemy's war-making capacity. Nor did they have an intercontinental bomber force capable of delivering bombs to the United States. Like Britain and the United States, however, they recognised the value of its potential as a political and diplomatic weapon. A Soviet Air Force officer, Major-General E. Tatarchenko, linked the emerging paradigm change with an earlier one, and the first recognisable nuclear arms negotiations.

> The Second World War was the first mechanised war or war of engines. But the Second World War was, along with that, a war in which the widespread use of atomic energy did not occur. However, two atomic bombs ... on Hiroshima and Nagasaki and also the experimental atomic bomb detonated in New Mexico ... were harbingers of new methods of waging war.
>
> Almost simultaneously with the birth of the atomic bomb appeared a new term – 'atomic politics'. The problem of utilising atomic energy is discussed in the Security Council of the United Nations Organisation ... In their

presentations eminent American scientists have quite rightly spoken of the very risky attempt to monopolise work in the area of atomic energy.[47]

Two other reports received by the Soviet government in 1946 also played down the effects of nuclear weapons. One covered the American tests at Bikini Atoll in July 1946, at which M.G. Meshcheriakov and Anatoliy Aleksandrov, both physicists, were present as Soviet observers. They wrote of 'general disappointment' with the results of the explosion, when a plutonium bomb was detonated over a group of warships. In August, the Allied Control commission for Japan visited Hiroshima and Nagasaki. A Soviet intelligence officer attributed many of the casualties to surprise and the lack of precautions.[48] In the longer term, however, the existence of the bomb was to influence the development of the Soviet Union's armed forces profoundly.

Even at the end of the 1940s, neither the Soviet Union nor the United States believed that a nuclear attack on the Soviet Union would win a war. The first US plan, dated 4 September 1945, envisaged 20 nuclear targets in the USSR and Soviet occupied territory. In 1949, the 'Dropshot' plan for war with the Soviet Union was formulated, envisaging an attack with some 300 atomic bombs. But in 1951, a Soviet colonel argued that the damage inflicted by the Allied air offensive against Germany was equivalent to 330 atomic bombs: that was more bombs than the United States possessed – and more than the Soviet Union thought they possessed. And that had not defeated Germany. In the first four months of war in 1941 the Germans had captured or killed millions of Soviet soldiers and seized 60 per cent of the coal, iron and steel production facilities – far more damage than an atomic air offensive *at that time* would inflict on the Soviet Union. The Soviet Union had survived and fought back, to win. The vision of a future war in 1950 looked very like World War II: an initial Soviet success, overrunning much of mainland western Europe, followed by a build-up of British-American strength in the United Kingdom, under cover of superior sea and air – including limited nuclear – power.[49]

The idea of 'deterrence' was clearly present in the early decisions by the Soviet Union and Britain to accelerate their own work on nuclear weapons. It was not enunciated as specifically as later, and had more of a 'they've got it therefore we must have it' tone. For a short time, the wartime Allies, placing faith in the new institution of the United Nations, stepped back from the commitment to total war they had pursued with such determination. The Soviet Union demobilised seven million of its eleven million-strong army: Britain and the United States demobilised more. But east-west tension rapidly emerged as a new source of potential war, as recognised in Churchill's 1946 'Iron Curtain' speech, and in 1947, Britain – the country which had so long resisted compulsory military service – reintroduced it, in 'peacetime'. Thinking about war was inclining even more towards totality.

The formal doctrine of deterrence was enunciated in the early 1950s. In 1952 the British government concluded it was the West's best bet in its confrontation with the vast armies of the East.[50] In January 1954, in one of the landmark speeches of the nuclear age, the US Secretary of State John Foster Dulles, announced that the United States intended in the future to deter aggression by depending 'primarily upon a great capacity to retaliate instantly, by means, and at places of our own choosing.' The doctrine became known as 'massive retaliation'.[51]

The subsequent development of nuclear strategy is an academic subject in itself, most succinctly – and graciously – summarised by one of its leading experts as the story 'of a gradual return to the simple view that, in conditions of nuclear stalemate, arsenals of these tremendously powerful weapons tend to cancel each other out.'[52] Whatever the shifts in strategic thought and technological development, the most astonishing thing about the four decades from 1945 to 1985 from *this* book's point of view is the amount of national effort and resources that went into the nuclear arms race, and the apparently clinical way in which the total destruction of developed civilisations was contemplated. Immediately after the United States exploded its first bombs, Stalin appointed his notorious secret police chief Lavrentiy Beria to run the Soviet nuclear programme, with free rein to draw on the natural resources of a sixth of the world's land surface and all its human resources, including the concentration camp network – the GULag.

Even more extraordinary than the effort by the wealthy United States, and the vast Soviet Union where resources and expertise could be commandeered, and did not have to be bought, was that expended by a small nation off the coast of Europe, shattered after six years of war. The development of Britain's first nuclear deterrent force, the 'V' bomber force, showed an astonishing single-mindedness. It

required almost 15 years of effort and the expenditure of almost £1,000 million [at 1945–60 prices]. It resulted from a conjunction of military, technical, political and psychological currents in 1952 that persuaded the Churchill government, newly returned to power, to adopt the nuclear deterrent strategy and accept the consequences. The evolutionary span of

15 years falls into two periods of approximately equal length, with the year 1952 as the watershed.[53]

As the historian of the V-force has pointed out, the investment was colossal. There were three new aircraft and the nuclear bombs, and the ten V-bomber bases, scattered to provide some chance of survival in a nuclear war. Then there was 'a large and high-quality human investment in aircrew and ground crew for the 33 new squadrons (30 bomber, two photographic reconnaissance and one "special signals") . . .'[54]

Until the mid-1950s, nuclear weapons were seen as a more efficient way of carrying out the strategic bombing of the Second World War. Three new factors then intervened. The first was the development of the thermonuclear 'hydrogen' bomb, which promised yields (the size of the bang) equivalent to hundreds of thousands or millions, rather than a few thousands, of tons of conventional explosive. The second was the development of ballistic missiles which could deliver the warheads faster and more reliably than lumbering, intercontinental bombers.

Thirdly, as nuclear weapons became more common, the possibility of using them as part of conventional land operations emerged. So-called 'tactical' nuclear weapons became an issue in the mid-1950s, and remained so through the debate on the 'enhanced radiation weapon' or 'neutron bomb' of the 1970s. Military thinking followed that on chemical weapons: except for certain, very special cases, nuclear weapons were likely to slow things down rather than be of any real military value. And nobody could be sure that the nuclear war would stay 'tactical'. This gave rise to complex theories of 'escalation', and to the structuring of nuclear forces on several levels so that the threat to respond with a slightly higher form of killing would remain credible – Nato's doctrine of 'flexible response'.

Once the Soviet Union also acquired nuclear weapons, and the means to deliver them, the bombing of enemy cities began to take second place to ensuring the survival of one's own nuclear force. In another seminal article early in 1959, Albert Wohlstetter introduced the ideas of 'first strike' and 'second strike'.[55] A first strike means not simply the first shots in a nuclear war but an attack directed at the enemy's means of retaliation. In the theological jargon of nuclear war, it is 'counter-force' (attacking the enemy's nuclear forces), not 'counter-value' (attacking his cities). The ability to mount a second strike implied being able to absorb an enemy first strike and still inflict devastating retaliation on him.

By the early 1960s, missile forces designed to survive a first strike were being introduced. Land-based missiles were placed in concrete under-ground silos and missiles were mounted in nuclear-powered submarines.

However, once a duel had taken place between the sides' nuclear systems, it was still necessary to threaten the fundamentals of national existence. Therefore, the ability to mount a second strike, against cities, had to remain. This led to the idea of 'mutual assured destruction', which entered the jargon in 1964.[56]

By this time, however, nuclear war was shearing away from the characteristics of 'total war' identified here. In 'total war' the entire population was exploited by the warring sides. In nuclear war, most of it was written off. The Soviet Union took active civil defence measures to try to prepare the population to survive a nuclear exchange, but it is uncertain how well this would have worked. With cities in ruins, food stocks destroyed, water supplies contaminated and nuclear fallout, the prospects for any survivors would not have been rosy. In the United States, underground shelters were constructed for the military and party officials, to ensure the survival of the government, even in the event of a nuclear holocaust. One, designed for the entire US Congress, beneath a luxury hotel in the Appalachian Mountains, was revealed in 1995. Increasingly, the means of conducting a nuclear exchange, and serious measures to help survive it, were divorced from the majority of the population. Only in small, rich and neutral countries – Sweden and Switzerland – were serious measures taken to enable a significant part of the population and national life to ride out a nuclear storm.

The absurdity of nuclear war as a means of achieving any realistic political objective and the costs of the arms race led to the first arms control negotiations. Much of the negotiating effort of the 1970s was designed to establish rough parity between the superpowers – to slow down and halt the arms race. The possibility of nuclear war had also influenced the configuration of conventional armed forces. Because a clash of arms in Europe was expected to 'go nuclear' at any time, armies trained to fight in both 'conventional' and 'nuclear' environments. The Soviet Army's great emphasis on armour, for example, owed as much to the fact that inside a tank is the best place to be if nuclear weapons are going off around you, as to the Soviet experience of World War II. Even the design of Soviet equipment – its very low silhouette, for example – owed as much to thinking about nuclear blast as thinking about camouflage.

The threat of nuclear war gave rise to three important developments which form part of the present, fundamental revolution in all aspects of

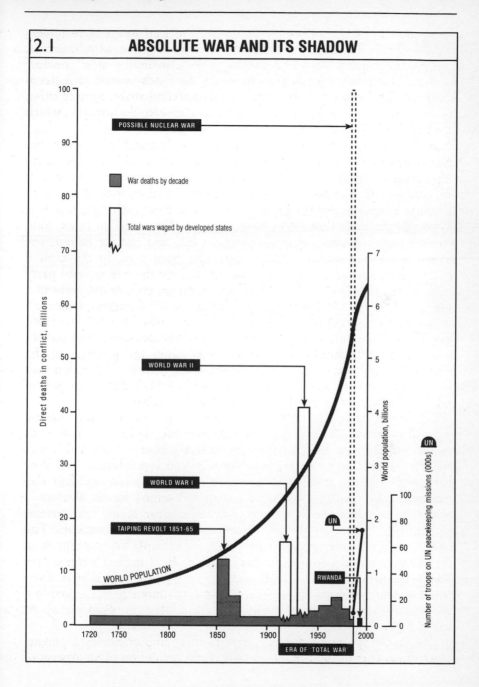

2.1   **ABSOLUTE WAR AND ITS SHADOW**

POSSIBLE NUCLEAR WAR

War deaths by decade

Total wars waged by developed states

Direct deaths in conflict, millions

WORLD WAR II

WORLD WAR I

TAIPING REVOLT 1851-65

WORLD POPULATION

UN

RWANDA

World population, billions

Number of troops on UN peacekeeping missions (000s)

ERA OF TOTAL WAR

war and peace. The first was the idea that it might be possible to overrun Nato before a decision to use nuclear weapons could be made – the 'conventional quick kill' idea of the late 1970s and early 1980s. Glancing back to traditional military ideas, some of them employed very success-fully by the Tsarist Army as well as by the Red Army, the Soviet general staff examined ways of getting their troops right in among Nato, so that nuclear weapons could not be used for fear of hitting their own side. This evoked a similar response from the Americans, who also had every reason to try to keep any major war in Europe conventional, and led to the emergence of 'AirLand Battle' doctrine. This process brought about a renaissance of traditional military thought, and recognition of the operational level of war, in the early 1980s, and formed the basis on which the Gulf War of 1991 was fought and won.

Then there was the development of much more accurate conventional weapons, notably laser-guided bombs, and new 'area weapons': weapons which could scatter submunitions across a wide area, or fuel-air explo-sives, which spread a cloud of petrol vapour over a big area and then set it off. These all opened up the possibility of achieving military objectives which would previously have required nuclear weapons. These weapons, developed under the mantle of plans for total war, again proved highly successful in limited wars – notably the Gulf and, most recently, the Nato strikes on the Bosnian Serb command structure. The high-precision weapons, with the associated means of pinpointing targets, will be crucial in the much more limited operations of the future.

Finally, in the early 1980s, the possibility of defending against incoming missiles, rather than deterring attack, was raised as part of President Reagan's 1983 Strategic Defense Initiative – 'Star Wars' – against a nuclear strike in total war. As such, it would probably have been impossibly expensive, and could not have provided the absolute guarantee that no incoming missile would get through. Nonetheless, the technology of Star Wars, developed in response to the nuclear balance of terror, is proving very useful in the new world order. Some of the people who may soon have nuclear weapons – and already have chemical and biological weapons – are not necessarily susceptible to deterrence. They may not care if their capital city is flattened as long as they happen to be in a tent in the desert at the time. More limited forms of 'Ballistic Missile Defence' will, in the author's view, form the principal guarantee of national security in the future.

The developments of the current revolution in warfare have their origins in the last years of 'total war'.

In February 1986, Mikhail Gorbachev alluded to a fundamental change in Soviet Military Doctrine, but it was bigger than that. Not only was further expansion of nuclear arsenals senseless. Whether 'absolute' in its physical destructiveness – it would wipe out the human race – or 'total' in terms of the (albeit unwilling) involvement of everybody in it, the idea of total war, consuming all the energies of the nation, had come to the limit. To the edge of the precipice.

> The contemporary world has become too small and fragile for wars and the politics of force . . . This means realising that it is no longer possible to win the arms race or nuclear war. The continuation of this race on earth, and even more its spread into the cosmos will accelerate the already critical rate at which nuclear weapons are stockpiled and developed. Not only nuclear war itself but also the preparations for it, in other words the arms race and striving for military superiority, cannot, objectively, bring political gain to anyone.[57]

The taut spring was about to recoil. There had been 162 conflicts which had started since 1951, none of them nuclear. In 1982 Britain and Argentina had waged a very old-fashioned, limited conflict over the Falklands, using some rather advanced technology. In the mid 1980s, strategists were stumbling in the mist, at the top of the total war crag, unsure of what would happen next. The Falklands sent signs, as one observer put it most astutely, that the world was about

> to take a step back into an older, more professional style of warfare. The new weapons need élite, highly trained soldiers to use them effectively. They do not need the mass armies that provided the cannon fodder of the two world wars . . . It seems that modern technology is taking us back toward the eighteenth century, toward the era when small, professional armies fought small, professional wars.[58]

Or, to return to Clausewitz, that after nearly 200 years, war was to be taken back from the people, who could no longer be trusted with it.

CHAPTER THREE
IN THE SHADOW OF
ABSOLUTE WAR

Small Wars

> There isn't a thing in Vegetius, Saxe or Jomini the Indian doesn't know and more besides. He is the greatest guerrilla fighter the world has ever known.
>   He doesn't know a thing about all that military balderdash of close order drill, military courtesy or parade ground soldiering. Everything he learns is by applying it that way. He's taught, sure, but he's taught to fight and to win and he wastes time on none of the fixings.[1]

Like many ex-regular officers of the US Army in the west just after the American Civil War, the fictitious Shalako would have been brought up on Jomini. But colonial wars tended to call on a different sort of knowledge. Large-scale warfare between great powers might be increasingly dependent on technology and the movement of huge armies and, therefore, paradoxically, more crude and imprecise, but in more primitive conditions the art of war as understood by Sun Tzu prevailed, and even flourished. For most of the nineteenth and early twentieth centuries, real soldiering for professionals of the developed nations (as opposed to *Kriegsspiel* or war games, interrupted by the occasional large-scale war), took place in Africa, India, central Asia, south-east Asia, China, or the American West. This kind of fighting was recognised as different by Major (later Sir) Charles Callwell of the Royal Artillery in his intelligent and meticulously researched book, *Small Wars*, of 1896. 'In a distant land, hedged round by dangers,' he wrote, echoing Shalako, 'the accepted code of strategy and tactics is of no avail and the maxims of the academic school of military thought have small significance.'[2]

Small Wars covered just about everything other than clashes between the major European armies: wars against 'savages and semi-civilised races', as well as campaigns undertaken to suppress rebellions and guerrilla warfare. It also alluded to the crucial role of sea-power in isolating and supplying forces in distant places – the naval dimension where the more developed states were unlikely to be challenged. We no longer share Callwell's certainties about the superiority of our civilisation, but if we can free ourselves for a moment to discard the different values of our times, *Small Wars* has a lot to teach us a hundred years later.

Amateur strategists and table-top soldiers tend to be preoccupied with technology. In big wars it can, of course, be decisive, but in most areas the armaments of major combatants tend to develop at roughly the same rate. A hundred years ago, Major Callwell noted that the latest breech-loading rifles were percolating through to what would now be called Third-World countries. We can say the same about ballistic missiles. What matters is their number, whether people can use them properly, and whether they are used with precision and discipline as part of some coherent, cohesive philosophy.

In these small wars, Callwell insisted, the fundamental thing, far more important than any transient technical advantage, was the principle 'of overawing the enemy by bold initiative and resolute action whether on the battlefield or as part of the general plan of campaign.' Callwell recognised the principle of moral influence or moral authority, hinted at by Sun Tzu, and which proved crucial in the UN's early intervention in Bosnia. For the 'enemy', let us substitute 'the warring parties'. He continued:

> The enemy must be made to feel a moral inferiority throughout. The spectacle of an organised body of troops sweeping forward slowly but surely into their territory unnerves them. There must be no doubt as to which side is in the ascendant, no question as to who controls the general course of the war; delays must not occur, they cause the enemy to pluck up courage; every pause is interpreted as weakness, every halt gives new life to the foe. Therefore it is essential that the campaign should not be commenced till there are sufficient forces on the ground to prosecute the work with vigour.[3]

Appearances matter. That was a principle which surfaced again and again in UN operations. Following the UN's loss of face in Bosnia, the Nato operation to enforce the peace plan thrashed out at Dayton in November 1995 and signed at Paris the following month followed these precepts, though more by accident, perhaps, than design.

In nineteenth-century colonial warfare the regular armies of developed states enjoyed superiority of firepower in a straight fight. The locals, more lightly equipped and knowing the terrain, could move faster.

Hence, 'tactics favour the regular army, while strategy favours the enemy – therefore the objective is to fight, not to manoeuvre.' Again, there is a parallel here with recent operations. The difference is that a modern commander, especially one in a wider peacekeeping operation, is unlikely to be allowed to bring the enemy to battle in order to capitalise on his superiority, much as he might like to. When straight battle is joined – as in the Nato air attacks on the Bosnian Serb command and control system – the results tend to be unambiguous.

The difference between conventional and 'small' wars lay partly in their battlefield character, notably in the relation of 'tail' to 'teeth' (the former applies to the effort expended on ensuring supplies and troops to guard them; the latter to the effort expended on the main striking force). The 'tail' tended to be relatively bigger in 'small' wars, because of the distances that had to be traversed and the number of depots or wells that had to be defended. Another aspect was that the terrain itself, and the climate, became adversaries – far more so than in the developed and relatively temperate country of Europe. 'Small wars are often campaigns rather against nature than against hostile armies. It is not the question of pushing forward the man, the horse or the gun . . . so much as the provision of the necessaries of life for the troops when they have been pushed forward,' wrote Callwell.[4] Logistics and the maintenance of a tolerable standard of living among professional soldiers with high expectations have acquired renewed importance in modern peacekeeping operations. But whereas the lengthening chain behind regular troops in a late nineteenth-century 'small war' increased its burdens with every step, air transport has now overcome many of the problems associated with supplies. Air transport, indeed, fulfils the function of sea transport in the colonial era – except that it can cover 100 per cent of the planet, not just 70 per cent.

The difficulties of the terrain in colonial warfare contributed to another break with conventional military wisdom. In conventional operations it was a cardinal sin to divide one's force. But in 'small' wars, in order to live off the land in arid country, to confuse the target nation, and to impress it with one's power and numbers, forces were often broken up into columns. Each column was meant to be strong enough to fend off anything the enemy might throw at it: the trouble was, commanders did not always know what forces the enemy had available. Callwell noted how the British invasion of Zululand in 1879, crossing the frontier in three places, threw the Zulu King, Cetewayo, into confusion. That did not stop Cetewayo annihilating one of the British columns, at

Isandhlwana, although in the long term the strategy could be said to have worked. The US colonel, George Armstrong Custer, faced the same fate at Little Bighorn in 1876. Modern peacekeeping forces are also likely to be forced to disperse across a territory, rather than concentrating as conventional military strategy would demand, increasing their vulnerability to attack, hostage-taking and so on.

Then there was intelligence. 'Small wars break out unexpectedly and in unexpected places. The operations take place in countries often only partially explored, if not wholly unexplored.' Even if there are no unexplored countries today, the difference between possessing maps (the details of which still often bear little resemblance to the ground), and an informed knowledge of what routes are really like and who controls what, remains vast. And, however inadmissible Callwell's late nineteenth-century racial attitudes may be now, no one who has been in a recent peacekeeping operation – for example, Bosnia – can fail to recognise his desperation in trying to gather intelligence from local people who seem to be pathological liars.[5]

Colonial wars gave commanders – sometimes quite junior ones – experience of public relations and politics as well as war. Britain, the United States, France and Russia all accumulated a vast and fascinating repertory of experience of colonial warfare – but it was never incorporated into a coherent theory of war. In Chechnya and Dagestan, the Russians fought one of the greatest guerrilla commanders of all time, the Imam Shamil (1797–1871). In the western United States, a series of Indian leaders, finishing with Geronimo, displayed a genius in combat that became legendary. The Russian experience in the Caucasus from 1817–64, in Central Asia, and operations against 'banditism' in the 1920s, ought to have provided a vast reservoir of experience and doctrine which could have been of immense value in Afghanistan in the 1980s and in Chechnya in 1994–95. Yet this area formed an astonishing hiatus in recorded Russian and Soviet military thought, which concentrated overwhelmingly on the great 'future war' (which a Russian general translated, revealingly, as 'World War III'), to the exclusion of all else.[6]

Even in Britain, the much-publicised campaign against the Turks by T.E. Lawrence, 'of Arabia', from 1916–18, which the scholarly Lawrence used as the basis for some very profound theory, was ignored or underrated after the First World War.[7] A ground-breaking seminar on 'modern strategy' in 1941 ignored revolutionary and guerrilla warfare completely.[8] The reasons for this are fairly obvious. At the time, massive, conventional interstate conflict was the overwhelming priority. In the nuclear age, however, revolutionary warfare has flourished. This is partly due to the fact that war between the nuclear-armed powers has become impossible or too dangerous, and partly because the vast investment necessary to prepare for a big war left the larger nation states vulnerable to alternative approaches. Another factor is the deliberate nurturing of 'national liberation movements' by the Soviet Union after 1945, in concert with the break-up of colonial empires, which provided fertile ground for 'revolutionary' – including guerrilla – war.

A Permanent UN Intervention Force?

As the end of the most destructive conflict in human history approached, in 1945, the representatives of the wartime Allies in San Francisco were looking ahead to a new international organisation that would prove more effective than the League of Nations in saving 'succeeding generations from the scourge of war'. The 'United Nations', at that time, meant the victorious Allied powers – not, as it later came to mean, the assembled representatives of all the countries of the world – and implicit in that title was the belief or hope that the wartime Alliance between the democratic and capitalist West and the Soviet Union would continue. It was not to be, and that was the main reason why a permanent, standing international peace force was never set up.

As we have already seen, in Chapter 1, the representatives' thoughts focused on international conflict. Chapter VII of the UN Charter authorised action in accordance with Articles 41 and 42. The former authorises the Security Council to impose sanctions; the latter, to 'take such action by air, sea or land forces as may be necessary to maintain or restore international peace and security.'[9] Article 47 provided for the establishment of a Military Staff Committee (MSC) 'to advise and assist the Security Council on all questions relating to its military requirements for the maintenance of international peace and security, the employment and command of forces placed at its disposal, the regulation of armaments, and possible disarmament.'[10]

The ultimate military sanction available to the UN has never been fully used. The phrase used to describe it, then as now, was 'enforcement'. The first head of enforcement was Brigadier Sir Edgar Williams, who had been Field Marshal Bernard Montgomery's Chief of Intelligence during the preceding war.

In May 1947 the Military Staff Committee started trying to put together a permanent UN military force. It was envisaged that most of the forces should come from the 'big five' – the five permanent members of the Security Council including, at that time, Nationalist China, although other nations were not necessarily to be excluded. On 25 June the Security Council asked the Committee to submit an estimate of the sort of forces that would be needed for peace enforcement operations. The proposed force structure envisaged 20 US divisions (the principal military formation including all the fighting arms – typically about 20,000 troops), 12 Soviet divisions (which were smaller) and, extraordinarily, 16 French and 8 to 12 British, being made available. The United States would, however, provide the majority of the air and naval forces.[11]

As the 'iron curtain' became more solid, the Soviet Union was understandably concerned at the prospect of a US-dominated UN wielding such military power with unchallenged supra-national authority. They looked at the US proposals, and wondered why such huge forces were necessary, unless they were to be used against a major power. The over-ambitious plans favoured by the US and Soviet concerns killed the idea. Edgar Williams resigned, frustrated by Soviet opposition to the creation of his international peace force. Only when the Cold War ended did the prospect of such a force re-emerge.

In the meantime, the search for international peace and security followed two other routes. The first was the delegation of responsibility to regional organisations: to the European Defence Community founded in 1948 which later became the Western European Union, and Nato, created the following year (it is sometimes forgotten that the European arm of Nato actually predates Nato itself). The second route, for which the UN charter did not include any specific provisions, was that of peacekeeping, to be carried out by people from countries which were emphatically *not* members of the 'big five'.

Big Wars, but not Absolute

Since 1945 there have been a number of major armed conflicts which would have been considered very significant in the pre-nuclear era. In all, up to 1985 there were 150 limited wars of the type that typically leads to military intervention, causing casualties estimated at 20 million. However, none of the major military powers waged what is now called a general war: a war involving all its resources. Total war is a general war waged towards unlimited objectives: general war has few restrictions, and still involves the full resources of the nation.[12] However, a general war can still be limited. None of the conflicts waged by developed countries since

1945 has even merited the classification of general war. They have all been limited, not only in their aims but also in the proportion of available resources poured into them. Developed countries have fought all their wars since 1945 – even the relatively big ones – on a 'peacetime' basis, apart from the drafting of troops.

Whilst direct conflict between the superpowers and their European clients was avoided, conflicts between surrogates in the Third World were frequent. Many military developments, especially in technology, were tried out. The Korean War, in which a US-led coalition intervened on behalf of the UN, provides an important and illuminating example for the command structure which might be used in possible future operations. Yet it was waged with World War II methods and World War II technology. Although nuclear weapons were available, they were not used – though only just.

The best known theatre was the Middle East, where Israel and the Arabs fought wars in 1948, 1956, 1967, 1973 and 1982 (the last being the Israeli invasion of Lebanon – operation *Peace for Galilee*). The American involvement in Vietnam from 1965 to 1975 was a defining phase in American national consciousness, and immensely costly, but it was still a limited war. Vietnam fulfilled the ideas of Mao and of traditional Vietnamese military thinking: what began as an armed insurrection moved remorselessly towards more conventional operations. In the end, it was not guerrillas but Soviet-style armoured columns that carried the day.

The second Gulf War, of 1991, waged by an international coalition on behalf of the UN to eject Iraqi forces from Kuwait, and the Falklands War of 1982, in which Britain expelled an Argentinian invasion force from British sovereign territory it had invaded, again under a UN mandate, were also limited wars. They were not even 'general' wars, although it is possible that Britain would have gone to general war had the Falklands operation not been concluded so swiftly. The 1991 Gulf War provides an outstanding example of a limited war, waged for clearly defined objectives yet using the technology and the command and control apparatus designed for general or total war.

The Soviet Union also shied away from general – never mind absolute – war. The invasions of Hungary in 1956 and Czechoslovakia in 1968 and confrontations with China in the 1960s were all very minor irritations for the superpower, which could handle them by alerting one of its military districts. So, it seemed, was the invasion of Afghanistan at the end of 1979 – though, like every invader of that country, the Soviet Union found it had bitten off more than it could chew. Russia's imperial past could have provided excellent guidelines, but these were ignored.

Other countries' wars moved closer to the Clausewitzian absolute. The longest conventional interstate conflict to have taken place since 1945 is the 1980–88 Iran-Iraq war – the first Gulf War. The conflict between Iran (41 million people) and Iraq (14 million) was limited only by the technology available. It was, essentially, waged along the lines of the First World War, complete with trenches, poison gas and massed, suicidal attacks, though there were a few pieces of new technology, notably ballistic missiles, which both sides used to bombard each other in the so-called 'war of the cities'. For the inhabitants of Iran and Iraq, it was a total war. If this war resembled World War I, the 1967 Arab-Israeli war, with the striking success of Israeli tanks and aircraft, closely resembled the early stages of World War II. In 1973, the armour-air combination, which had given rise to the journalistic term blitzkrieg, ran into trouble, and the very existence of the state of Israel was threatened. Had Israel's conventional forces not been able to hold the line, nuclear weapons would almost certainly have been used.

During this period, British preparations for World War III referred to 'general war', not total. The political objective – halting the Russians and some sort of negotiated peace – embodied a degree of limitation.

Special Forces

During the Second World War, there was a reaction against vast, impersonal armies – millions of pressed men and women who practised 'massive and collective destruction'.[13] Besides being a natural human response to grey monotony, it was also a reflection of the increased complexity and scope of military operations. Increasing numbers of élite units emerged, and so-called 'special forces'. The former were selected units which nevertheless practised warfare in much the same way as others – the armoured units of the Waffen-SS, for example. The latter were small, highly motivated volunteer units with special training or expertise: the US Rangers, the British SAS, Special Operations Executive, Paratroops and Commandos. Many opposed the creation of special forces units, believing, with good reason, that fit, disciplined, intelligent soldiers should be able to do most things – that, as one British general put it, a man does not need to belong to a special tree-climbing unit in order to climb a tree to observe the enemy. Ordinary infantry units were trained to parachute from aeroplanes, and did it just as well. The key point about special forces, or members of ordinary units undertaking special tasks (like the Chindits, who operated behind Japanese lines in Burma), was that they were *volunteers* for the special duties they undertook, and that they depended less on a rigid chain of command and more on self-motivation. Much of the selection process for the British special forces, for example, centres not so much on the final physical standard achieved but on the ability to carry on thinking, and to do it *on your own*.

During the next fifty years special forces would become more prominent, and their particular expertise in handling small arms, explosives, signals, intelligence and languages would prove of particular value against guerrillas, or in liaising with friendly resistance movements. They were also used in delicate internal security or urban situations. Where the bulk of the forces were particularly mediocre, special forces acquired a disproportionate prominence. During the Soviet campaign in Afghanistan, special counter-insurgency units were developed, and from 1983 these units, which came to form about a fifth of the total Soviet force, bore the brunt of the fighting.[14] The ordinary Soviet conscripts were not fit enough, could not shoot well enough, could not read maps well enough . . . In Chechnya in early 1995 the grey, urban camouflage and older faces of soldiers of the *Spetsnaz* – the Russian special forces – were often in evidence. In the author's experience, they were the only Russian troops you could trust to act with discipline.

The importance of 'special forces' is likely to continue to increase.

Guerrilla and Revolutionary Wars

These are two different categories of war, which may or may not coincide. Not all guerrilla warfare is revolutionary, and revolutionary wars need not necessarily use guerilla methods. The word 'guerrilla' – Spanish for 'little war' – entered the English language during the Napoleonic Wars when Spanish *guerrillas* acted in loose cooperation with Wellington's armies in the Peninsula against the French. Guerrilla warfare is probably best defined as harassing the opponent without presenting a cohesive target or front for him to attack. Traditionally it has coexisted and interacted with conventional warfare. Mao Tse-tung, whose views on the subject have been widely studied (although they draw much on the work of Sun Tzu), stressed this point: guerrilla war was the refuge of the weaker side, and their aim was always to shift to conventional operations as soon as it became expedient. Guerrilla warfare was not the preferred strategy: it was the only strategy that remained available.

In spite of the occurrence of 'guerrilla' and 'revolutionary' war throughout history, they were not considered as subjects worthy of serious study until after 1945. The post-1945 revolutionary movements grew mainly out of resistance to domination and oppression during the Second World War. The most successful example of resistance in Europe, which has particular relevance to more recent events, was the resistance in Yugoslavia following the German invasion of 1941. Two resistance movements, hostile to each other, emerged: General Draha Mihailovic's royalist Chetniks, and Tito's Communist Partisans. One resistance movement was thus conservative, linked with the old, defeated order, the other revolutionary, seeking to replace it with a new order in parallel with resistance against the invader. The twenty-five year IRA campaign in Northern Ireland from 1969–94, which had a revolutionary agenda as well as seeking to end British rule, had more in common with the latter.

Clausewitz gave 'The People in Arms' cursory treatment in *On War*. He noted that some objected to the idea of the people taking up arms against an invader and not resigning themselves to the results of the big battles 'on political grounds, considering it as a means of revolution, a state of legalised anarchy that is as much a threat to the social order at home as it is to the enemy.'[15] He acknowledged that the first side to employ these methods would enjoy an advantage, and that those who used them intelligently would naturally be in a better position than those who did not. A 'general uprising' could be effective in a large country that was rough and inaccessible because of mountains, forests, marshes or other local peculiarities, and where the character of the people was suited to that kind of war.

Clausewitz might have been writing about Yugoslavia. Within seven months of the German invasion in 1941, which took just eleven days to seize key cities and roads, but never established control over the more difficult terrain, Chetniks and Partisans were fighting each other. Ironically, in the recent conflict in former Yugoslavia, the Serbs are always referred to by their Muslim and Croat opponents as Chetniks, although the Serbs' quest for a 'greater Serbia' arguably owed as much to Tito's creation of a Serb-dominated Communist state as to pre-Communist Serb nationalism. The memory of Tito, and his Partisans, is still regarded with some respect, even affection, by non-Serbs. Although Allied support initially went to Mihailovic, it was subsequently switched to Tito, with a British mission in 1943 and US and Soviet missions in 1944. The close proximity of the advancing Red Army helped further sway events in Tito's favour. A revolutionary objective, and the taut discipline of Communist organisation, had focused Yugoslav resistance.

The Yugoslav experience also highlighted two technological innovations – the radio and the aircraft – as important components of any revolutionary or guerrilla war, and as links between guerrillas inside a country and supporters outside it. Although both were at a primitive stage of their development, their use provided a foretaste of the role of long-range communications, the media and air transport in the humanitarian aid and wider peacekeeping operations of our own time.

Yugoslavia was the only European country where events conformed to this pattern. It was more common in Asia. In Burma, Vietnam, Indonesia and Malaya movements arose during the war to oppose the Japanese invaders who had overthrown earlier colonial governments. These movements then reappeared to oppose those governments when the Japanese were defeated.

Mao Tse-tung (1893–1976) gained his experience of revolutionary war during the 1930s, against the Chinese Nationalists led by Chiang Kai-shek. In the face of a determined offensive, the Communists withdrew in the famous 6,000 mile 'Long March', to the borders of Tibet. Having found safety, Mao wrote his treatise on *Guerrilla Warfare*, drawing on sources as diverse as Sun Tzu and Lenin. After Japan invaded China in 1931, the Communists opposed them as well. Writing in 1937, Mao predicted 'the guerrilla campaigns being waged in China today are a page in history that has no precedent. Their influence will not be confined solely to China in the present anti-Japanese struggle, but will be world-wide.'[16] With hindsight, Mao's writings are not so radical: he placed a premium on intelligence, readily provided by a sympathetic population, the use of deception, mobility and surprise – all classic aspects of 'conventional' operations.

By 1970, it had become respectable to predict that internal warfare, usually of a guerrilla character, would be the most common form of conflict. A nation's armed forces should therefore be shaped as much for this sort of conflict as for conventional interstate war. From 1959 to 1966 there were 164 conflicts, 149 of them internal. The vast majority were in poor countries, where a poverty-stricken and exploited populace provided an ideal breeding ground for revolt. (The alienation of people in western inner cities today, and the growth of a 'sub-culture' cut off from enfranchised society in western democracies, could play a similar role in the future.) Guerrilla warfare seemed to fall into two categories: urban – as advocated and practised by Lenin (1870–1924) and Trotsky (1879–1940) – and rural, on the Mao model. Both, however, shared an important characteristic: they depended on organising the population as a prelude to armed revolt. A second model, practised by Che Guevara (1928–1967) and Fidel Castro in Cuba, suggested it was not necessary to wait for all the revolutionary conditions to arise and that the insurrection could of itself create the conditions for armed revolt.[17]

Responding to the New Challenge: Counter-Insurgency and Low Intensity Operations

The established nation states met the spate of challenges which sprang from resistance movements established during World War II, sometimes incited by Communism and sometimes not, in a pragmatic, case-by-case fashion. There might have been a common doctrine to follow, based on British and French experience in the colonies, if they had looked for it – but one of the lessons we have already imbibed is that theory about war and peace dies unless someone makes a conscious effort to keep it alive. There is too much else to learn.

A quarter of a century on, in 1970, Frank Kitson wrote in his seminal book on *Low Intensity Operations*

> The British Army gives separate definitions of Civil Disturbance, Insurgency, Guerrilla Warfare, Subversion, Terrorism, Civil Disobedience on the one hand and of Counter-Insurgency, Internal security and Counter-Revolutionary operations on the other. Elsewhere conflicts are variously described as Partisan, Irregular or Unconventional Wars and the people taking part in them have an even wider selection of labels attached . . .[18]

Between them, Kitson observed, the terms covered everything up to the threshold of conventional war. That was what made these operations different, and also linked them with another evolving kind of operation – UN peacekeeping. One was under national command, and purely in the interests of national security, the other under the UN mandate, but the two categories were essentially similar. Both involved impartiality and obedience to the rule of law.

> Peacekeeping does not involve the activities of an army which fully attacks one or both parties to a dispute in order to halt it, because although this

might be done with a view to reestablishing peace, the activity itself would
be a warlike one and would be of a totally different nature to a peacekeeping
operation.

Counter-insurgency, or whatever you called it, also mirrored a key
characteristic of what it was designed to counter:

> The second main character of subversion and insurgency is that force, if
> used at all, is used to reinforce other forms of persuasion whereas in more
> orthodox forms of warfare persuasion in various forms is used to back up
> force.

Kitson called these operations 'low intensity war'. This phrase is no
longer used, as operations other than war or operations short of war may
nevertheless be very 'intense', and use equipment designed for 'high
intensity' conflict. His specific prescriptions are, perhaps, less important
than his cardinal recognition of the link between this type of operation
and UN-style 'peacekeeping'.

Such operations, he said, 'genuinely did break new ground':

> Not *keeping the peace* (aid to the civil power) – a polite term used to describe
> a mild form of countering subversion. Peacekeeping is *different* because the
> peace force acts on behalf of and at the invitation of both sides to a dispute
> and is supposed to prevent violence without having recourse to warlike
> actions against either of them.

The peacekeeping force in Cyprus from Christmas 1963 to March 1964,
for example, was British, and at the time it was supposed that they might
be replaced by a Nato or a Commonwealth force. The fact that it was
ultimately relieved by a UN force 'should not be taken to mean that in
future all peacekeeping operations will be associated with this body'.[19]

Peacekeeping and counter-insurgency operations were critically
dependent on good political judgement at the start: a single rash word
could ruin everything. A classic error occurred with Aden in February
1966, when the British government made it clear it would pull out in
1968 – whether or not the insurgency then in progress was defeated and
whether or not the replacement government looked likely to be able to
handle the situation. Thus, the prime target in any counter-insurgency
operation – the people – was lost. They knew the British were going to
pull out, anyway. All they had to do was keep their heads down and make

life as difficult as possible for the withdrawing colonial power in the meantime.

Sir George Erskine, the Commander-in-Chief in Kenya during the Mau-Mau uprising, put his finger on another important principle when he wrote,

> If the Army is required to intervene it should do so in such a way that it does not prejudice the natural progressive development of the territory. No lasting results will be obtained by the unintelligent use of force in all directions . . . to do this you must have a very good intelligence service. You must not be surprised to find that it is inadequate and your first task should be to build it up.[20]

Confluence with the 'natural progressive development' of the territory has been established as a key principle in wider peacekeeping and even peace enforcement operations. By 1994, in Bosnia, officers were talking about the war 'running its natural course'. The principle had emerged during decades of counter-insurgency warfare: steer here and there, use your power, but, like the cox of a rowing eight, use the 'stream' as well: go with the flow.

The counter-insurgency warfare thinking of the 1970s, however, was not, by and large, so well attuned to a new problem: the emergence of religious fundamentalism and increasingly extreme terrorist groups, often linked with religious fundamentalist ideas. The problem was highlighted in 1983, when a suicide bomber carried out an attack on the US Marine base in Beirut, killing 231 Marines. As a result the US 'peacekeeping' force, sent to stop the Lebanese civil war was withdrawn shortly after. The problem became more apparent during the 1980s and early 1990s. The latter have seen the growth of extremism in Algeria and in Egypt, traditionally one of the more moderate and westernised Arab states.

Kitson and other writers on counter-insurgency presupposed an opposition which shared much the same values and attitudes to life as they did. The revolutionaries depended for sustenance and support on the population: therefore, the 'hearts and minds of the population became the first target of counter-insurgency forces'. The return to what most Europeans and Americans would consider medieval attitudes to death and the after-life (that is, that every combatant who dies in the service of the cause will go straight to paradise), poses enormous problems for western security policy. At best, the new brand of terrorists, motivated in part by religious fundamentalism, may be largely isolated from the rest of the population, operating, as far as possible, independently of it, and unconcerned about any casualties it may suffer – even if 'it' belongs to the same broad religious persuasion. At worst, for the western security agencies, the terrorists will take the population with them.

In Malaya, or Kenya, fairly basic amenities and modest improvements to the lifestyle would win 'hearts and minds'. Among more extreme and fundamental opposition, as the US encountered in Vietnam, they will not. Such trifles will be of no concern to people who have become profoundly disillusioned with – or have never experienced – western materialism. Nor can the objectives of the terrorist groups themselves be understood in straightforward economic or political terms: Marxist revolution, after all, was all about improving the material lot of the masses and the greatest good for the greatest number. A profound disillusionment with materialism and a reaction against anything western are becoming more apparent as we approach the millennium. A similar, though less pronounced trend, is also developing within western societies, among an increasingly disenfranchised underclass. The latter may not be so difficult for western governments to counter, as the people affected have been brought up in a society which craves comfort and material possessions: the danger of insurgency lies in their unwillingness to undertake traditional work to pay for them. The counter-insurgency strategy outlined by General Kitson and others would work here, as it seems to have done in Northern Ireland, which has been the recipient of vast aid from the British Government over the past quarter of a century. In the Middle and Far East, however, the newer form of terrorism will be more difficult to counter. The population – the 'pool' in which the fish swim – may also be broadly sympathetic. And if it is not, the fish can survive very well anyway.

The increased vulnerability of modern information-based society, and the availability of more lethal weapons – like nerve gas, used in attacks on the Tokyo underground in April, 1995, or devices to scatter nuclear material using conventional explosives, or even primitive nuclear devices – will tend to make terrorist groups more independent. Not only can they do more damage, but the nature of the weapons used will tend to isolate them and their activities from society.

Conventional thinking about insurgency and counter-insurgency may have dated very quickly. Rather than winning the 'hearts and minds' of the population, the solution will be to go straight for the terrorist cells using greatly improved surveillance and targeting methods.

UN Peacekeeping

Nothing in the UN charter authorises it to carry out peacekeeping operations, nor is there any official definition of what peacekeeping is or even when the first UN peacekeeping operation took place. Its origins can be traced back to the delimitation commissions which redrew European frontiers in the early 1920s after the Great War. The prevailing view in the UN is that the UN Truce Supervision Organisation (UNTSO) in Palestine, which arrived there in June 1948, was the first UN peacekeeping force. A similar force was sent to Kashmir a few months later. The UN Palestine Organisation proved helpful in implementing the Arab-Israeli Armistice Agreements of 1949 and that led to further demands for its services.

The role the UN could play in defusing international tension became apparent in 1956, when it provided Britain and France with a way out of the embarrassing situation they had got themselves into over the Suez Canal and the invasion of Egypt. Although they were opposed by the United States and the Soviet Union – two other permanent members of the UN Security Council – and most of the other member states of the UN, had they withdrawn and let the Egyptians reoccupy the entire canal zone it would have been highly embarrassing and precipitated a political crisis in both countries. Considerations of domestic politics and national interest have never lurked far below the surface in the machinations of the UN. In the view of Sir Anthony Parsons, later a British permanent representative at the UN, this was the 'finest hour' of the UN General Assembly. A UN Emergency Force (UNEF) was established to replace the British, French and Israeli forces in the Canal Zone and Sinai. By March 1957, the situation had been restored to what passes for normal in the Middle East, and UNEF kept the peace for the next ten years with a force of about 6,000 troops from ten nations. It was the first occasion the UN had acted as a ladder down which countries perceived as 'great powers' could climb, having become stuck in isolated and uncomfortable positions. It was also, as Sir Anthony points out:

> the first time ever that an armed peacekeeping force (as opposed to unarmed observers) had been deployed; the first time that blue helmets had been used; the first time that the UN had taken military action with the consent of the parties to a conflict, an eventuality not envisaged in the charter. It was the precedent for what has become the most familiar of UN activities.[21]

During the next fourteen years only one new UN operation was started – that in southern Lebanon. Although there was no formal provision for peacekeeping in the UN charter, and the Soviet Union occasionally complained about peacekeeping therefore lacking legitimacy, a body of custom and practice grew up.

Firstly, in spite of the early Cyprus precedent, peacekeeping was a UN affair. It was thus distinguished from the enforcement operations in Korea, and, later, Kuwait in 1991 and Somalia in 1992, which were authorised by the UN Security Council but under national command. Peacekeeping operations were under the command of the UN Secretary-General, and their costs were met collectively by the member states as 'expenses of the UN Organisation', under Article 17 of the UN Charter.

Secondly, UN peacekeeping operations could be set up and proceed only with the consent of the parties to the conflict. This could be a weakness: in May 1967, for example, Egypt withdrew its consent to the presence of the UNEF troops on its territory.

Thirdly, peacekeepers had to be impartial. Peacekeeping operations were, by definition, interim arrangements, set up while the parties were still arguing about something. There was a natural conflict between the requirement for impartiality, and the fact that the UN troops had to be drawn from member states of the UN because the UN could not afford to maintain its own, supra-national standing army. The arrangement for member states to provide the Security Council with troops to help resolve disputes came under Chapter VII of the UN Charter – 'Action with Respect to Threats to the Peace, Breaches of the Peace and Acts of Aggression' – in other words, conventional interstate war. There were no such arrangements with regard to peacekeeping as it had evolved.

The final principle which had emerged concerned the use of force. More than half the UN operations before 1988 had comprised unarmed military observers. Force should only be used to the minimum extent necessary and for the defence of the UN force only – not, initially, to impose some vague concept of international justice on one warring party which might be raping, pillaging and looting another warring party.

After 1973, however, self-defence came to include situations in which UN peacekeepers were prevented from fulfilling their mandate by armed members of the other parties. In practice, UN commanders in the field rarely took advantage of this wider definition of 'self-defence'. This principle of restraint was almost universally followed in Bosnia. You might overpower the first local roadblock, but not the second, or the third, for to do so would cause the 'consent' on which the UN presence depended to evaporate.

In practice, UN peacekeeping operations take several forms. The first – and ideal – type is relatively new: the preventive deployment. In his pamphlet *An Agenda for Peace*, the UN Secretary-General at the time this book was written, Boutros Boutros-Ghali, advocates the use of preventive deployments to 'alleviate suffering and to limit or control violence . . . [to] save lives and develop conditions of safety in which negotiations can be held.'[22] The Secretary-General recommended that, if the Security Council decided that the likelihood of hostilities between neighbouring countries could be prevented by such a deployment, such action should be taken. A preventive deployment should also take place, he said, if one country feared an attack. UN troops would be put on their side of the border – at their request only – as a 'deterrent', or 'tripwire'. The one and only example of such a preventive deployment up to the time of writing has been in Macedonia – to try to prevent the wars of the Yugoslav succession spilling over. What would happen if the other party in a potential dispute of this kind ignored the deterrent, and tripped the wire, is unclear – but it would presumably start a UN-blessed response under Chapter VII of the Charter. The question, as always, is where would the troops come from and would they get there quickly enough?

The second category, traditional peacekeeping, aims to support diplomatic efforts to secure peace – known as peacekeeping – by creating conditions in which negotiations can proceed. It therefore involves monitoring ceasefires and controlling buffer zones. This is the mission with which Nato forces were sent into Bosnia at the end of 1995; however, the previous history of the area and the particularly flammable nature of the situation might make the heading 'wider peacekeeping' more apposite. But the Nato mission was emphatically not one of 'peace enforcement'. Traditional peacekeeping is by definition an interim arrangement, but it can last an awfully long time if peacemaking efforts are slow to bear fruit. The Palestine force, UNTSO, was deployed for more than forty-five years and the Cyprus force for more than thirty. Other examples are unarmed military observers as in the Middle East, Kashmir and the Western Sahara and armed forces, mainly infantry, not only in Cyprus but in Syria and southern Lebanon. Operations like those on the Iraq-Kuwait border since 1991 do not fall into this category: they are a consequence of earlier intervention operations, without the original consent of the parties, though they rely on their tolerance to some extent.

Operations to implement a full-scale settlement form a third type.

These have become more prevalent since 1988. Examples include Namibia in 1989–90, El Salvador, Angola, Cambodia and Mozambique.

This category involves not only monitoring cease-fires but demobilising local troops, 'decommissioning' (identifying, collecting and sometimes destroying) weapons, and even forming armed forces and police for new states. It also involves monitoring the observation of human rights, and supervising and conducting elections. Again, the Nato operation in Bosnia authorised at the end of 1995 falls into this category, and because of its complexity, the UN must be involved as well as the Nato presence to supervise the merely military aspects.

This type of operation takes place *after* negotiations are concluded. That could cause problems over impartiality: if one of the parties refuses to comply with the settlement, how can the UN (or any other peacekeeping) force remain impartial? It should take action against the offending party to enforce compliance with the agreement. But that party is likely to contend that it *is* complying with the agreement, and so, in real terms, the peacekeeping force has to make a judgement – to be the arbiter. This dilemma, which involves taking sides, will in practice differ little from that encountered in peace enforcement. This could be a potential problem for the Nato implementation force in Bosnia.

Protecting humanitarian relief constitutes a fourth category of 'peace-keeping' operations. The need for such operations arises from the absence of authorities on which the UN can rely to allow the passage and impartial distribution of aid, as in Somalia and Bosnia-Herzegovina. While it is possible that a mission of this kind could be required in circumstances which otherwise conform to traditional UN peacekeeping criteria, the need to protect humanitarian aid with armed troops implies a degree of chaos and lawlessness which suggests it is more likely to be part of a 'wider peacekeeping' operation than a traditional peacekeeping one.

Two other categories of operation need to be mentioned here, although these almost certainly lie outside the realm of traditional peacekeeping. The first is the deployment of a UN force in a failed state, where institutions have collapsed and the UN is the only law in a lawless land. The second is cease-fire enforcement, which is a variant of traditional peacekeeping but might include firing on ordnance that has violated an agreed cease-fire, for example. Both these categories imply a level of disorder that suggests a 'wider peacekeeping' context – a context that may be highly volatile. Yet the principles of consent and impartiality still apply.

The difference between traditional peacekeeping and 'wider peacekeeping' is, from the analysis above, and the evidence, largely – though not entirely – a difference in degree.

CHAPTER FOUR
INTERVENTION

Russia, 1918–19

'What are our boys doing in Russia?' That question was asked in December 1918, a month after World War I ended, by a candidate in the British General Election.[1] The turn of phrase, and the circumstances, would have been profoundly familiar seventy-five years later. Why had the victors of World War I sent troops to the edge of the former Russian Empire – an unknown, chaotic landscape, with its vast, dark, unknown heart, a frozen version of Conrad's Congo? They would not have dreamt of doing so seventy-seven years later, when Russia stood, still armed with thousands of nuclear weapons, and lashed out with its steel-shod paw against the Chechen rebellion. But in 1918 what had been the Russian Empire was now a failed state.

My great-uncle was there, as a sergeant in the newly formed RAF, disembarked at Archangel in north Russia, to service seaplanes. His diary, scribbled in coloured pencil, became a family memento. He noted what the Bolsheviks (the 'Bolos') did to captured officers, and thanked God he was not an officer. And he told an extraordinary story of how a Scottish unit had headed inland, up a railway line – for it was, in many cases a one-dimensional war, fought from armoured trains – and disappeared. All they found later were some kilts, nailed to telegraph poles. I have not been able to verify the story from other sources: most likely it was hushed up.

In fact, it was not just 'our boys' who were there. So were boys from the United States, France, Italy, Japan, Serbia, Poland, Greece and the newly created state of Czechoslovakia. All these countries had sent troops to intervene in the Russian Civil War – except in the case of the Czechs. They had mostly drifted into Russian territory after deserting from the

Austro-Hungarian Army, and then coalesced into a coherent fighting force.

The Russian Civil War (1917–1920) had started sporadically in December 1917 and erupted across Russia in May 1918. The intervention forces sided with the 'White' – counter-revolutionary – forces against the 'Reds' – the forces loyal to the Bolshevik government which had taken power in Petrograd and Moscow in the 'October Revolution' of 1917. All told, there were 30,000 intervention troops in northern Russia. Another 9,000 Americans and 70,000 Japanese were in the far east, at Vladivostok. Then there were the 70,000 Czechs scattered along the Siberian railway, two British forces in Transcaucasia, and a few hundred British, French and Italians at Omsk.

By late 1918 the intervention forces were clearly fighting the Bolshevik government. Obnoxious and incomprehensible though the Bolshevik regime was to the ruling classes in the West, its destruction was not the original reason for intervening. Until 1917, the Russian armies, for all their faults, had tied down half of the armies of Germany and Austria-Hungary – 160 divisions – and bled them mercilessly, sometimes skilfully. When the Bolsheviks took Russia out of the war in November 1917, Britain was bearing the brunt of the fighting against Germany. France had been crippled by a series of mutinies and the US forces were not yet in Europe. The Allies – especially Britain – faced the nightmare prospect of the efficient but increasingly starved German Army pouring east from the line they already held into Ukraine to tap Russia's unlimited reserves of grain, oil, coal, iron and maybe even people, too. The intervention was to restore and prop up the eastern front against Germany.

The defeat of Germany did not end the problem. The night before the Armistice, 10 November 1918, the British war cabinet was concerned that events in Germany were following the same course as those in Russia the year before. The idea of German and Russian Communists collaborating to overrun exhausted western Europe was horrific to contemplate. No sooner had Germany been destroyed in the first 'total war', than Winston Churchill was demanding its Army be rebuilt against Bolshevism.

The Allied intervention in Russia provides many lessons for modern interventions in 'weak' or 'failed' states, and there are many parallels. The US President, Woodrow Wilson, played a leading role in the arguments about whether to intervene, even though the Americans were relatively new to war-torn European politics. His famous 'Fourteen Points', which inspired the League of Nations, stressed national self-determination, and he strongly resisted pressure for intervention from the British and

French. When he finally approved the commitment of US troops in July 1918, they went 'to guard military stores' and to 'make it safe for Russian forces to come together in organised bodies'.[2] A speech was written for him justifying intervention on the grounds that the Bolsheviks did not represent the true will of the peoples of the Russian Empire, but he never delivered it.[3] And, anyway, this was not an intervention by any supra-national body. It was, like the Kurdistan operation in 1991, an action by an ad hoc alliance, and a continuation of a preceding conflict.

Intervention meant taking sides, with local forces of varying quality and at best, dubious legitimacy. In north Russia, the Allies expected a million men would join them: they got about 3,000. The White Russian generals were sometimes militarily competent, but their regimes were brutal in the extreme and there was little to choose between them and the Bolsheviks on grounds of taste or morality. By establishing a toehold in north Russia and attempting to recruit local support, the Allies found they were taking on responsibility for feeding the population of the entire, vast area – something they were quite incapable of doing.

The Allied intervention almost certainly stiffened Soviet resistance. There is nothing like a foreign invasion to get people going. The foreign intervention also had a profound effect on subsequent Soviet attitudes. It permitted the Soviet regime to establish a link with Russian nationalism, which it used to good effect for seventy years thereafter.

The intervention was also hugely expensive (estimated at £150 million a year for Britain, a colossal sum for the time), and profoundly unpopular in the countries which intervened. Exhausted and sickened by the 'war to end war', and prone to sympathy with the Bolshevik government, public opinion – notably that of trade unionists and intellectuals like E.M. Forster – was largely against intervention. By April 1919 the British press was in full cry against further involvement in Russia. The decision to withdraw US troops had been taken in February, and that to withdraw the British had followed in March, even though it would take until autumn for them to pull out completely. Therefore, the 'hands off Russia' movement did not actually develop until the British had withdrawn their own troops – an indicator of the lack of public understanding and public information.[4] There was an important lesson to be learned here: no intervention can be maintained by a modern, democratic state in the face of public hostility and indifference.

The intervention failed to re-establish a second front against Germany – it was too slow, disorganised and half-hearted. Nor did it establish any long-standing independence in Transcaucasia or central Asia: all the states there were under the Soviet wing by the early 1920s. Its only tangible achievement was to secure the independence of the Baltic States for twenty years, until 1940, following a British naval victory over the Reds in the Baltic. From today's point of view, with Baltic independence re-established, it looks more significant than it did in, say, 1985, when the Baltic States had been part of the Soviet Union for forty-five years. But it is hard to avoid the conclusion that the intervention was uncoordinated, inept, and lacked detailed understanding of the peoples and concerns of the country intervened in. Anybody contemplating intervention in a chaotic or 'failed' state now should study it. And learn.

The Congo, 1960–64

The Congo was totally unprepared for independence from Belgium on 30 June 1960. Right up to the last minute, Africans had been excluded from government posts and even from commissioned officer posts in the armed forces: there were just seventeen Congolese graduates, and no doctors, lawyers or engineers, for a country with 14 million inhabitants. Having pulled out of the Congo, Belgium promptly sent troops back in to protect the European residents who remained. On 11 July the leader of the mineral-rich Katanga province announced he was seceding. In order to keep control of the mining industry, Belgian interests supplied Katanga with armaments and 500 foreign mercenaries to lead its army. Then the President dismissed the Prime Minister, who refused to step down and attempted to join his deputy, who had set up a rival regime in Stanleyville. In August, the Baluba of South Kasai also proclaimed independence, so the country was now split into four rival camps.[5]

President Joseph Kasavubu and Prime Minister Patrice Lumumba had requested UN assistance on 12 July to repel 'aggression' – the redeployment of Belgian troops. That request formed the basis for what became the biggest and most complex civil and military operation mounted by the UN until Cambodia in 1992–93. At its peak, the UN force in the Congo (ONUC) numbered 20,000, of whom 234 died. It was an early, and extraordinary, manifestation of a paradigm which gelled thirty years later. Korea in 1950–54, the Gulf in 1990–91 and Somalia were bigger undertakings, but they were all UN-blessed operations led by the United States. The Congo operation was conducted from start to finish by UN Secretary-General: Dag Hammarskjöld and, after he died in a plane crash on 17 September 1961, U Thant. It was also successful. The UN extricated itself from the morass of civil war and brought stability to the country before the last UN troops and civilians left, four years after independence, on 30 June 1964.

Hammarskjöld laid down a set of principles for UN forces in civil wars which hold to this day. It was a temporary deployment, until local forces were ready to take over, and had to remain impartial. Its work included not only traditional peacekeeping, but also policing, disarmament and peace enforcement. It was responsible for restoring law and order, preventing civil war, training Congolese security forces and securing the withdrawal of foreign mercenaries. In its campaign against the Katangan mercenary forces, the UN force carried out air attacks – the only UN force to do so with its own aircraft – although the UN's calling on Nato planes in Bosnia had the same effect.

The Congo operation also saw the first use of the term 'Military

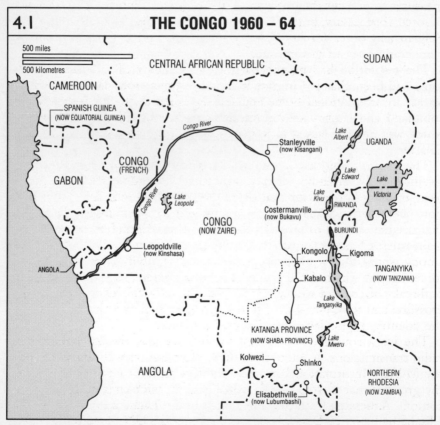

4.1   THE CONGO 1960 – 64

Information' as a euphemism for intelligence. In 1960, Secretary-General Hammarskjöld had refused to countenance setting up a permanent UN intelligence agency, saying the UN 'must have clean hands' – a function of the shady undertones of the word 'intelligence'.[6] In practice, an operation of this size and complexity needed good intelligence – as the British had learned in Kenya – but it took six months to create an organisation to provide it. At the end of 1960 the first commander of ONUC, Swedish Major General Carl von Horn, urged 'the setting up of an information gathering and processing agency' along with a huge increase in personnel and firepower.

After the murder of Patrice Lumumba in February 1961 by the Kantangan rebels, the UN mandate was revised. The new Security Council resolution authorised the UN force to take 'all appropriate measures to prevent the occurrence of civil war . . . including . . . the use of force, if necessary, in the last resort.'[7] It also urged the evacuation of all Belgian and other foreign military personnel, and the restitution of a democratic form of government.

The resolution had no precedent. The mandate of a 'peacekeeping' force had been changed to give it an enforcement role, even though no 'threat to international peace and security' then existed. It also left the command and control of the operation to the UN Secretary-General, which was not the way it should have been done according to the UN Charter.

The more ambitious mandate brought with it the creation of an intelligence organisation. Memos were circulated ordering the use of the term 'military information', although the first chiefs of military information, lieutenant colonels Bjorn Egge and N. Borchgrevink, called themselves 'Chief of Military Intelligence'. The 'Milinfo' branch had four main roles: to assess threats to UN personnel from the various factions among whom they worked; to provide detailed intelligence on non-UN forces against which the UN might need to operate; to warn of possible outbreaks of conflict which might catch the UN and Europeans in the crossfire; and to monitor arms traffic and movements of mercenaries into the country, particularly into Katanga province.

The main source of battlefield intelligence was the interception of radio transmissions. A radio monitoring organisation was established for the Military Information Branch of the UN force in February 1962, on the grounds that it would be 'invisible' and therefore not upset the local factions. A message from the commander of the Katangan forces to bomb Elisabethville on 29 December 1962 triggered the UN operation to enter

Katanga and remove the foreign mercenaries, establish freedom of movement and end the Katangan rebellion. *Operation Grand Slam* was completed in January 1963.

Air reconnaissance was not invisible, but the UN force was in fact extremely weak in this important area. A 'UN Air Force' with Ethiopian and Swedish jet fighters and Indian Canberra bombers was instituted in October 1961. Its prime role was to incapacitate the Katangan air forces; a secondary role was reconnaissance and Close Air Support – attacking ground targets on behalf of UN ground forces. The Indian Canberras were not well equipped for reconnaissance of targets and troop movements, having been fitted out to assess bomb damage. On one occasion, for example, a hospital at Shinkolobwe, north-west of Elisabethville, was attacked by UN fighters. Had air photographs of the area been available beforehand, the UN chief of fighter operations said, this unfortunate error would not have occurred.

Lastly there was 'human intelligence' – the interrogation of prisoners and the use of informants and agents. The former often produced useful results, revealing the names and whereabouts of mercenaries and the origin and routes of arms imports. The use of informants and agents was described as 'comic'. For example, a Greek ex-policeman in Elisabethville passing information to the UN was known to the Katanga militia as 'Chief of the UN Intelligence Services in Katanga'.[8]

Nevertheless, the evolution of the UN intelligence operation revealed the necessity of having a comprehensive intelligence apparatus in any future UN intervention of this type. In particular, given the sloppy radio procedure used by the local factions, much intelligence could be gained by listening in, and the presence of the UN in a peacekeeping role provided many opportunities for gathering intelligence quite openly.

By February 1963, the Secretary-General could report to the Security Council that civil war had been averted and that the foreign mercenaries had been removed. The UN force was then scaled down: a small detachment remained for six months of 1964 at the Prime Minister's request. It finally withdrew on 30 June.

The Congo therefore provides an example of a full-scale military operation under command of the UN Secretary-General, and of taking a 'peacekeeping' force committed in a non-threatening fashion and ordering it to switch to peace enforcement. One view is that, occurring in the era before Vietnam, when Britain and France were still strong colonial powers in Africa, the Congo operation exemplified a combination of idealism and colonial arrogance which could not be repeated later, after the blood-letting in Vietnam made western states more wary of getting involved in 'other people's wars'. It was, perhaps, as close to Conrad's *Heart of Darkness* as it was to the new UN operations of thirty years later. The UN's robust seizure of the task also owed much to the personal energy and determination of Dag Hammarskjöld, who gave his life in the process. History will probably not see all Secretaries-General in the same light.

Kurdistan, 1991

The new wave of UN and UN-blessed interventions might never have begun – or might have begun differently and rather later – were it not for an old-fashioned military victory by the US-led coalition in the 1991 Gulf War. The operation, a classic limited war, had been spectacularly successful in driving the Iraqis out of Kuwait with minimum Allied casualties. It also finished Iraq as an offensive force in the region for some time. But it had failed in one of its key objectives: the destruction of Saddam Hussein's Republican Guard, much of which escaped north-wards, across the Euphrates. At Safwan on 3 March 1991, the Iraqis agreed surrender terms, including a ban on all flights by their fixed-wing aeroplanes. The ban did not extend to 'rotary wing' helicopters. Within a month the Kurds in northern Iraq, encouraged by what appeared to be a decisive defeat of Saddam's regime, had begun another rebellion as part of their long and tragic quest for an independent territory in what are still Iraq, Iran and Turkey. The Iraqis moved some of their battered but unbowed divisions which had fought in the Kuwait Theatre northwards – the 10th Division, for example, which we found north of the 37th parallel by 10 April. The surprisingly intact Iraqi ground forces, supported by helicopters – which were allowed to fly under the surrender terms – began to harry the Kurds, who fled northwards into the icy moonscape of the mountains on the Turkish border.

The media, which had had so much practice during the Gulf War, was probably instrumental in galvanising opinion in favour of renewed intervention by the victors of the war under the UN's auspices. The pictures of barefoot refugees struggling through the snow undoubtedly contributed to public pressure on governments. And the by now household figure of Saddam Hussein was a ready-made villain. It was easy to feel pity for yet another group of Saddam Hussein's victims.

UN Resolution 688 of 5 April was a historic watershed because it demanded action within a sovereign state against the wishes of that state's authorities. Like the intervention in Russia in 1918, it would not have happened if Iraq had been on its feet. Severely mauled and with its national command and control systems virtually destroyed, Iraq had to comply with any instructions from the UN – more or less. Resolution 688 was careful to affirm Iraq's territorial independence and sovereignty and to stress the threat to *international* peace and security, before demanding access for humanitarian organisations. In spite of its attempts to mollify criticism from every direction, the resolution only just scraped through.

On 8 April, the British Prime Minister announced his plan for 'safe havens' for the Kurds in northern Iraq, right up against the Turkish border. Unlike the later 'safe haven' fiasco in Bosnia, the area was at least relatively accessible from Turkey, a Nato power, and, *in extremis*, defensible – a requirement for any safe haven. Clearly the Turks, who had

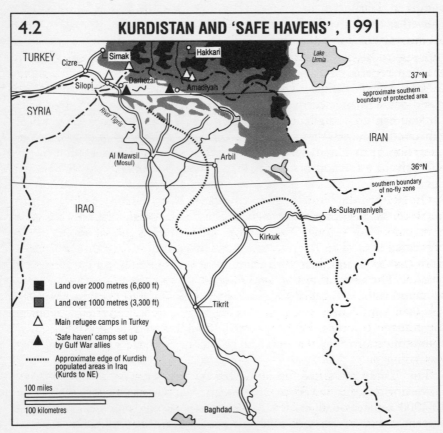

4.2   KURDISTAN AND 'SAFE HAVENS' , 1991

TURKEY Cizre
Silopi   Sirnak
Darhozar
Amadiyah   Hakkari   Lake Urmia

37°N

approximate southern boundary of protected area

SYRIA

River Tigris

IRAN

Al Mawsil (Mosul)   Arbil

36°N

southern boundary of no-fly zone

IRAQ

As-Sulaymaniyeh

Kirkuk

■ Land over 2000 metres (6,600 ft)

▨ Land over 1000 metres (3,300 ft)

△ Main refugee camps in Turkey

▲ 'Safe haven' camps set up by Gulf War allies

.... Approximate edge of Kurdish populated areas in Iraq (Kurds to NE)

100 miles

100 kilometres

Tikrit

Baghdad

and continue to have a major problem with the Kurdish independence movement in their own territory, had reason to be profoundly uncomfortable with camps which might turn into guerrilla bases just on the other side of the border. In the interests of humanity, however, they put a brave and polite face on it. As in any wider peacekeeping or humanitarian operation, they kept an eye on the 'aid' going across from Turkey into the camps in northern Iraq, to check the Turkish Kurds were not smuggling weapons into the camps.

Operation *Provide Comfort* or *Haven* tried to keep Western intervention in Iraq at arm's length. Based in Turkey, the Allied forces carrying out the UN mandate would overfly northern Iraq to deter any Iraqi air activity and take photographs, and would drop supplies by parachute to isolated groups of refugees in the mountains. They would also supply camps at Darhozan and Armadiyah just over the border, overland. I arrived as the initial RAF drops were starting, in an operation which had all the traits of 'something must be done'. Groups of refugees, huddled on mountainsides, were the targets for plastic sheeting (for shelter, which is the first requirement of mountain survival), for blankets, and for high-calorie 'compo' rations. It was hasty, but what was the alternative? 'You could come in and set up your forces and miss a week of feeding people. Or you can go straight in but have no infrastructure,' one RAF officer explained. They went straight in, and probably rightly. In a relief operation of this kind, speed is of the essence, and action – any action – will galvanise further, better organised action. That was one thing they did right.

On 10 April the United States told Iraq not to fly aircraft or helicopters north of the 36th parallel, the latitude south of Mosul. The area north of here embraced a good deal, though by no means all, of the Kurdish populated area. The Iraqi ground forces were not expected to withdraw from that area, and their 10th and 38th divisions were north of the 37th parallel. The aim was just to keep them away from the refugees who were squeezed right up against the Turkish border. In some places they were less than a mile away and Iraqi special forces almost certainly infiltrated the refugee columns. With no air flights allowed and no sophisticated communications left, that was the only way Baghdad could know what was going on.

The Turks protested that they could not manage all alone. The Governor of the Diyarbakir region in south-east Turkey said that 300,000 refugees had arrived in Turkey in the ten years preceding the present crisis, which was likely to produce another 600,000 refugees straddling the Turkish-Iraqi border. In mid-April, the British 3rd Commando Brigade was deployed to help patrol the Turkish border and secure sites for 'safe havens' in northern Iraq, while US forces screened the eastern edge of the area, known as 'happy valley'. The commitment of large numbers of ground troops – the Marines' presence peaked at 4,500 – inevitably led to friction when, within two months, they were pulled out. The decision to withdraw them was in fact taken on 15 May. The Kurds feared Iraqi death squads, which they thought would pursue those who had helped the Allied intervention forces. By mid-June, the Kurds were protesting outside the US base at Dihok, begging the Allies not to leave. Some of the Allied soldiers were outraged at what they saw as a 'betrayal' of the Kurds.[9] With hindsight, the decision to intervene should have been accompanied by much more careful consideration of the extraction of the force, another key rule. But 'something must be done' – and to do something, however hasty, may be better than to do nothing.

The constant patrols and occasional reminders to Iraq have enabled the Kurds to maintain a degree of independence in northern Iraq. This has caused problems for the Turks, who in 1995 launched an attack to pursue Kurdish guerrillas operating in Turkey to their sanctuaries across the border. The separation of genuine refugees or displaced persons from guerrillas using them as cover is a key problem with any such operation. They cannot be easily distinguished: sometimes there is no distinction. The only way that countries with their own problems can be persuaded to accept the establishment of safe havens by the international community is for refugee camps to be under firm and undisputed UN or other international control and for refugees to be screened rigorously. This, in turn, leads to tension with the refugees. As in all operations in the new art of war and peace, a delicate balance has to be maintained.

Somalia, 1992–94

Somalia came into existence in 1960 from the fusion of former British and Italian territory. Its position on the Horn of Africa, dominating the southern end of the Red Sea, made it of immense strategic interest to the superpowers, which courted the Somali factions and neighbouring Ethiopia with arms. Despite the dictatorship of Siad Barre from 1969 to 1991, the division into six clan groupings survived. A destructive war with Ethiopia in 1977–78 was followed by civil war from 1981 and a decade of famine. In January 1991 Barre fled and fighting between the factions multiplied. Among them were factions led by President Ali Mahdi and

General Farah Aideed. In May 1991 the Somali National Movement, based in the north, broke away from the south. International aid agencies had been active throughout the 1980s but by 1991 it was estimated that 80 per cent of the aid was failing to reach the people at whom it was aimed and bandits had begun to attack the aid workers.

In early 1992 the UN imposed an arms embargo, and then arranged for observers to monitor a ceasefire agreed in March. In June General Aideed consented to UN troops guarding aid convoys but then accused the UN of bringing arms to his opponents, under Ali Mahdi. The UN response was slow and gradual: in mid-August it prepared to despatch 500 troops to protect aid supplies, at the end of August 3,500 were authorised. The troops, from Pakistan, began to arrive in Mogadishu in September but were only authorised to use force in self-defence and the local warlords treated them with contempt. Finally, in November, the United States offered to command and control an operation on behalf of the UN. This was one of five options put to the Security Council, and the one chosen. Resolution 794 of 3 December 1992 effectively authorised 'a Member State' – the United States – to make the necessary arrangements. It did so under Chapter VII – 'threats to international peace and security'. In fact, it had very little to do with international peace and security: it was about concern at the starvation, bloodshed and anarchy within Somalia. Built into the wording of the resolution was a link with the Secretary-General and the Security Council. This linkage differentiated the operation from those carried out in Korea and the Gulf, where full authority to run the operations had been passed to the United States. In Somalia, a 'slight restriction', in Sir Anthony Parsons' words, was placed on the United States as the UN's sub-contractor.[10]

The plan for operation *Restore Hope* was that a US force of 28,000 (8,000 of them at sea) would form the core of a multinational force, the Unified Task Force (UNITAF), with another 17,000 troops from twenty countries. It consisted of four phases: first, US troops would secure the airport and seaport of Mogadishu, and then move out to Baidoa and Baledogle; second, they would reinforce the US forces in Baidoa and expand further to the west; third, they would move to the south and secure Kismayo with its airport and seaport and the airport at Nardere; and, fourth, transfer humanitarian relief to UN forces, to be called UNOSOM II, after six months (UNOSOM I had been the observers deployed in 1992).

The US forces began landing on 9 December and at first the operation seemed to go well. However, the planned transfer from the US to the

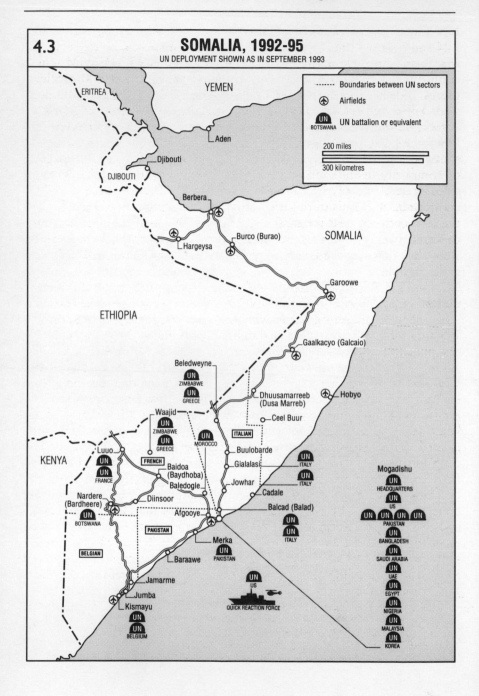

4.3 **SOMALIA, 1992-95**
UN DEPLOYMENT SHOWN AS IN SEPTEMBER 1993

UN forces caused problems. Aideed's faction had little respect for the UN and resented the UN force's more active attempts to disarm them. In March and April alone the two forces – UNITAF and UNOSOM – had confiscated 1,100 small arms, 50 armoured vehicles and 400 artillery pieces. Aideed's forces responded. On 5 June 1993, 25 Pakistani soldiers were killed and 40 wounded in a massive shoot-out with the Somalis. Attacks on the UN continued through September, and on 3 October the US forces, led by Rangers (Special Forces) launched an operation in south Mogadishu to capture several of Aideed's aides who were suspected of complicity in the ambush of 5 June. This was the decision – taking sides against one of the warlords – which Sir Michael Rose, the UN commander in Bosnia during 1994, called 'crossing the Mogadishu line' – the line between peacekeeping and peace enforcement. The Americans captured twenty-four suspects but in the fighting two US helicopters were shot down and the bodies of dead US troops were displayed in a grisly fashion.

As the US Rangers withdrew with those they had arrested, they came under fire, and troops from the UNOSOM force went in to rescue them. The operation therefore began with US troops acting in support of the UN mandate: only when they had to be rescued did the UN-commanded troops become directly involved.

On 9 October one of the factions agreed to cease hostilities against the UN and in November the Security Council abandoned the hunt for Aideed, with whom there was still no sign of reconciliation. The UN force's mission would not be considered complete until elections had been held and a government with genuine popular support had been elected. By January 1994 it was clear this was a distant prospect. To continue the policy of trying to disarm the heavily armed factions would have required an increase of the force to 32,000, but several countries had decided to withdraw their contributions, so that by this time the force was down to 26,000. The policy of disarmament was therefore abandoned, and the UN force concentrated on protecting key points and routes and escorting humanitarian aid – much like the force in Bosnia. Over the next year, responsibility for security, law and order was gradually transferred to local authorities including a reconstituted Somali police force. The last UN troops withdrew in March 1995.[11]

The operations in Somalia demonstrated the difficulty of enforcing peace in a divided country where at least one major warlord, enjoying considerable support, refused to cooperate. There were too many objectives, necessitating far bigger forces than those made available.

Following the decision (rash, with hindsight), to 'cross the Mogadishu line', Western governments and the public also faced the prospect of seeing their people killed for aims which were going to be more demanding than just peacekeeping and protecting aid and yet were clearly not in their own national interest. Those governments were not prepared to pay that price and make more forces available. In the end, the UN in Somalia had to revert to an old Warsaw Pact military principle – adjust the ends to the means.

Rwanda, 1994–96

Tension between two major groups in Rwanda – the Tutsis, who filled many of the professional positions, and the Hutus, who dominated the armed forces and the interim government in Rwanda in 1994 – had been evident since 1990. A small UN force had been sent in to supervise the return of refugees, oversee elections, protect aid, and help with mine-clearing. The death of the Presidents of Rwanda and Burundi on 6 April 1994, when their plane was brought down by a surface-to-air missile (probably fired by disaffected troops of the Presidential Guard), precipitated an orgy of blood-letting.[12] Hutu extremists used the death of their President as an excuse to begin a purge of Tutsis and moderate Hutus, which was obviously pre-planned. They targeted professional people, including doctors and teachers, and also the church. Fighting broke out immediately in Kigali, the capital. The woman Prime Minister, Agather Uwilingiyimana, who was pregnant, was killed. Her ten Belgian UN guards were disarmed and taken to the barracks of a Hutu regiment. They were stripped naked, and paraded on the square in front of the assembled regiment. The Hutu commanding officer told his troops the Belgians were responsible for killing the President, and walked away, leaving them to be hacked to bits. If the peacekeepers had had any clue as to their fate, they would never have let themselves be taken alive. They followed standard peacekeeping procedure, allowing themselves to be disarmed without too much much resistance, attempting to maintain a degree of trust. And suddenly they found themselves being treated with primeval savagery. The effect on public opinion in Belgium of this gruesome episode was predictable. Returning Belgian UN troops threw their blue berets on the ground in disgust.[13]

The UN commander, Major General Dallaire, has been criticised for not doing more to stop the ensuing massacres, but he can, perhaps, be excused for putting his own troops' safety first. On 9 April, unannounced

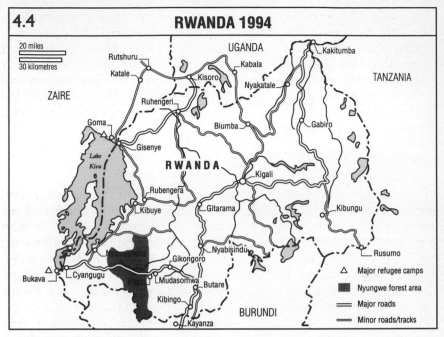

to Dallaire, French troops arrived in Kigali to help evacuate any Europeans who wanted to go. They left three days later, by which time the killings had reached a frenzied peak of ferocity.

The Hutus used terror to force the UN to withdraw, and the tactic worked. Brussels announced it was pulling its troops out on 14 April, and they began to withdraw on the 19th.

The horror inflicted on the Belgians was but a prelude to the slaughter that followed. The Tutsi-dominated Rwandese Patriotic Front (RPF), moving down from the north, clashed with Hutu government troops, who in the meantime began butchering any Tutsis they could find. The Security Council decided to withdraw the small UN force on 22 April, as it was powerless in the face of fierce fighting and atrocities on a mass scale. In all, it is estimated that a million people – mainly Tutsis but Hutus also – out of a population of eight million, died in the slaughter. The heavily edited TV reports only hinted at the horror of people slowly hacked to death with machetes or burned or buried alive. My colleague Richard Dowden watched the bodies floating downriver across the Zaire border, and could only describe the spectacle as being like brown Windsor soup.

At this stage the Security Council considered intervening, but, following the US experience in Somalia, the United States strongly resisted pressure for more action. They were guided by a new doctrine which, until July, thwarted any move to stem the tide of genocide. American diplomats were ordered not to describe the mass killings as genocide but as '*acts of genocide*', thus avoiding any legal obligation to do anything under the 1948 UN Convention.[14]

The Tutsi RPF began to push the Hutu population south and west. Fearing reprisals for the massacres Hutus had inflicted on the Tutsis and on those Hutus – and there were many – who had tried to protect them, the population fled. The speed of the RPF success is difficult to explain: one theory is that the Rwandese Armed Forces (FAR) had 'used up so much ammunition killing civilians [the luckier ones] that they did not have enough to fight the RPF.'

By early July the defeat of the FAR had turned into a rout. The French announced their intention to intervene militarily in late June and the RPF intensified its attacks on Kigali in order to win before the French could freeze the battle lines. Although there may have been occasional revenge killings by the RPF, it was largely due to their advance that the genocide came to an end in July. In some cases, such as the camps at Kigayi, the killings by extreme Hutus intensified in the face of the RPF advance. But had the RPF not taken Kabgayi, there would have been more. Most of the killings by Hutu extremists, however, were in areas well away from the front line.

As soon as news of the genocide began to leak out, international agencies began to demand the commitment of UN forces. It took the UN itself far too long to reach that conclusion. The original UNAMIR force had been far too small to keep an eye on Rwanda, because of the nature of the terrain, and could not intervene effectively in the civil war which erupted on 6 April. According to one assessment;

While an expanded UNAMIR force with an enlarged mandate could certainly have stopped some of the killings, it could not have stopped them all by any means. A UN force would certainly have been unwilling to take significant casualties. Moreover, the forces would have taken some weeks or months to arrive, and the human rights record of UN troops on missions elsewhere in the world leaves much to be desired. Thus there is no reason to suppose that UN troops would have been any more effective than RPF soldiers in stopping the killing and upholding human rights. Almost certainly it would have been far less so.[15]

In effect, the RPF became a sort of humanitarian intervention force itself. The quickest way to halt the genocide was by military advance. The UN would have had the advantage of 'neutrality', but if it could not get there, in time, what was the point?

The UN forces in Rwanda at the start of the killings might have done more to prevent them. As soon as the slaughter began on 7 April, many educated Rwandese sought protection from the UNAMIR troops. The Belgians based at the Eto Eto school drove away, leaving hundreds of people to their fate. As one witness said later, 'people were dying because of the massacres, not the war. Some of the areas most affected by large-scale massacres, places like Butare, Cyangugu and Kibuye, have seen no battles whatsoever. And UNAMIR knew this perfectly well. What was required was to change their mandate as soon as the massacres started, to enable them to protect civilians.'[16]

Marc Rugenera, the Minister of Finance, concurred. 'UNAMIR did very little to help people when the crisis began. People telephoned them in desperation. They had armoured carriers and tanks. What did they bring these weapons for if they are going to stand by when people are being butchered in front of their very eyes? . . . They had the capacity to stop people being killed and they did nothing.'[17]

There is little doubt that, given the right mandate, and assured of some back-up, the UN forces could have saved perhaps tens of thousands of lives. A handful of Tunisian soldiers protected 600 threatened Tutsis and moderate Hutus in the Milles Collines hotel. Major General Dallaire, the Canadian UN commander, said that, 'if I had the mandate, the men and the equipment, hundreds of thousands of people would have been alive today.'[18] He may have overstated UNAMIR's potential somewhat, but not in principle.

While the UN and the United States dithered (the latter refusing to invoke the Genocide Convention of 1948), France, the old colonial power with a long involvement in Francophone Rwanda's past, decided, belatedly, to act. Operation *Turquoise*, launched on 23 June 1994, has been criticised as making a mockery of UN principles. While UNAMIR had been starved of resources which could have made a difference, labouring under the limited rules of UN Charter Chapter VI, France was given Chapter VII authorisation to use force. As in the case of Kurdistan, the Security Council vote was close – ten in favour and five abstentions, with France as a permanent member voting for its own intervention.

As with all international mediation in crisis and civil war up to the present, national interests and agendas were close to the surface. France's influence in Africa, associated closely with the use of the French language, would suffer if the English-speaking RPF, which had coalesced in English-speaking Uganda, achieved total dominance. Even General Dallaire, a French Canadian, was wary of the French plans. Asked if the French troops could make a contribution, he said, 'I flat out refuse to answer that question. No way.'[19]

The French would create a security zone in the south-west of the country, around Cyangugu and Gikongoro. The area included the Nyungwe forest, a secure area which could be resupplied from Zaire. At least the French understood the military principles applying to 'safe areas'. They should be accessible, sustainable and defensible.

By the time the French got there, the RPF advance had already ended much of the genocide. The French troops had been told that the Tutsis had been killing Hutus, and the Hutus were the 'victims' – not the other way round.[20]

Whatever the motives behind the commitment of the French force, it dragged the UN behind it. In August 1994 the UN operation *Gabriel* began. Ethiopians took over from the French in the south-west, with battalions from other African countries (Ghana, Malawi, Nigeria, and Tunisia) around the country. The British moved into Kigali, and thence to Ruhengeri, where Canadian medical staff were also based, to Kitabi and Byumba. They were there for six months to help rebuild the infrastructure and create something people might want to come back to. The people did not want to return. The Hutus who had fled to Goma and Bukavu in Zaire feared reprisals, and made themselves relatively comfortable in numerous large camps surrounding both cities. The camps concealed perpetrators of the genocide, alongside genuine refugees whom the western aid agencies were trying to help. These refugees were a drain on the resources of Zaire, which was a poor country, too. A year later, the Zairean forces attempted to drive the refugees out, with more bloodshed. The refugees fled, but up into the surrounding hills, not into Rwanda, and then came back to the camps. The UN then provided buses to take them back into Rwanda, but very few would go.

The UN was not entirely to blame for the failure to act decisively to prevent the massacre of a million people in Rwanda. But if it had read the signs, which were there from 1990, and had more people in place on 6 April 1994, that would have helped. So, too, would an immediate and robust reaction: a decision, taken on the ground, to save lives, confident in the knowledge that the UN had the will and could make the resources available to support that decision. That is the kind of confidence an officer in a national army expects to enjoy. 'If I make the decision, based on my knowledge, experience and judgement, my people will back me up.' It is the way the media tries to work, too. For the UN, Rwanda was another case of too little, too late.

Cambodia, 1991–93

In November 1991 a small Dutch Marine UN patrol approached the Cambodian border, guarded by a boy armed with a Kalashnikov. After twenty years of civil war and Vietnamese invasion, a Comprehensive Political Settlement had been signed on 23 October 1991. To help implement the peace agreement, signed by the Khmer Rouge, who ruled large tracts of Cambodia, and other parties, a 200-strong UN Advanced Mission to Cambodia (UNAMIC), including 50 military observers, 40 signallers and 20 people to teach the locals about the pitfalls and perils of mines, was ordered into the country.

The boy, from the Khmer Rouge, was expecting the full might of the combined nations of the world: instead, he saw a tired UN officer who asked permission to cross the border. The boy refused. The UN patrol called for orders, but the relevant commander could not be found. So it turned round and drove away. The mighty UN had failed to assert its moral authority. And like the flapping wings of a butterfly, which can affect vast weather systems, it was such a minor incident. The Khmer Rouge resolved to resist. The party and its armed elements refused in many cases to recognise UNAMIC as a legitimate agency of the UN. This was a 'major obstacle', as the work of the UN force would require cooperation from all the parties in Cambodia, and, in particular, freedom of movement around the country.

There is no doubt that perceptions matter. This act of diffidence on the border could have ruined everything, like a small tremor in the air currents that might lead to a hurricane. Fortunately for the UN, this manifestation of chaos theory played itself out, and Cambodia, in the end, proved to be one of the UN's most successful missions.

UNAMIC became operational on 9 November. The 'mine awareness' programme was expanded to include mine-clearing by a UN resolution of 8 January, and a second Thai battalion, of engineers, joined the force. The mines were perhaps the most distinctive problem. Cambodia has a higher proportion of amputees – mainly people who have lost feet and legs to mines – than any other country in the world: one person in 236, as against one in 20,000 in western countries. Lieutenant General J.

Sanderson, the UN commander, reckoned it would take forty years to clear most of the mines.

On 28 February 1992, the larger UN Transitional Authority in Cambodia (UNTAC) was set up. Among its tasks was preparation for democratic elections, to be held by May 1993. All non-UN foreign troops – namely, the Vietnamese, who had invaded Cambodia in 1978 – were to be withdrawn. Reconnaissance in November 1991 had established that 203,000 armed personnel from four parties would need to be supervised and, after the election, three quarters would have to be demobilised. The UN force, UNTAC, would need to be 16,000-strong, including 12 infantry battalions and 32 naval vessels, the last to patrol and monitor traffic on the watery maze of rivers so characteristic of the territory.

The 'cantonment' of the local forces – putting them in specified, monitored areas – was due to begin on 13 June, when eight battalions were supposed to have been deployed. In fact, due to the poor state of communications in the country, only half had been. The Khmer Rouge, claiming that the Vietnamese still had troops in the country, refused to cooperate. Nevertheless, by 21 September more than 50,000 troops from the other three parties had been cantoned and 115,000 refugees returned to where they had come from. The UN condemned the non-cooperation of the Khmer Rouge in July, and directed that aid for reconstruction should only go to those parties cooperating with the UN forces.

As the elections scheduled for May 1993 approached, time began to run out. The Khmer Rouge controlled such a vast area that it was impossible to enforce the UN restrictions on, for example, petrol supplies, although UN patrols and checkpoints did have some effect. The civilian teams preparing for the elections were escorted by UN forces into the more dangerous areas. In spite of the difficulties, in particular the Khmer Rouge's refusal to cooperate and to demobilise its forces, the elections were held, with an 83 per cent turnout, and were certified as free and fair by international observers. The successful fulfilment of the mandate was confirmed on 24 September when Cambodia became a constitutional monarchy with a legislative assembly. The plan for the withdrawal of the UN force was put into effect, although there was still a deal of low-level 'banditry' in outlying areas. A small UN presence remained, to give the public confidence in the new administration and to help pull out UN equipment, until the end of 1993.[21]

Cambodia was an even bigger operation than the Congo. It was meticulously planned, with attention to all aspects of the country's life, from mine-clearing to elections. The UN Security Council and Secretary-General remained firmly and incontestably in charge, without individual nation states substituting their own agendas. It is hard to disagree with Sir Anthony Parsons, who said Cambodia 'should be the basic text for UN operations in analogous circumstances.'[22]

But are there ever any 'analogous circumstances'?

'Cease-fire imminent. Heavy fighting.' Ex-Yugoslavia, 1991–96

As we awaited news of a possible cease-fire in Bosnia (the thirty-somethingth) on 5 October 1995, the daily foreign news list of the *Independent*, which consists of brief headings outlining that night's planned stories, cynically recorded our expectations. 'Cease-fire imminent. Heavy fighting.' As it turned out, this cease-fire would last some time.

Following the election of national governments in Croatia, Slovenia and Bosnia-Herzegovina in 1991, the Federal Yugoslav authorities endeavoured to dissuade them from seceding using the Yugoslav People's Army (JNA). There was fierce fighting in Slovenia from June and Croatia from July. Initial attempts by the EC to broker peace failed, and on 25 September 1991 the UN Security Council imposed sanctions and an arms embargo on the whole of former Yugoslavia. Fighting between Croatian and Serbian forces continued, with the shelling of the historic city of Dubrovnik in November. At the end of the month Croatia and Serbia agreed to the deployment of UN peacekeepers in disputed areas – primarily those areas of Croatia where the majority of the population were Serbs. The Croats saw the UN as a means of recovering those territories: the Serbs as a means of keeping them out of Croat hands.

It was not until February 1992 that the Security Council passed resolution 743, establishing four UN protected areas in Croatia and supervision of the local authorities. The force was to be called UNPROFOR – the UN Protection Force. The UN went into Croatia primarily to protect Serbs in the Serb-dominated areas, known as the Krajina. When the Croatian armed forces became strong enough, they drove the Serbs out of one of the UN protected areas in May 1995 and two more in August. The UN forces could do nothing to prevent them, and tried to get out of the way, although they lost several men in the process. The fourth area, the rich arable land of eastern Slavonia in the far east of Croatia, remained under Serb control. The peace deal signed at Dayton,

Ohio in November assumed it would return to Croatian administration in between one and two years.

Until the end of 1991 the multi-ethnic Republic of Bosnia-Herzegovina had avoided civil war. The international recognition of Bosnia-Herzegovina in April 1992 led to a sharp polarisation of the three main groups, commonly described as 'ethnic', although the divisions are in fact political and religious arising from the historic position of the country on the 'fault line' between the Austro-Hungarian and Ottoman empires. The majority – 43 per cent, who paid lip service to Islam – tended to favour a unitary Bosnian state. They included many of the urban professional classes in Bosnia. The 25 per cent who were Croats (Roman Catholic), who tended to live in the southern part of the country, Herzegovina, favoured union with Croatia. The 32 per cent who were Serbs (Orthodox) similarly favoured union with Serbia, as part of a 'greater Serbia'. At the time, Presidents Tudjman of Croatia and Milosevic of Serbia also favoured and encouraged such a division. Civil war broke out, between the Bosnian government army (BiH), the Bosnian Croat HVO and the Bosnian Serb army (VRS). The Croats were closely interlocked with the forces of Croatia proper (HV), the Serbs with the forces of 'rump' Yugoslavia (JNA). At first the HVO and the BiH just tolerated each other, but in April 1993 they began to fight in a war that lasted for nearly a year. Muslim-Croat fighting was responsible for one of the worst sieges and the most appalling destruction of the war: the Croat investment of the Muslim enclave in east Mostar and the destruction of the historic city and its famous Ottoman bridge. After a peace deal between them in February 1994, brokered by the British UN commander, they joined forces again against the Serbs.

The Serbs in Croatia had their own force, known to the UN as the Army of the Republic of Serb Krajina (ARSK). To add to the complexity of the situation, one corps of the Muslim-led BiH under the leadership of Fikret Abdic in the extreme north-west of Bosnia later broke away and fought against BiH forces still loyal to the Sarajevo government; and small groups of more extreme Muslim Mujaheddin appeared, some from North Africa and the Middle East. The BiH used these as storm troops.

In mid-September 1992 a separate UN command for Bosnia-Herzegovina – UNPROFOR 2 – was established to protect aid convoys and assist the movement of wounded and refugees. Overall command continued to be exercised from Zagreb, by a 'four-star' general, with the 'three-star' general in charge of Bosnia-Herzegovina reporting to him from Sarajevo.

The initial strength of Bosnia-Herzegovina command was 7,800, including troops from Britain, France, Spain and Canada. The British assembled as winter approached, and escorted their first aid convoy north to Tuzla on 18–19 November.

The UN also issued a ban on military flights by the local parties in Bosnia. Whereas in the Congo the UN had acquired its own, small air force, the number and quality of the aircraft and air defence missiles available to the warring sides in Bosnia (particularly the Serbs, who regarded the UN as unfriendly) necessitated a different response. Nato, the regional security organisation which had deterred World War III and won the Cold War without firing a shot, would act as the UN's sub-contractor to police the no-fly zone. Although some military helicopter flights slipped through (a Croatian helicopter from Split regularly dropped supplies to the Croat enclave round Vitez), the Nato patrols effectively ended combat flights by the warring parties.

The complex physical and human geography of Bosnia affected the military and aid operation profoundly. The initial idea was that the aid routes would 'go with the ethnic grain', and avoid crossing the confrontation line between Serbs and non-Serbs (see map). Routes to

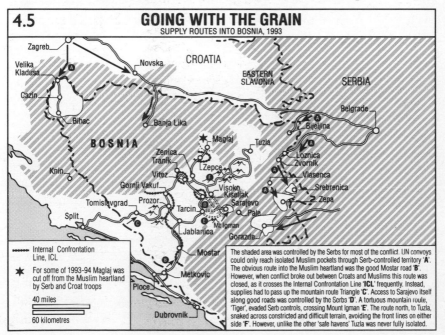

4.5 **GOING WITH THE GRAIN**
SUPPLY ROUTES INTO BOSNIA, 1993

The shaded area was controlled by the Serbs for most of the conflict. UN convoys could only reach isolated Muslim pockets through Serb-controlled territory 'A'. The obvious route into the Muslim heartland was the good Mostar road 'B'. However, when conflict broke out between Croats and Muslims this route was closed, as it crosses the Internal Confrontation Line 'ICL' frequently. Instead, supplies had to pass up the mountain route Triangle 'C'. Access to Sarajevo itself along good roads was controlled by the Serbs 'D'. A tortuous mountain route, 'Tiger', evaded Serb controls, crossing Mount Igman 'E'. The route north, to Tuzla, snaked across constricted and difficult terrain, avoiding the front lines on either side 'F'. However, unlike the other 'safe havens' Tuzla was never fully isolated.

supply Serb-controlled Bosnia passed through Serbia; those to supply non-Serb areas branched out from a single route from Split. The main metalled roads on either side were within range of Serb gunfire and threatened by Serb forces. Therefore, a logging track east of Tomislav-grad became the main route into central Bosnia. Over the next three years the Royal Engineers widened, straightened, drained, cambered and surfaced it to became a fine two-way gravel road. The routes further north also snaked through forest and mountain to avoid the front lines: on the way up to Tuzla, the first British-escorted convoy came under small-arms fire from Serbs just a mile to the east.

'Going with the ethnic grain' was fine until the ethnic grain suddenly changed. There had been sporadic fighting between Muslims and Croats at the end of 1992. But in April 1993, following the massacre of Muslim civilians by Croats at Ahinici, near Vitez, a bloody guerrilla war erupted between the Muslim-led BiH and Croat HVO. The main route into central Bosnia and northwards now crossed no less than three front lines: from Croat to Muslim at Gornji Vakuf, from Muslim back to Croat on entering the Vitez pocket, then back to Muslim on leaving it and heading north for the big Muslim cities of Zenica and Tuzla. There was no question of using the good, Mostar road, which the Croats had closed to help the Serbs in their attempt to starve Sarajevo.

The position of several Muslim enclaves also created insoluble problems. Three – Srebrenica, Zepa and Gorazde, in the east of the country – were virtually inaccessible. The former two were eventually wiped out in summer 1995; a corridor to Gorazde was one of the sticking points in the final peace plan. In the far north-west, the Bihac pocket also remained largely isolated, although once the Croat-Muslim federation was formed, supplies were taken in by Croatian army helicopters from Zagreb. The Croatian reconquest of the Krajina in August 1995 ended Bihac's isolation.

The biggest and most important 'enclave' was Sarajevo itself. The Serbs never managed to cut it off entirely. For much of the civil war, UN aid flights could land at the airport and access was permitted by road through a series of efficiently manned checkpoints known as the 'Sierras' (S – for Serb). Even when these links were cut, a tortuous mountain track over Mount Igman, south of the city, known as 'Route Tiger', permitted access, though it was hazardous. The Serbs were close to the road and as it descended into the city they could, at points, fire right along it. Vehicles travelling at night, without lights, sometimes went over the edge.

Tuzla had a difficult but secure road linking it with the Muslim heartland of central Bosnia, and although there were Serbs, some distance away, on three sides, it was not an 'enclave'. However, any aircraft trying to use its excellent runway (the longest in the former Yugoslavia) would need guarantees from the Serbs that they would not try to shoot them down. Agreement was finally obtained in March 1994 and on 22 March the first UN flight landed at Tuzla, carrying the UN Special Representative, Yasushi Akashi, and the commander in Zagreb, General Jean Cot. However, little subsequent use was made of the airport and it did service as a refugee camp until the Dayton peace accord at the end of 1995, when it became the point of entry for US Nato forces who would be based around Tuzla.

In May 1993 the UN Security Council passed resolution 824 naming Srebrenica, Zepa, Gorazde, Tuzla, Sarajevo and Bihac as 'safe areas'. According to General Sir Michael Rose, the UN had a four-hour military briefing which argued the proposed 'safe areas' were unsustainable, indefensible, and should not be declared as 'safe'. They ignored this recommendation.

On 4 June, resolution 836 extended the mandate of the UN protection force to deter attacks on 'safe areas'. A further resolution, 844 of 19 June, authorised reinforcement of the UN to enable an extra 6,500 troops to be sent to the 'safe areas'. It never happened. However, the UN presence was steadily increased elsewhere. By September 1994 the total presence in former Yugoslavia (mostly Bosnia) numbered 38,000.

In February 1994 the new UN commander in Bosnia, General Sir Michael Rose, succeeded in negotiating a cease-fire in Sarajevo, to take effect from 25 February. All heavy weapons were to be placed in UN-monitored collection points, or pulled back out of range of the city: mortars to a distance of 10 kilometres and all artillery pieces and tanks to a distance of 20 kilometres (12 miles). This was supported by a Nato declaration of 10 February which threatened air attacks on any weapons not complying with these conditions.

The Sarajevo cease-fire and the conclusion of the Muslim-Croat peace, negotiated by the commander of UN sector south-west, Brigadier John Reith, who had set up his headquarters at Gornji Vakuf on the Muslim-Croat front line, led to a brief burst of optimism. This evaporated in March and April as the UN 'safe area' of Gorazde came under Serb attack and there were reports, which later proved exaggerated, that it had fallen. British UN troops in the area were engaged in fierce gun battles with the Serbs and one 'Joint Commission Observer' – probably a euphemism for an SAS man marking targets for Nato planes – was killed. In accordance with the stiffened UN mandate, Nato planes carried out their first small-scale air attacks, and at the end of April the Serbs agreed to pull back 3 kilometres from Gorazde town and to a 20-kilometre exclusion zone for artillery.

The Muslim-Croat cease-fire took effect and UN troops, who no longer had to be on the alert all the time for hostilities from either side, began to divert their energies into reconstructing the local economy. John Reith was absolutely clear about the importance of restoring amenities. If people did not see a rapid and unequivocal improvement in their lot as a result of peace, they would go back to war. Or to put it another way, you had to give them something they really did not want to lose. Electricity and water gradually returned, and in the course of the next year petrol stations, cafés and restaurants started opening again. It certainly seemed as if the Muslims and Croats of central Bosnia preferred peace, though the war with the Serbs continued.

The early part of 1995 was dominated by a sequence of events beginning with the Croatian offensive to recapture one of the Serb-controlled areas of Croatia, western Slavonia, in early May. The Croatian attack, from both sides of the small pocket, was successful. The Krajina Serbs responded by firing long-range rockets (from the *Orkan* launcher, maximum range 50 kilometres or 30 miles) at the Croatian capital, Zagreb.

Meanwhile, further uses for the UN troops in central Bosnia were being considered, and the success of the Muslim-Croat cease-fire had freed the powerful British contingent in central Bosnia for other tasks. In mid-May the UN Secretary-General, Boutros Boutros-Ghali, hinted that the British UN troops at Vitez and Bugojno might be redeployed to help replace French troops in Sarajevo, who were being withdrawn in response to domestic pressure in France. At the same time, it was clear that the UN might be planning to abandon the isolated enclaves in eastern Bosnia, where it had been unable to fulfil its mandate, and concentrate instead on the central region. In central Bosnia, the UN had been very successful. It was maintaining the Muslim-Croat cease-fire, its forces were relatively safe and it might withdraw relatively easily down roads which, by now, had been greatly improved if its presence in Bosnia was no longer wanted.

On Thursday 25 May, following continued violation of the heavy weapons exclusion zone around Sarajevo, Nato planes attacked Bosnian Serb ammunition dumps near Pale, the nearby Bosnian Serb 'capital'.

More attacks followed the next day. Whereas individual tanks and guns had proved difficult and unprofitable targets, large static installations like ammunition dumps, at one remove from the actual weapons that were violating UN conditions, seemed a sensible target. They were easy to find and hit and their destruction would eventually starve the guns of ammunition. At the same time, Serbs disguised as UN troops captured 12 French UN peacekeepers at the Vrbanja bridge, in central Sarajevo. French patience finally ran out and they stormed the bridge on the morning of Saturday 27th, killing four Serbs, wounding three and taking four prisoner.

The Serbs' reaction to the Nato air strikes – defined as attacks on important targets, not directly in support of UN operations on the ground – was uncompromising. They immediately took more than 200 UN peacekeepers hostage. On 26 May, following the second Nato 'air strike' – an attack on ammunition dumps which was not directly connected with the activities of UN troops – 8 were seized and another 200 confined to their quarters. The spectacle of one of the unarmed UN observers, Canadian captain Patrick Rechner, chained to a lamp-post at a Bosnian Serb ammunition dump as a 'human shield', caused outrage. On 28 May a further 33 UN troops, from British observation posts around Gorazde, were also taken prisoner although another 24 managed to escape.

The UN's first priority was to extract the 200-plus hostages – who became 400 by the end. It was by now abundantly clear (as it had been to military planners for some time) that unarmed observers dispersed through potentially hostile territory were incompatible with robust military action against elements in that territory. By the end of May plans for a hard-hitting Franco-British Theatre reserve force which could be used to punch a route through to Sarajevo were well advanced, and the first British reinforcements for the force began arriving in Split, en route for central Bosnia, at the beginning of June.

On 3 June the formation of a new, 10,000-strong UN 'Rapid Reaction Force' was announced. One of its two brigades would be the British 24th Airmobile Brigade (infantry carried in helicopters); the other would be a Franco-British brigade, comprising two Task Forces: Alpha, the British, based on British troops already in Bosnia plus reinforcements including artillery, and Bravo, a French force. It is now clear that nobody really knew what the RRF was for. There were doubts over whether it was strong enough to punch a secure route through to Sarajevo, and although the UN and western leaders said it was there to 'enable the UN to perform its mandate more effectively', it was clearly also there in case the UN had to pull out. The 24th Airmobile Brigade, consigned to an insect-ridden swamp on the Adriatic coast, was later pulled out, not to return. Lightly armed infantry in vulnerable helicopters were not what the theatre demanded.

As the UN negotiated to rescue its hostages, the Rapid Reaction Force began assembling and training. Attention then switched to Srebrenica, where on 11 July the Serbs bulldozed their way in from the south. Now committed to defending a declared UN 'safe area', the UN requested Nato air strikes. The Serbs shrugged off two air attacks, which destroyed two Serb tanks but were otherwise ineffective against infantry moving through the woods. The Dutch peacekeepers in Srebrenica made an attempt to fend off the Serbs but, under threat of being outflanked, withdrew. It was the UN's biggest humiliation. Later, like the peacekeepers in Rwanda, they stood by while Muslim women and children were separated from the men. There had been about 37,000 people in Srebrenica town and another 12,000 in villages in the Muslim enclave. Thousands of fighting men, and the wives and families of senior Bosnian Army officers, had chosen to trust themselves to the forests and mountains. Many died attempting to escape. The women and older men who were allowed out by the Serbs waited for their menfolk to filter in from over the hills and through the minefields. They told us of a terrible ambush at Konjevic Pole, in which thousands were killed. Over the next few weeks some of the soldiers arrived. Many never made it.

Following the fall of Srebrenica, the Serbs turned their attention to neighbouring Zepa. Relations between the BiH and the UN reached an all-time low, as the Bosnian government forces blamed the UN for deserting and betraying the inhabitants of the enclaves. But then the UN Rapid Reaction force moved on to Mount Igman in a development which clearly favoured the Bosnian government forces, and relations began to improve. And the London conference at the end of July promised swift and disproportionate retribution for any further attacks on safe areas – though that was too late for Srebrenica and Zepa.

At the same time, the Croatian and Bosnian Croat forces in Herzegovina were enjoying some success in overrunning Serb-held territory in the west of the country. From now on, the military successes of the Croatian and Bosnian Muslim-Croat forces became intertwined with the progress of UN and Nato operations. On 4 August the Croatian Army launched operation *Storm*, a large offensive against the Serb-held Krajina area of Croatia, overrunning UN sectors north and south within a few days.

Most of the 150,000 Serbs in Krajina headed east, through Bosnian Serb territory towards Serbia proper.

The Croatians halted at the Bosnian border, having opened the way to the Bihac pocket. The developments of the previous two months had resulted in a remarkable tidying up of the map. The indefensible Muslim enclaves in eastern Bosnia had gone. So had all but one of the Serb-held areas of Croatia. It might not be right; it should, perhaps, never have happened; but a tidier map makes a viable peace easier to achieve.

The defining moment came at the end of August. On Monday 28 August a Serb mortar bomb fell on Sarajevo, killing thirty-eight people. It took a while for the UN to be sure it was fired by the Serbs – it could have been a 'provocation', by the Muslims. According to a UN spokesman later, the commander of UN forces in Bosnia, Lieutenant General Smith also withheld news of the 'provocation' for twenty-four hours – to the fury of the Muslims – while the last of his UN peacekeepers were extracted from the Muslim enclave of Gorazde, where they would have been vulnerable to Serb reprisals. Only when the British UN troops were safe did he authorise escalation.[23]

Then, on 30 August, Nato planes and the UN Rapid Reaction Force guns on Mount Igman launched attacks of unprecedented intensity against Bosnian Serb gun positions, ammunition dumps, factories, and anti-aircraft gun and missile sites around Sarajevo. Instead of single attacks on single objectives, Nato planes flew more than 200 sorties in the biggest and most sustained operation in the alliance's forty-six-year history. Nato and the UN were not just retaliating against attacks on 'safe areas' or attacks on UN personnel. For the first time in four years of war in the Balkans, the West intervened with all the force at its disposal, not just to stop the slaughter in Sarajevo but to force an end to the conflict. This was a concerted attempt to destroy Serb military power. In terms of the then current British doctrine, it marked the transition from 'wider peacekeeping', with all its complexity and danger, to 'peace enforcement'. But the results actually threw the British emphasis on that sharp divide into question. After the UN and its Nato agent crossed the 'Rubicon' to peace enforcement and facilitated a Serb collapse, the parties moved to the negotiating table. They agreed a peace, and consent – to a different operation – was re-established.

But for the moment, the air attacks continued. On 10 September Nato also launched thirteen Tomahawk cruise missiles with conventional warheads from US warships in the Adriatic. They were fired at air defences around Banja Luka – targets deep inside Bosnia which it would still have been risky for manned aircraft to attack. American F-117 stealth fighters – the angular planes virtually invisible to radar used to attack the centre of Baghdad in the Gulf War – were next on the list, but they were not needed.

Nato air attacks were suspended on Thursday, 14 September, after 3,400 sorties of which 750 were attack missions against ground targets. Nato had struck at a total of 56 targets, within which there were 350 'aiming points' – individual sheds, bunkers, radars and so on. Officially, these attacks had nothing to do with the renewed Croat and Muslim advance against the Serbs, which started as the Nato bombing ceased. Indeed, Nato avoided hitting Bosnian Serb front-line troops, partly because troops in the field are difficult for aircraft to hit and partly to prevent accusations that they were directly helping Bosnian government and Croat forces.

However, Nato did take out the Bosnian Serbs' ammunition depots and armaments factories – their most obvious advantage over the more numerous but less well-armed Muslims. More important still, they punched out the Serbs' eyes and nervous system. One of the areas they concentrated on was around Banja Luka, the area where the Croats and Muslims now renewed their offensive. Although the prime Nato objective was to disable the air defence network, that meant cutting the communication network more widely. Aid workers confirmed that the attacks had also dislocated the telephone network. Nato had disabled not only the air defence system but the entire state structure, such as it was, of the Bosnian Serb Republic. One of my colleagues was having difficulty getting permission from the Bosnian Serbs to work in their area and suggested they telephone a higher authority. 'Unfortunately, your planes destroyed the telephone exchange this morning,' was the reply.

Paralysed and weakened by the Nato attacks, the Serbs fell back again, until they were close to Banja Luka – their main stronghold in north-west Bosnia. The advancing Muslims came to an exhausted halt. The battle lines froze in an uneasy stalemate. Within two weeks, a US-brokered cease-fire was agreed, which was maintained until the signature of the Dayton peace agreement on 21 November, confirmed in Paris on 14 December. Although presented as a triumph for US diplomacy, the Bosnian peace was really a result of the military defeat of the Bosnian Serbs.

The later stages of the Bosnian war are highly instructive. For nearly three years, the UN forces had fulfilled their mandate heroically. They

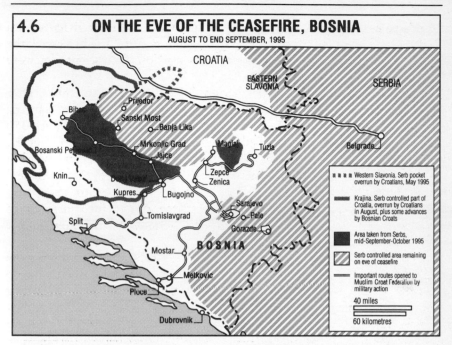

4.6 ON THE EVE OF THE CEASEFIRE, BOSNIA
AUGUST TO END SEPTEMBER, 1995

undoubtedly prevented many atrocities and much slaughter. The Muslim-Croat cease-fire was an important, though neglected UN success. Yet it was only when the UN and Nato began to move with the flow of events that their presence became decisive. The UN has been, and will be, severely criticised for not saving more lives in Srebrenica, and perhaps rightly. But to criticise the UN for condoning 'ethnic cleansing' – the eviction of people from a different faction – is perhaps over-sentimental. The only way to obtain peace and a viable settlement was to tidy up the maps. The war did not only produce 'ethnic cleansing'; it was designed to facilitate 'ethnic cleansing'. Moral scruples probably got in the way of doing the best for the people evicted.

In November 1992, shortly after the UN involvement in Bosnia began, the UN High Commissioner for refugees, Sadako Ogata, summarised the continuing dilemma:

> To what extent do we persuade people to remain where they are, when that could well jeopardise their lives and liberties? On the other hand, if we help them to move, do we not become an accomplice to 'ethnic cleansing'?[24]

The problem continued even after after the November 1995 peace agreement, by which time 'ethnic cleansing' had shifted large numbers of people into areas adjacent to their co-religionists and eliminated the isolated enclaves. The Dayton agreement specified the return of a large area overrun by Croat forces in the summer offensive to the Bosnian Serbs – a desolate and by now unpopulated tract of 700 square kilometres sticking southwards towards the Croatian border which the British Army called the 'anvil' and the Serbs the 'kidney'. Ironically, the Croat population of one village, Majdan, had remained there during the years of Serb control largely unmolested. But when it became clear the Croatian forces would withdraw under the supervision of British troops, now part of the peace implementation force, IFOR, they began packing. During the period of Croatian control, neighbouring Serb villages had been torched and now they feared revenge from the returning Serbs. One freezing Sunday in January 1996 the British commander, Brigadier Richard Dannatt, addressed the congregation in the catholic church, pleading with them to stay, but few did. The irony was obvious, and we headlined the report 'Peace sends village fleeing for safety'.[25]

The Brigadier was doing his duty but he was resisting the flow of events. It is a sad fact that once a complex patchwork of religions, ethnic origins and allegiances starts to dissolve into internecine slaughter, then large-scale movements and exchanges of population, into areas separated by clear boundaries that can be monitored, may be the only realistic way of ensuring that peace and stability finally return.

Rather than obstinately refusing to acknowledge such regrettable facts, it may in some cases be better to respond to, or even anticipate them.

Rather than distribute the Muslim refugees to dozens of grim camps around central Bosnia, for example, a more imaginative solution such as that suggested by Larry Hollingworth, formerly the UN High Commissioner for Refugees' representative in Zenica, might have been employed. He suggested creating a replica Srebrenica, and a replica Zepa, in central Bosnia. Those people, after all, were not going to go back, and the same is true of the Krajina Serbs.

The principle of following the inexorable flow of events also applied to the military course of the war. The problem is identifying that course. For years, the Bosnian Serbs seemed invincible, unless massive intervention took place on a scale which no western government would support. Then, after the Muslims and Croats stopped fighting each other, the tide began to turn. There were a few limited Muslim successes in central Bosnia. Then Croatia proper launched its unexpectedly successful attack in May and early August. In between, the UN reinforced its troops in the

Sarajevo area. Following the seizure of UN hostages at the end of May and their subsequent release, and the loss of Srebrenica and Zepa in July, the UN, at least, had few potential hostages in Serb-held territory. The Croatian attack on Krajina in early August stunned the Serbs and dealt their morale a terrible blow. Nato air strikes at the end of August, following a very ill-advised Serb provocation, disabled their command and control, and further Croat and Muslim advances capitalised on that weakness. These advances came as no surprise to Nato, but it avoided actions which helped the Muslims and Croats too obviously. The West tried to stay impartial, but in the end, one lesson of the Bosnian conflict may be that the best hope for peace is to back the winner – and help him win more quickly.

CHAPTER FIVE
CAUSES OF FUTURE
CONFLICT: NEW FACTORS
AND NEW ROLES

Clausewitz did not touch on the work of one of his contemporaries, the Englishman Thomas Malthus (1766–1834), on population growth and movement. Malthus, an economist and demographer, is best known for his cheerful proposition – which seems to have held good – that population will always tend to outgrow the available food supply. There was probably no need for Clausewitz, who was dealing with man's very deliberate and premeditated violence towards man, to concern himself with such issues. The world was still big enough for the people in it, and although Malthus's work had possible implications for revolt and guerrilla warfare in the crowded cities, which were attracting large numbers of people from the country as the Industrial Revolution got underway, those cities were still very small by our standards. However dark and grim they seemed, fields, light and air were never very far away. Population growth was not an issue for military thinkers. In 1850, the world's population was 1,200 million: in 1992 it was 5.4 billion.[1] In 1850 the rest of the world seemed extremely large, and much of it was still unexplored. Nearly seventy years later, by the time the Allies intervened in Russia in 1918 (a landscape in which armies could, and did, 'get lost'), most of the world had been explored to some extent.

The vulnerability of the human condition to factors beyond its control was highlighted by the great influenza epidemic, which killed more people that year than had died in the entire First World War. But for the governments of the time that was not a security issue. It was a sad fact of life. In 1918 there were no antibiotics, no blood transfusions. People who got ill died. Only the tough survived. Advances in medical science and improvements in living conditions have accounted for the dramatic growth of population since then. It was not that people bred faster. They stopped dying so fast.

In the 1990s, some scholars have focused their attention on what have been called 'soft security' issues – population growth, refugee movement, global warming and the availability of natural resources. These factors affect security in two ways. First, they may precipitate conflicts of a traditional type. Second, they are in themselves 'security issues' in that they threaten our lives, our well-being and our prosperity. Moreover, measures to tackle harmful changes provide potential new areas, such as humanitarian aid, disaster relief, civil engineering and rapid action to forestall geological and agricultural catastrophes, where the armed forces' expertise in dealing with big problems in the open air can be very useful.

A cynic might argue that the increased interest in 'soft security' issues simply fills a gap left by the end of the Cold War and the vast armed confrontation it represented. There is, at the moment, no direct and credible military threat of the traditional, 'hard security' kind to most of the developed countries in the world. There is no shortage of wars, however; indeed, the number of wars has increased. But, as we have seen, they do not directly threaten the European Union, North America or Japan. Furthermore, the issues involved in these small wars do not always lend themselves to detached academic analysis. Understanding them requires field work, to which strategic studies is something of a stranger.

'Soft security' is a misleading term. The movements of refugees and displaced persons are a real security issue and are already the reason for military operations, such as those in Rwanda and Bosnia. Oil was and will remain for some time a real strategic and security issue, over which wars have been fought. The 1991 Gulf War and the Russian destruction of Grozny in 1995 were both, in large part, about oil. Water is now replacing oil as the most precious strategic commodity in the Middle East. That is not a 'soft' issue, either. Libya's leader, Colonel Gaddafi, succinctly highlighted key areas, in a speech he gave to students in 1987:

> The Arabs must possess the atom bomb to defend themselves until their numbers reach one billion, until they learn to desalinate sea water, and until they liberate Palestine.[2]

Nuclear weapons, population growth, water, and traditional political arguments about territory and national self-determination. A pretty hard-headed summary of some of the main issues, in fact.

A 'Clash of Civilisations'?

The peace of Westphalia in 1648 marked the beginning of the modern international system. From that point, the conflicts which affected the western world were – unsurprisingly perhaps – between western states, even though they might be conducted overseas. The 'cabinet wars' of the late seventeenth and eighteenth centuries mutated into the more nationalistic wars of the nineteenth and twentieth. But they were all conflicts *within* western civilisation. In a much-cited article of 1993, 'The Clash of Civilisations', Samuel P. Huntington, a professor at Harvard University, suggested this phase had now come to an end, and that future wars would be caused by clashes *between* civilisations.[3] In his view, 'the West' now faces the prospect of a clash with a Slavic Orthodox civilisation, an Oriental Confucian one, and a Middle Eastern Islamic one. Many of these issues recall those of the Middle Ages – not only the long and bitter clash between Christianity and Islam, but the nomadic 'invasions' of the so-called 'Dark Ages', which were, in fact, large-scale movements of displaced populations, much like those we may expect in future. This view is consistent with, though not entirely the same as, the widespread view that future conflict will tend to be between 'North and South', rather than between 'East and West'.

Huntington is right to stress the importance of the Treaty of Westphalia 350 years ago as a key watershed. We are now facing actors and factors which recall times before then. Westphalia also coincided, it may be remembered, roughly with the seventeenth-century scientific revolution and an acceleration of western technological superiority over any potential adversary which has lasted to the present. Technological dominance undoubtedly played a big part in ensuring increasing western influence over costume, manners, and the education of the ruling élites of non-western countries. Huntington may be right when he says that these countries are no longer willing to accept that influence: they now want to be modern, and technologically advanced, but not western. The Japanese have so far been the only people to achieve conspicuous success in this regard, but others will follow.

Like all paradigm changes, the origins of the renewed prospect of the 'clash of civilisations' are obscure and fuzzy. The Second World War and the Cold War arguably involved clashes of civilisations: from 1941–45, Imperial Japan proved a very alien civilisation indeed. And although Soviet Russia was heavily overlaid with western ideas – like Communism – and was part of a common, central European totalitarian framework, which had something in common with Nazi Germany, it was by appealing to historic Russian nationalism that Stalin motivated the great eastern empire to defeat Hitler. The Cold War was an even clearer conflict between western values, as they had grown up since the Renaissance, and a civilisation which had missed out on the Renaissance and got Ivan the Terrible (1530–1584) instead, and was rather different, even though its declared political ideology was a western product. Since the end of Communism, that important link with the western intellectual tradition has gone.[4] A clash between the Jewish civilisation and the Islamic one has also been underway in Palestine since before the Second World War, though it has recently calmed down, as has a continuing conflict, punctuated by several wars and continuing unrest, between Muslim and Hindu in South Asia.

Huntington noted the 'kin-country syndrome' which in some cases appears to be supplanting traditional allegiances based on political ideologies. The Russians' and Ukrainians' friendly – or less unfriendly – relations with their fellow Slavs, the Serbs, in the recent Bosnian conflict is a case in point. Perhaps they forgot that Panslavism was invented by a Croat.[5] And in other cases the 'kin country' idea falls down. In the Gulf in 1990–91, Arab states ganged up with the United States against Saddam Hussein, whose objective was to be leader of the Arab world. Yet all his attempts to rally Arab states against the United States failed.

To talk of a grandiose clash – one between the West and a 'Confucian-Islamic' alliance, for example – may be stretching the point. China has, indeed, supplied Saudi Arabia with CSS-2 missiles, the longest-ranged and biggest ballistic missiles in the Middle East, and probably helped Pakistan with its nuclear weapons programme. But these connections may be purely pragmatic. Both China and Islamic countries benefit from the exchange: Middle East money for Chinese technology, especially in the field of ballistic missiles and 'weapons of mass destruction' (nuclear, biological and chemical). Neither China nor the Middle Eastern countries would expect to have such exchanges with the West. Huntington is probably right to foresee an era of 'the West versus the rest', rather than 'the West versus something in particular'. 'The West' is used here as a shorthand device: it is really the western half of the northern hemisphere: perhaps we should say the 'north-west'. People are understandably resentful and jealous of western dominance of the world's affairs. And as distances – measured in travel and communication time – get ever shorter, the scope for conflict increases.

However, it is unclear how the rivalry and resentment between different civilisations will translate into actual armed conflict, especially as the various 'civilisations' tend not always to share land borders. At the time of writing, the most likely source of conflict in east Asia is widely considered to be between China and Taiwan, and warning signs emerged when China conducted major naval and military exercise off Taiwan in March 1996. Although Taiwan is a westernised, industrial economy, and Communist China is not, the archetypal model of different 'civilisations' hardly applies. Here, and in the dispute over the Spratly Islands in the South China Sea, conflict will probably only involve naval and air forces, which is likely to keep it limited. The 230 islands, lying between China and Malaysia, are important for mineral resources, and strategically, as they lie between the Indian and Pacific Oceans. China, Taiwan and Vietnam each claim all of the islands; the Philippines, Malaysia and Brunei lay claim to some of them. China has garrisons on seven of the islands, the Philippines on eight, Malaysia on three, Taiwan on one and Vietnam on twenty-one.[6]

The potential for maritime conflict over the Spratly Islands is obviously very great, especially between China and Vietnam, which also share a land border. The potential for conflict between states in the Muslim Maghreb and the European Union is less great, and they only face each other across a fairly wide stretch of sea – the Mediterranean.

Where 'fault lines between civilisations' exist on land, as in ex-Yugoslavia, the civilisations concerned are likely to become involved as supporters of the fighting factions, rather than as direct actors. This has been seen with Muslim states supporting the Bosnian Muslims with arms and money, while the Croatian Army was rearmed with help from former Warsaw Pact countries in central Europe, and trained and equipped with necessities like radios and field rations by Americans.[7]

Finally, there is the dilemma of 'torn countries', like Turkey and Mexico. The élites in these countries tend to be pro-western; the population, and certain opposition factions, tend not to be. The same applies to Russia, at the time of writing, where the pro-western reform movement led by Boris Yeltsin is under increasing pressure from Russian nationalists. This conflict mirrors that between slavophils and western-isers in the nineteenth century: a French-speaking, westward-looking aristocracy and court out of touch with very different traditions and undercurrents among the people.

It does not take a great deal of historical insight to establish where the 'fault lines' between civilizations lie. The circumstances that lead to conflict on the edges are likely, as throughout history, to be local, driven by immediate self-interest, perhaps even trivial. Such conflicts will need to be watched very carefully – as has been the case with western concern over Bosnia – to stop them spreading into a more grandiose clash between 'civilisations'. Although the 'clash of civilisations' could be presented as the grinding of tectonic plates, which produce earthquakes, the situation in human affairs suggests the opposite. It is as if the earthquake comes first, and that makes the plates move.

Weapons of Mass Destruction: a Cause as well as a Means of Conflict?

It is fairly remarkable that, up to the time of writing, only six states have developed nuclear weapons arsenals and a seventh claims to have developed one and voluntarily destroyed it. The six are five declared nuclear powers – the United States, Russia, Britain, France and China – and one 'nuclear opaque' state, Israel. The seventh was South Africa, which claimed to have had six bombs – recognised as the minimum viable nuclear arsenal for a state which wants to hold a few in reserve in case of retaliation. India let off a 'peaceful' nuclear explosion under the Rajasthan desert in 1974 and, like Pakistan, could probably build a nuclear arsenal very quickly but, again like Pakistan, has voluntarily eschewed it.

There have been occasions when nations' attempts to develop nuclear weapons and other 'weapons of mass destruction' – chemical and biological – have actually caused conflict. In 1981, Israel launched an air strike on the Iraqi nuclear reactor at Osiraq to pre-empt its development of nuclear weapons. During the 1991 Gulf War, ostensibly waged to eject the Iraqi Army from Kuwait, the first targets of the strategic bombing campaign were Iraqi nuclear, biological and chemical warfare facilities. Subsequent investigations by officials from the International Atomic Energy Authority confirmed the Iraqis were not far off completing development of a nuclear device. They already had biological and chemical weapons in large numbers. Attacking the Iraqi facilities was therefore prudent, and you could argue that conflict might, in future, be motivated by a desire to destroy such facilities before it is too late. Such attacks, however, are likely to be limited as states involved in the clandestine development of nuclear and other exceptionally nasty weapons tend not to admit the fact, they will protest and sulk but not launch reprisals.

At the time of writing the clandestine development of nuclear weapons may be getting easier. Traditionally, to produce a nuclear weapon with a known 'yield' (the size of the bang), you need to test it. Computer simulation techniques have now advanced to the stage where, for the most developed countries, testing is no longer necessary. The international outcry about France's nuclear tests in 1995 centred on the belief that they were not really necessary. In the old days, a total nuclear test ban would have been a good way of impeding nuclear proliferation. In the future, with reliable computer codes, testing may be completely unnecessary, and a sophisticated military nuclear arsenal – not a crude nuclear 'device' of unknown power – could be developed in secret.

New Actors, New Stars

Traditional military thinking dealt with a limited number of human actors, who were almost exclusively nation states. In recent years, the number of actors – national, multi-national, supra-national and internal – has multiplied. This is partly due to the development of economies in Asia and the Pacific rim, and in the Middle East, and partly to the breakdown of European empires and, now, of the Communist empire. Some of the new actors are on the traditional nation-state model, and some are of a totally new kind.

The first example of the former was the emergence of Japan as a great power at the end of the nineteenth century. A more recent arrival on the world stage is India, which exploded a nuclear device in 1974, and has some of the world's largest armed forces, and a space programme. Any 'developing country', such as Pakistan, Iran or Iraq, would shoot to stardom straightaway if it acquired nuclear weapons. The Ukraine is one of the new and powerful actors arising from the break-up of the former Soviet Union and other Communist countries. And a new form of European state, small but powerful, is re-emerging. After Croatia's victories over the Krajina Serbs in May and August 1995, some made comparisons between Croatia and Israel. A small country the size of Scotland, Croatia had used the four years away from direct confrontation with Serbia proper to develop armed forces which, whatever their limitations and faults, were untypically tough, aggressive and independent for a modern, European state of that size. With its sharp business sense and military tradition, Croatia might become a little Balkan Sparta, punching well above its weight in south-east European politics.

But new nation states are not the only new actors. The number of multinational companies has snowballed, from 7,000 in 1970 to 37,000 at the time of writing.[8] Some of these are very large, with wealth and resources rivalling smaller nation states. Business is conducted across state boundaries and beyond state control. The existence of satellite TV channels and the computer internet cuts across national laws on what people are allowed to watch or read. National controls are becoming increasingly irrelevant to such organisations, which are also acquiring increasing power to control or affect the key business of our time – information transfer. Short of casing an entire country in lead, or employing an impossible army of spies, detectors and informers, these developments cannot be stopped.

Drug cartels are also new 'actors'. With drug money they can run substantial armed units, and possibly buy the expertise of a new generation of high-tech mercenaries, or condottieri, as the Italian 'freelances' of the late middle ages were known. It was possibly threats of this kind that the British Defence Secretary, Michael Portillo, was contemplating when on 16 November 1995 he alluded to the possibility of diverting 'defence' resources to countering international crime and drug trafficking.[9] A large, well-armed yacht, perhaps adapted to carry rapid-firing cannon and missiles, engaged in a multi-million pound or dollar drug operation is unlikely to surrender to a policeman in a small motorboat, or even a well-equipped customs and police team, without a serious fight.

The availability of weapons and people trained to use them is a key factor in the multiplication of actors. The break-up of the Warsaw Pact, and the dramatic reduction in the service personnel of all European countries and North America, plus the prevailing economic climate, all makes weapons and expertise widely available to multinational cartels with money to spend. And, relatively speaking, they are very cheap.

Weapons of mass destruction also mean that very small groups within nation states can be disproportionately effective. The nerve gas attack on the Tokyo underground in March 1995 linked to the Aum Shinri Kyo cult was a warning as to what small, dedicated groups could achieve. The activities of extremist groups, either those motivated by religious belief, or the growing band of 'animal rights' extremists and others who believe these methods may achieve environmental improvement, have much in common with traditional insurgency or guerrilla war. But their significance as opponents for national security forces will have to be measured in terms of their potential effect, not their small size. A nuclear bomb, or a device to spread radioactive fall-out over a wide area, can cause destruction on a massive scale, regardless of the size of the organization responsible.

The last group of new actors is the supra-national authorities which increasingly are supplanting some of the traditional functions of nation states. Because military power of any great import has tended to be concentrated in the hands of national governments for most of the last 350 years, it is no surprise that national governments remain the most efficient organisers of military operations and the most credible 'units of deterrence'. However, if supra-national authorities like the European Union are to take over many of the legislative and regulatory functions of nation states, some transfer of military command to those authorities will inevitably follow, albeit slowly. Since 1945 the United Nations has preserved a monopoly on dispensing justice – and punishment – under international law. It follows that it should have its own enforcement agency.

Population Growth and Movement

The coming anarchy: nations break up under the tidal flow of refugees from environmental and social disaster. Wars are fought over scarce resources, especially water, and war itself becomes continuous with crime, as armed bands of stateless marauders clash with the private security forces of the élites.[10]

Robert Kaplan's gloomy prediction of the first decades of the twenty-first century was credible enough to be cited in 1995 by the UN High Commissioner for Refugees in an authoritative report which estimated that there were about 50 million people who were displaced within their own country, or were refugees who had crossed borders – one in 110 of the world's population.[11]

In 1950, world population was about 3 billion: it is predicted it will be 6.3 billion in 2000, 7.2 billion in 2010 and 8.5 billion in 2025. Even assuming efforts to control the population are made, a median prediction for the year 2100 is 11 billion, and a high one is 14.2 billion. Even if the population was controlled at 'replacement level' – one birth for every death – it would take 75 years before population growth ceased.[12] But overall population growth is not the most potentially dangerous factor. Whereas population growth in Europe and the developed world has, in fact, almost ceased and in Germany and Hungary the population is actually declining, 90 per cent of births take place in the 'developing' or 'third world'. Not only do the figures for the next century suggest the world's resources will be stretched, but those born into the 'developing world' will expect at least some of the comfort and amenities currently reserved for the developed world. Energy consumption levels in Europe and the United States are tens of times those in Africa.

The potential for explosive competition and confrontation is clear. As a senior British civil servant wrote in a Cambridge study, 'failing a tolerable way of life for the masses of humanity, the affluent minority can have no assurance that it will continue to hold and enjoy its present benefits, even if it is prepared to close its mind to the moral issues involved.'[13] However, as Norman Angell pointed out in his work on the difficulty of 'capturing' wealth or trade, it is not immediately obvious how the rest of the world might 'capture', or limit, the wealth of the developed nations. The division arose, in the first instance, from exchanging manufactured goods, produced in the north-western segment of the planet, for raw materials, which came from elsewhere.

But since Norman Angell wrote, that system has broken down. Manufactured goods are produced more cheaply in Asia and on the Pacific rim than in Birmingham or Detroit, and office work for some firms in London is now done by computer operators in Calcutta or Bombay, who earn a fraction of the wages. A global economy, and global communications, may enable the poverty-stricken masses to 'take' the wealth and privilege of the north-west directly.

Even the business of finance, traditionally centred on London and New York, is now also centred on Hong Kong and Singapore. The ability of a single trader, Nick Leeson, to break Britain's oldest merchant bank in 1995 from Singapore, is a concrete example of how the deprived 'third world' could, in a very real way, *take wealth away* from the north-west. In the case of Baring's employees in London, they were made redundant. Leeson was British, working for a British bank in Singapore. But it is not a far step to see how the developing world can and will gradually take more of the non-productive work (accountancy, filing, financial services) on which the north-western economies rely to fuel the process of circulating money which drives them.

Norman Angell's ninety-year-old thesis that there is not very much that traditional military power can do about this sort of thing clearly applies to the new situation. In extremis, a north-western power, or powers, desperate to regain business of this type to forestall mass-unemployment, alienation and internal disorder, could use electronic 'soft-kill' devices spread through computer networks to disable a south-east Asian business powerhouse. The same could happen in reverse. But such a confrontation is unlikely to take a traditional military form. It would be a strategic conflict fought with non-military means.

The main military implication of population growth is, quite simply, the spread of population across borders. In the nineteenth century, the overspill of people from Europe spread rapidly into the vast expanses of South Africa, Australia and the American west. In many cases they clashed with local peoples. At the end of the twentieth century, with the whole world enclosed and borders defined, the opportunities for such free movement are fewer.

The UN High Commissioner for Refugees (UNHCR) has pointed out, rightly, that most migrants move within states rather than across borders, and that when they do move they are more likely to do so from one low-income country to another.[14] It is natural for people to migrate, and modern-day controls on movement across borders are a relative innovation. Many of the main refugee emergencies have been directly attributable to wars: 2.7 million people displaced in Bosnia-Herzegovina; 1.5 million by the conflicts in the Caucasus; 3 million people from Afghanistan who, in 1995, were still in neighbouring Pakistan and Iran; and 2.2 million people displaced within Rwanda or in neighbouring countries.

The increase in the number of UN peacekeeping operations and the number of people employed on them (from about 10,000 in 1988 to 75,000 in 1994) has helped the UNHCR in its efforts to resettle refugees. By demobilising local militias and identifying and removing land-mines – of which there are an estimated 100 million scattered round the world – peacekeeping troops have assisted the UNHCR in its efforts to get refugees to return home. Their success has been greatest in Cambodia, Somalia and Mozambique. More than 1.6 million people returned to Mozambique from neighbouring countries between 1992 and 1995. But the UN has had little success in Rwanda.

The main area of concern for western Europe is the southern Mediterranean. Between 1990 and 2010 the littoral population from Turkey to Morocco is expected to have grown from 219 million to 330 million. The European population on the north shore will only have grown from 190 million to 196 million. The total population of Europe, including Ukraine plus the Russian Federation, will have grown from 723 million to 741 million. Western Europe will be a destination for many people from the southern Mediterranean. In the early 1990s there were fears of large migrations – in the order of 10 million people – westwards from the former Soviet Union and eastern Europe but these have not materialised. Apart from refugees from the war in ex-Yugoslavia, there has been relatively little pressure on the European Union from the east. There were peaks in migration from ex-Yugoslavia in 1992–93, but migration from eastern Europe is expected to have gone back to zero by 2010.[15]

One of the main areas of migration is within the Russian Federation, from the Caucasus and central Asia. It has been suggested some 25 million Russians may seek to return to mother Russia from outposts in the 'near abroad'. This demographic factor, combined with the political instability of the southern rim of the Russian Empire, and with the drying up of large tracts of central Asia and the Aral Sea, makes it a likely location for armed conflict and crisis.

To date, the 'threat' of floods of immigrants into western Europe from the east has not materialised, but the situation in the southern Mediterranean is serious. Of 10 million migrant workers in Europe, 2.4 million originated in North Africa and 2 million in Turkey. The continuing pressure on Europe from these directions is driven by poverty and not, specifically, by population growth. The level of illegal immigration from North Africa is expected to rise. Once again, specific military responses – apart from naval patrols – are not the answer. Investment and aid to increase the prosperity of the countries from which the migrants come probably are. The United States has been facing the same problem with large numbers of illegal immigrants from Mexico and Cuba but its attitude to Cuba has been self-defeating. Rather than trying to destroy the Cuban economy, it needs to help it.

The biggest problem is that the indigenous European population is not only virtually static (no bad thing in itself), it is getting older. By 2025 it is estimated there will be a 30 per cent shortfall in the European labour market. Even if current retirement ages were adjusted upwards, it would not solve the problem. Some jobs require people who are youthful, physically fit and robust. There will be a particular shortage in the unskilled and semi-skilled labour categories – those traditionally filled by immigrants.[16]

An ageing population in the north-west may have important military implications. Military personnel are young, and most leave to undertake other jobs well before middle age (the medical profession still defines 'late middle age' as starting at 40!). In general terms, the shortage of young people will have multiple effects on the armed forces, who will be competing for them with every other employer in the job market. This suggests that the armed forces of developed countries will have to place greater reliance on technology and on older people, and use younger people for very specific tasks.

In the developing world, the population appears to be focusing on the cities. By 2000, it is estimated that the largest will be Mexico City, with 25 million people. Tokyo, the largest in 1985 with 19 million, will have slipped to third with 20 million after Sao Paolo, with 24 million. Calcutta and Bombay will be fourth and fifth, with about 16 million each.[17] The centripetal movement into cities – or the vast areas of shanty towns around them – will reinforce the trend towards states becoming less preoccupied with international conflict and more preoccupied with internal conflict, drug trafficking and crime.

Population growth will undoubtedly create the potential for more conflict – though the conflicts triggered, will not necessarily be 'hot' wars, but movements of people requiring international aid and supervision. They may well give rise to the type of military operations known as 'wider peacekeeping'.

Global Warming, Global Warning ...

There is little doubt any more that the earth is getting warmer as a result, in part, of chemical emissions. By 2020 the earth is expected to be 1.3°C warmer than now, rising to 3° warmer by 2070.[18] That will cause icecaps to melt, sea levels to rise, *arid areas to expand both northwards and southwards, away from the equator*, a reduction in rainfall in the most productive parts of the northern hemisphere, and an extension of the process of 'desertification' which is already underway. The most dramatic effects are likely to be associated with rising sea-levels. Some studies suggest that 18 per cent of Bangladesh, which is sinking anyway, because of the drilling of boreholes to extract drinking water, could be under water by 2050. Its teeming population will have to go somewhere.

The exact extent of sea-level rise is difficult to predict and has probably been exaggerated. It may be only a metre in the next century, which would not have too much of an effect other than on Bangladesh and the coastal cities of the Nile Delta. In the next fifty years it might be less than half a metre. However, some 70 per cent of the world's population lives within 100 miles of the sea, and even a modest rise in sea levels is bound to cause flooding and profound disturbance, which will take place in concert with population growth.

Global warming is also expected to cause an increase in famines, floods and storms. At the very least this will increase the number of military-type operations associated with natural and human disasters.

Desertification happened without appreciable global warming, primarily as a result of agricultural practices. The 'fertile crescent' of Mesopotamia, one of the cradles of civilisation, is now desert – mainly because of over-grazing, intensive farming and irrigation techniques which were damaging in the long term. Deforestation has been another factor: when jungle is cleared, the terrain reverts to savannah, or desert. Deserts can spread surprisingly quickly: in Mali, by 1992, the Sahara had spread 350 kilometres southward in just twenty years, and in southern Sudan it has advanced 100 kilometres in seventeen years.

In Uzbekistan in central Asia the Aral Sea is drying up as a result of two irrigation schemes based on the Amu Darya (Oxus) and Syr Darya rivers. The two rivers normally flooded twice a year, filling the sea with 47 billion cubic metres of water. It is now 30 billion cubic metres short, and is drying up. This has led to a shortage of water in the Fergana valley, which could lead to conflict between the three countries which share access to the Syr Darya there: Kyrgyzstan, Tajikistan and Uzbekistan. The associated process of desertification also threatens land in Turkmenistan and Kazakhstan.

Global warming could conceivably come to the rescue of the Russian Federation to the north, however. Much of Siberia's mineral wealth is locked in sub-arctic, frozen permafrost – ground frozen solid, permanently. A modest warming of the climate could thaw huge areas, making the vast national resources concealed beneath more accessible. For the Russians, a general warming of the environment would be welcome.

Water

A Central Intelligence Agency paper for the US government has estimated that war could erupt over limited and shared water resources in at least ten places in the world. Most are in the Middle East. In 1992, when the Pentagon was undertaking its 'Bottom-up Review' of conflicts that might require American intervention, it was no coincidence that one of the first conflicts studied was between Syria and Turkey, after Turkey's completion of the South-East Anatolia or GAP project to divert the headwaters of the Tigris and Euphrates for its own purposes, with the potential to parch Syria and Iraq.[19]

Four-fifths of the world's available (fresh) water is used for irrigation, which in turn produces 40 per cent of the world's food. In China, 87 per cent of water is used for irrigation; in India, 93 per cent. Israel uses 50 per cent of its water for irrigation, and 40 per cent for domestic use, which is close to European levels and more than four times that of neighbouring Arab states. But the small proportion of the world's water that is drunk is not always clean, and dirty water is responsible for four fifths of disease in the developing world. Land is scarce, fertile land is scarcer, but people need two litres of water a day to survive. The most critical area is currently the Middle East, where the population is expected to double in between seventeen and twenty-four years, and where water is in shortest supply.[20]

There are three main river systems in the Middle East, all of which are shared and all of which are sources of potential conflict. The first is the Jordan, which has its sources in Lebanon and Syria and flows into northern Israel and then down the 1967 cease-fire line between the Palestinian West Bank territory and the State of Jordan to the Dead Sea. Then there are the Tigris and Euphrates, which rise in Turkey, and water Syria and Iraq. Finally there is the Nile, which originates in central Africa, in Lakes Victoria, Albert and Keoga, and then flows through Sudan and Egypt. In all, it affects life in nine countries – partly because, at 6,800 kilometres (4,266 miles) long it is one of the longest rivers in the world. There are other water systems in the Middle East, too: a deep system of subterranean rivers and cracks, the courses of which are unclear; and vast aquifers – underground 'fossil' water, trapped from the Ice Ages, before the area became dry. The Saharan aquifers contain 60,000 cubic *kilometres* of water – each cubic kilometre is a billion cubic metres – but it can be mined only once.

The water of the Jordan was one of the direct causes of the 1967 Arab-Israeli war. An Arab plan to divert its waters led to Israel's pre-emptive attacks on Egypt and Syria. The capture of the West Bank and the Golan Heights, which shield the Jordan water as it enters Israel, were strategic bonuses from that war, both of which improved the security of Israel's water supply. There are also 170 springs in the Golan Heights which currently provide a third of Israel's water, and Israel draws water from aquifers under the West Bank, one of the few areas in the region which gets adequate rainfall.

In 1975, after Syria built its Thawrah dam, Iraq claimed the loss of water put the livelihood of three million Iraqi farmers at risk. However, this interruption to the flow of the Euphrates was trivial compared to what the Turkish South-East Anatolia (GAP) project would later threaten to do to both countries. It began in the 1960s as a simple plan to irrigate a

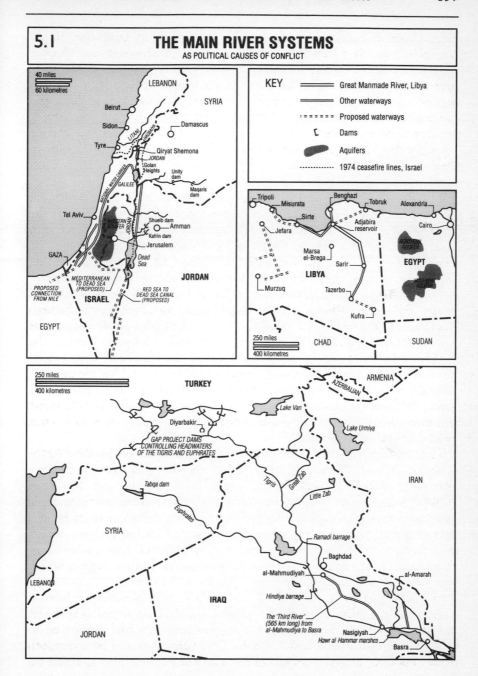

5.1   **THE MAIN RIVER SYSTEMS**
AS POLITICAL CAUSES OF CONFLICT

KEY
Great Manmade River, Libya
Other waterways
Proposed waterways
Dams
Aquifers
1974 ceasefire lines, Israel

plain along the border with Syria. After 1980, against the background of a guerrilla war with Turkey's 12 million-strong Kurdish population, the plan escalated into a vast project to double Turkey's output of hydroelectric power, increase the amount of water available and transform the whole south-east of the country. New wealth, the immigration of urban professionals from western Turkey and a new infrastructure would make it impossible for the guerrillas based among the mountain Kurds to operate. At this stage, water was not the cause of a war; it was a way to stop one, although Turgut Ozal, the head of State Planning and a hydrological engineer by background, clearly saw the GAP would also give his nation power and influence over the states downstream.

Syria and Iraq were soon aware of the plan and, in addition to the guerrilla war against the Kurdish rebels, the Turks anticipated attacks by Syrian or Iraqi commandos. In 1986 there were reports that Turkey had uncovered a plot to blow up the Ataturk dam, near Bozova. The Turkish engineers said it would take an atomic device to breach the Ataturk wall, 169 metres high and two kilometres long. By this time, the GAP plan was to use the water and power from the dams to irrigate and transform an area the size of the Netherlands. Much of the water would be diverted and remain in Turkey.

The Turks made an informal agreement that they would allow Syria a flow of 500 cubic metres a second down the Euphrates. They pointed out that the flow of the Euphrates could vary from a relative trickle of 100 cubic metres in summer to 7,000 in spring when the mountain snows melted. A regular flow of 500 cubic metres was surely preferable, they said. But it would be totally dependent on the goodwill of the Turks.

The first part of the GAP project only involved the Euphrates, but when it is finished, in about 2010, with its twenty-two dams, it will control the Tigris as well.

The Turkish plan is to extend irrigation and new towns right across Turkish Kurdistan to the borders of Iran and Iraq. The Kurdish guerrillas are unlikely to let that happen without a fight. Kurdish exiles say that unless political reforms – which means a high degree of autonomy – take place, eastern Turkey will remain as it is: rugged and lawless with the guerrillas dominating the mountains. It is another potential area of conflict.

Such conflict would probably not manifest itself as large-scale warfare. That is seen as too dangerous and expensive and does not always suit the terrain or the objectives. Attacks by commando teams on dams, the tunnels which divert water round them, pipelines, power stations and desalination plants are more likely.

The oil-rich states of the Gulf depend heavily on desalination plants, which take sea water and turn it into fresh. These proved particularly vulnerable during the 1991 Gulf War. Oil slicks from installations wrecked by the Iraqis drifted down the Gulf and threatened to choke two desalination plants at al-Jubayl which supplied three quarters of Riyadh's requirements.[21] Saddam Hussein of Iraq has also used water as a weapon. During the 1980–88 Gulf War, large lakes and moats were constructed as part of a defensive network against Iranian attack from the east. After that war was ended, work continued on the great 'Third River' project which ran from near Baghdad to near Basra, linking the Tigris and Euphrates. The 'Third River' also helped drain the marshes in southern Iraq, ancestral home of the Marsh Arabs and a refuge for opponents of Saddam.

The Nile is a final possible source of conflict. It was the cause of a four-day war between Libya and Egypt in 1977. Colonel Gaddafi had sent guerrilla units to Sudan, which sparked Egyptian sensitivities about the Nile, on which the nation is utterly dependent. Egypt had always made it clear that any threat to Nile water would be a cause of war, and President Sadat sent planes to bomb Libya. The excuse was the plight of Egyptian workers in Libya but there was little doubt that the threat to Egypt's southern, watery lifeline, was the real reason. The Egyptians accepted offers of international mediation, and the action was called off. The dispute between Egypt and Colonel Gaddafi over water continued, however: the Libyan leader planned to extract water from the great sub-Saharan aquifer down a huge pipeline known as the 'Great Man-Made River' to the coast. The Great Madman's River, as the Egyptians called it unkindly, took seven years to build, from 1984 to 1991. The Egyptians relied on aquifers of their own to water the Qattara depression, and said the Libyan plan threatened to suck water out of their own aquifers, which appear to be connected in some way.

Ethiopia has traditionally taken very little of the water from the Nile, but if it is to develop and agriculture is to be improved, Ethiopia will not be content to remain as the 'water tower of Africa'. It will have to draw off some of the water that currently flows on to Sudan and Egypt. Sudan now has an Islamic government, which constitutes a potential threat to Egypt, and to its vital water supplies. Egypt has problems with Islamic extremists of its own. However, up to the time of writing, the political disagreements have not been allowed to interrupt technical cooperation and the management of the vital water on which both countries depend.

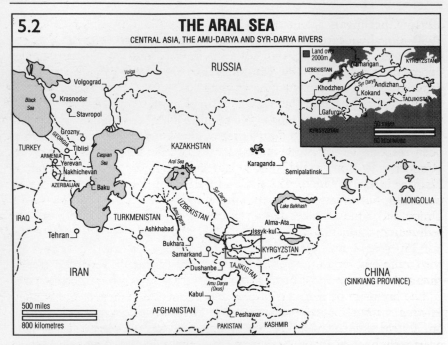

5.2 **THE ARAL SEA**
CENTRAL ASIA, THE AMU-DARYA AND SYR-DARYA RIVERS

Although water could therefore be an immediate and direct cause of future wars, King Hussein of Jordan, President Ozal of Turkey, President Sadat of Egypt and Boutros Boutros-Ghali have all noted it could be an excellent focus for international cooperation. Engineers all speak the same language.

New Factors, Old Factors

The above factors focus attention on certain places, notably the Middle East and central Asia, where population growth, global warming, water conflicts and desertification all coincide. When new and as yet untried political disputes are added, it is clear that the southern rim of the old Soviet empire, the stamping ground of Genghis Khan and Tamerlane, is a prime candidate for numerous conflicts.

It will be clear by now that the new factors outlined above are likely to act as catalysts, sparking conflict in the next quarter of a century or so. In the case of water, its influence may be more obvious and direct. Conflict never – or very seldom – arises from just one cause, however. Recent wars and interventions by the developed world have been about oil (the Gulf in

1991, Chechnya), about religion (Bosnia, Chechnya, the Gulf in 1980–88), about territory and strategic waterways or possessions (the first Gulf War, again, the Falklands), about territory and national self-determination (the Middle East wars, Bosnia, Chechnya), about ethnic differences and power struggles within a state (Rwanda, Bosnia, Somalia, Cambodia). They have been devices to divert attention from internal problems (the Falklands, the 1991 Gulf War).

National self-determination – or the quest to become a nation – has been responsible for most internal conflicts. The principle was cited by Woodrow Wilson in 1917 and adopted enthusiastically by the United Nations in 1945. The break-up of colonial empires led to a wave of new countries, but usually within old boundaries. The break-up of the Soviet Union and Yugoslavia created more. But the UN does not take kindly to redrawing national boundaries, with good reason. Most of the wars of the last 350 years have occurred when national boundaries did not coincide with religious, linguistic or ethnic divisions. Those boundaries usually changed after the wars, not necessarily for the better.

The break-up of the Soviet Union and Yugoslavia followed the lines of existing internal boundaries – Ukraine, Belarus, Croatia, Bosnia and so on. Those boundaries tended to be fairly arbitrary, of course. They were previously lines of administrative convenience, which were less important and emotive when they were merely internal, within a powerful and cohesive nation state. Inevitably, the realignment caused dissension. An extreme example was the struggle over the Crimea, which was historically Russian, but had been given to Ukraine by Khrushchev. While they were all part of the great Soviet Union it did not matter. When Ukraine became a fair-sized state by itself, including Crimea and the former Soviet Black-Sea fleet, it caused a terrible problem. Croatia had a good boundary, along the Sava river, coinciding with the old frontier of the Austro-Hungarian Empire, but there were still Serb communities in Croatia and Croats in Bosnia.

The break-up of nation states has caused endless problems. The emergence of supra-national entities like the European Union has not, so far, lessened the problem, although it ought, in theory, to be easier for Scotland to become independent of London knowing that it would still be part of the European Union.

Most people do not want to fight wars. Almost invariably, the blame can be laid principally on the ambitions of individual people and small cliques around them: Presidents Milosevic of Serbia and Tudjman of Croatia, who let their surrogates in Bosnia actually fight most of the war; Saddam Hussein; Dzhokhar Dudayev, who led the Chechens into a war of independence from Russia which many of them did not want.

From that, it is easy to see why the emergence of warfare, as an organised activity, coincided with the emergence of powerful and authoritarian states. Although most people want peace, they are also fearful of those in power over them, and this makes them more biddable. Once hostilities have begun, the circumstances in which they find themselves make them frightened, bitter and vengeful, and thus turn them against the declared 'enemy', and reinforce their willingness to do as they are told.

The role of the ambitious and charismatic individual in starting and sustaining conflict is undeniable. It is easier to confirm and understand than 'clashes of civilisations' or the 'pressure' of uprooted populations. It is one reason why the thesis put forward by Immanuel Kant (1724–1804) in his *Perpetual Peace* (1795) that war is unlikely to occur between democracies seems valid. Whatever its faults and its tedium, modern democracy does tend to exclude the extreme, and a system of checks and balances, including a free media, works to prevent the accession of extremists to positions of great power. It also limits adventures of the type that, in recent history, have been largely confined to authoritarian or fascist states: Hitler's Germany, General Galtieri's Argentina, Saddam Hussein's Iraq. Whether the fledgling democracies of countries like Russia are yet able to do that is uncertain.

Democratic states respond when attacked and because they are less 'militaristic' they may fight more clumsily, perhaps even more unrestrainedly, as the Allies did with their strategic bombing and use of nuclear weapons in the Second World War. But unless their own survival is unequivocally threatened, democracies try to keep conflict at the lowest possible level of violence. The aim is not usually to move to a more 'absolute' form of war or to amass overwhelming force to deal a crushing surprise blow – although that would be the logical aim of traditional military theory. It is to keep racking up the pain in a controlled progression, until the other party says 'stop'.

Proper Soldiering? New Roles for Armed Forces

Not so long ago, the Chief of Staff of the UN forces in Cyprus, Brigadier Michael Harbottle, asked the departing commander of a Canadian UN contingent how he had found the peacekeeping role.

'All right, but it will be good to get back to *proper soldiering*,' the Canadian replied.[22]

Brigadier Harbottle used the phrase in a pamphlet which has been used at the British Army Staff College and by several other countries' ministries of defence. 'He seemed totally to have missed the point that his period of UN service had helped keep the peace in that violence-torn island and had made a contribution far more positive than he would achieve by training for war,' Brigadier Harbottle later wrote. Or maybe the Canadian was joking. Maybe he understood *this* was proper soldiering – and not the pretence of practising for full-scale conflict, for something that was unlikely to happen.

While national security, in the conventional sense of weapon power, remains the most immediate and exclusive role of armed forces, it is no longer the only one. In fact it never was. 'Peace' and 'security' are not just the absence of conventional war: that is better summarised by the Russian word for security, *bezopasnost* – 'absence of [immediate] danger'.

The officer who wanted to go back to 'real soldiering' was unusual. The role of armed forces in international peacekeeping is now firmly established. Their experience goes beyond recognisably military roles, to medical assistance, rebuilding amenities, communications and not just the protection but the supply of aid.

One of the most important tasks of a peacekeeping force is safeguarding the rights and needs of the civilian population. In conventional war, whilst the Geneva conventions specify reasonable concern for the populace, and prohibit abuse, concern for those caught up in the war is extraneous to the main business in hand. Peacekeeping is therefore closely linked to disaster relief – indeed, it is a form of disaster relief. The only difference is the disaster is man-made.

In recent years the armed forces of many countries have been used for both sorts of disaster relief and for reconstruction. Their great advantage over other emergency services is that they have a great deal of advanced and specialised technology – ships, aeroplanes, helicopters – and a ready-made organisation to get relief to where it is needed fast. Navies have repeatedly attended flooding in the Bay of Bengal and Bangladesh, and the speed of reaction is particularly important in attending to earthquakes, where most of those buried will be dead within forty-eight hours of immolation. The provision of communications when the civil telephone networks are cut and of engineers to clear blocked routes are also areas where the military can offer particularly relevant expertise. As we witnessed in Kurdistan – a man-made disaster – they can also deliver supplies by helicopter and even by parachute. The US Air Force's successful attack on the breached oil manifolds at the Sea Island terminal off Kuwait in 1991 with precision weapons is another example. Again, it was a man-made environmental catastrophe; it could equally have been an accident.

There has been opposition to the employment of military resources in disaster relief, largely because of outdated perceptions of the way the military operate. There is a suspicion that they will react insensitively to humanitarian problems, but the performance of what is normally the British Army's most aggressive brigade in Rwanda suggests that fear is misplaced. The International Red Cross has been concerned that a military presence alongside its relief efforts may jeopardise its impartial status, as defined in its charter, but recent experience in ex-Yugoslavia, Rwanda and Cambodia suggests it would be ludicrous *not* to cooperate in such circumstances. The principle of 'impartiality' which is cardinal to any peacekeeping operation should remove that concern: another reason why it is not feasible to mix peacekeeping and peace enforcement.

In future, armed forces should go beyond merely reacting to disasters to providing 'environmental security': conserving the planet's environment and ecology. It is not their most immediate task, but there will be plenty of time when standing armed forces are not involved in more traditional military business, and it is very good training. Such a role should come naturally to soldiers, who are more familiar than most city-dwellers with the patterns and appearance of the landscape, the weather and the seasons. The military own, or have exclusive access to, vast tracts of land that are frequently of unusual environmental and scientific interest, but their potential to use their forces to conserve and improve the environment goes beyond that. The Russian Army has a tradition of helping with the harvest and could in future be used to try to repair some of the environmental damage suffered by Russia in the past fifty years.

The most imaginative and far-sighted use of armed forces for 'environmental security' has taken place in India, which has the world's fourth largest armed forces (1.15 million in 1995, as against 1.5 million each for the United States and Russia, and 2.9 million for China).[23] Each Indian Army formation (brigade, division and above) has an environmental team to monitor and coordinate the activities of its troops in this field. Tree planting and restoring arid landscapes are high on the list of priorities. Many millions of trees have been replanted over the past five years.

At the time of writing Indian Army Engineers are completing a water control 'barrage' (similar in principle to the Thames barrier which defends London) at Kutch in north-west India. It aims to divert monsoon floods which currently wash into the Indian Ocean towards the Rajasthan desert, for irrigation. The use of troops for these purposes in the developed territories of Europe and North America would be inefficient and politically unacceptable, but those rules do not always apply elsewhere.

The Indian Army is also experimenting with the use of solar energy both in barracks and when in the field, to cut down on wood consumption for cooking. The use of solar energy also has military advantages: electrical power available anywhere, and no tell-tale smoke. Military and environmental requirements often coincide. The Indian Navy has assumed responsibility for monitoring pollution in coastal and inshore waters and lakes. Finally, reservists who are called up to undergo refresher training split their time between military exercises and environmental work.[24] The latter can also help military fitness training: manual work in the open air is a far more productive form of physical exercise to keep soldiers fit than the nugatory business of 'pumping iron' or running round a track. That is not a new idea. John Ruskin, the Victorian philanthropist, was appalled to see Oxford undergraduates wasting their energy propelling themselves up and down the river, and put them to work building roads.

India was one of the countries which submitted a draft resolution to the UN General Assembly in October 1990 calling on the Security Council to explore the use of military resources to support civil efforts to protect and restore the environment. The other countries were Austria (which has used military resources to construct defences against avalanches), Brazil, Bulgaria (where the army has been used for afforestation), Mexico, Venezuela and the then USSR.

Another important advantage enjoyed by armed forces is that, unless actually at war with each other, the armed forces of different countries enjoy a common ethos and ways of doing things. The author participated in a 'confidence-building' mission and arms control inspection to Czechoslovakia, immediately after the end of the Cold War and another to Russia in 1996, and noted how extraordinarily well military personnel from different countries with different political systems got on. The growing experience of multinational operations lends support to the idea that armed forces could act as a valuable catalyst to initiate international cooperation on environmental projects which inevitably affect several countries. Clearing the River Danube of pollution, which affects seven countries, is one example.

In the next half century, the first and overriding role of armed forces will continue to be the defence of national sovereignty or that of a group of nations. However, it is increasingly unlikely that they will be called upon to do this. They will be used, in the main, to support national foreign policy objectives, probably under the umbrella of international organisations and according to international law, which is likely to reside with the United Nations. They will also be used increasingly to back up police and customs organisations, and to fight crime and other threats to national security, both internationally (under UN or other auspices, again) or internally. National Foreign Policy objectives are likely to include peacekeeping, wider peacekeeping, humanitarian aid and disaster relief, and environmental security. The latter is a valid and natural role for organised, disciplined forces able to react (and this should be their crucial advantage) very swiftly. Such roles dovetail naturally with the traditional roles of the military, and can enhance its preparedness for more conventional operations.

CHAPTER SIX
BETWEEN PEACEKEEPING AND WAR: A WHOLE NEW MIDDLE GROUND?

On 19 March 1994 light reconnaissance tanks – Scimitars – of the British Light Dragoons, working as part of the UN force out of Zepce in central Bosnia, reported Bosnian Serb troops moving west, out of positions they had held for months. The Serb forces, who had been helping the Croats cut off the mainly Muslim 'Maglaj finger', were slipping away from their former allies. It was as if a steel door was sliding open, revealing a long-locked, finger-shaped room. Maglaj had been isolated for months, with Serbs to the east and hostile Croats, collaborating with and stiffened by the Serbs, to the south. The UN High Commissioner for Refugees' representative in the Muslim town of Zenica, still further south, the charismatic, white-bearded Larry Hollingworth, had been trying to get a relief convoy into Maglaj since October. But, as I discovered on a visit to Maglaj shortly afterwards, the only aid to get in had been dropped by parachute.

The Muslim-Croat cease-fire of February was now clearly taking effect. The Serbs found themselves among Croats who were increasingly hostile, and between two facing groups of Muslim forces. They thought better of it, and quietly began to move. A message flashed to the headquarters of the British Army reconnaissance troops – known as the 'cavalry battalion' – at Zepce, at the foot of the 'finger', and back to the headquarters of the UN's Sector South-West at Gornji Vakuf. The UN commander, Brigadier John Reith, had brokered the Muslim-Croat cease-fire the month before. This was good reconnaissance, combined with good intelligence ('military information') about the situation on the ground and the implications of what the Dragoons had seen. A *window of opportunity* was opening. The British Army made contact with Larry Hollingworth, who alerted his aid trucks.

During the 1980s, western strategists had shown much interest in Soviet plans to insert 'operational manoeuvre groups' in conventional war, exploiting any break in the enemy front line. The 'OMG' would move in, slipping behind front-line formations, and destabilise the enemy defences. In the Gulf, the Allies had done something similar with the British armoured division, and British commanders explicitly acknowledged that their division was an 'OMG'.[1] Recognising the 'window of opportunity' in time and space was critical. Now, just like an OMG, this aid convoy, escorted by Scimitars, moved into the 'window'. But they were not trying to destabilise anybody's defences or to bring armed assistance to one side in the war. They wanted to take desperately needed aid to the civilian population of Maglaj, and to find out what had been happening there, for no one knew. By moving swiftly to exploit the opportunity, they succeeded.

That night, something very bizarre occurred. This was not a 'war' for the UN, either for the UN Protection Force or the UN High Commissioner for Refugees, with whose organisation they planned, consulted and controlled the operation. Nobody was launching an OMG into the rear area of an enemy army to tear it apart. But the way the operation was conducted was much the same. Find the moving window, and move through, as swiftly and silently as possible. The division between soldiers and aid workers disappeared. Was this a military operation? It was for the soldiers. It was planned and run just like that. But there was clearly something new here. A new mixture of combat and compassion for which there were no manuals, and no accepted rules. They did the only thing they could. They had a job to do. They made it up as they went along. There were, as yet, no manuals for the new sort of operation.

A Clash of Doctrines

The events of 1991, starting with the intervention in Kurdistan, began a new era, in which armed forces were most likely to be used for operations of this new type. General war was most unlikely. A limited war was also unlikely, but might occur perhaps once in ten years – the Falklands in 1982, the Gulf War in 1991. Some experts in the field predicted there would not be another one before 2000 (although I suggest there might be). At any time, they predicted there might be eight traditional peacekeeping operations underway and thirty of the new type – something between peacekeeping and limited war.[2]

What sort of animal was this new and prolific breed of operation? An extension of peacekeeping, on the traditional UN model; limited war of a very special and constrained kind; or something between? At the time of writing, there is still no agreement, and a polite row smoulders on. A bewildering range of descriptive terms has been suggested: 'chapter six-and-a-half operations' – a reference to the inadequacy of the UN Charter (see below); 'multifunctional operations'; 'second generation peacekeeping' or 'second generation operations'; and 'extended peacekeeping', which Lieutenant General Rose was using in Sarajevo in early 1994. Only one thing was certain. Whereas soldiers and scholars in Europe and the United States had been writing volumes about war for 200 years, there was no manual for this vast new area which had suddenly opened up. There was no doctrine, no instruction book. Creating a doctrine was the most important task for soldiers and scholars since at least the appearance of the atom bomb. Nobody would expect the first attempts to be perfect: the debate continues.

The British Army eventually decided to call the newly prominent type of operations 'wider peacekeeping', defined in its manual of that name, published in 1994, as 'the wider aspects of peacekeeping operations carried out with the general consent of the belligerent parties but in an environment that may be highly volatile.'[3] Wary of defining the animal wrongly, the manual went on to say what it looked like, rather than attempting to pin down its species. 'Wider peacekeeping' was concerned with 'UN-mandated multinational military operations covering the broader aspects of peacekeeping which, post-Cold War, are receiving greater emphasis than hitherto.'[4]

The British view is shown simply in figure 6.1. 'Wider peacekeeping' was an extension of peacekeeping – expanded by the different circumstances in which it had to be carried out. To take the animal analogy further, it might be a big, swimming crocodile rather than a small one basking on the bank, but it was still a crocodile – albeit more dangerous in the water.

'Wider peacekeeping' was quite separate from 'peace enforcement', which was defined as 'operations carried out to restore peace between belligerent parties who do not all consent to intervention and who may be engaged in combat . . .'[5] The line between wider peacekeeping (including peacekeeping) and enforcement was the line of consent. As shown in

6.1

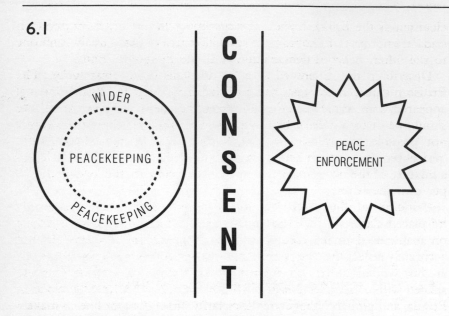

figure 6.2 once the consent line was crossed, it might be impossible to go back.

At this stage the British view – and the British diagram – differed profoundly from the American, set out in early drafts of *FM 100–23 Peace Operations*. The US manual saw a continuum of operations, distinguished only by the level of violence and the means employed. The Americans thought you could move up the continuum and then back down again. To the British, this looked terribly dangerous, and in 1993 they made a determined attempt to convince the Americans they were wrong. A British team from the Army's Headquarters for Doctrine and Training, which had been formed in 1991, visited the US Army Training and Doctrine Command to persuade them so, armed with visual aids – including the photograph on the back of this book's dust jacket. The British view prevailed, but probably as much because of the US Army's disastrous experiences in Somalia in autumn 1993 as because of British experience and persuasiveness.

In Somalia the Americans crossed the 'Mogadishu line' – the consent line. The final version of *FM 100–23*, published in December 1994, marked this very important shift, although, fortuitously, it was never as clear cut as the British manual. Peacekeeping and peace enforcement, it said, 'are not part of a continuum allowing a unit to move freely from one to the other. A broad demarcation separates these operations.'[6]

Describing the difference as a 'broad demarcation' was lucky. The British manual, in contrast, had a distinct line. After the British manual appeared, some critics said the line should more correctly be a zone, and should be 'fuzzy'. Indeed, fuzzy logic had an obvious value. It was surely not possible to say whether the Bosnian UN operation was either 'peacekeeping' or 'peace enforcement' with 100 per cent certainty. It was a mixture of the two – fuzzy set – perhaps 70 per cent the former and 30 per cent the latter.

Criticism of the exact way the ideas were presented is probably misplaced. After all, the boxes with crosses, and even boundaries drawn on maps, used to represent battalions, brigades and divisions, do not accurately reflect the way people are dispersed across the landscape. They are just symbols. That said, there is no doubt that *Wider Peacekeeping* was shaped with a heavy emphasis on the British Army's own experience in Bosnia, and perhaps exaggerated the clarity of the consent line to make a point. It was seen as vital to deter commanders in the field from

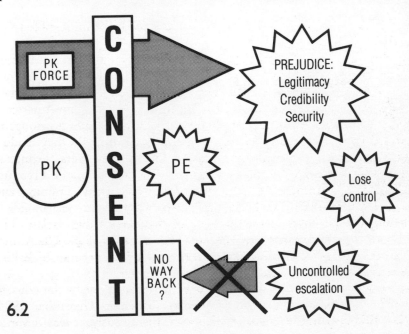

6.2

inadvertent escalation and 'mission creep' – a term which linguistic purists find distasteful but which gets the message across rather well. Commanders must try to avoid being dragged into new commitments from which they may find it difficult to withdraw.

Yet while *Wider Peacekeeping* laid down the law that 'consent' had to be maintained broadly, at the operational level, it also allowed commanders to breach the consent line at the lower, tactical level. The argument, which looks persuasive, is that at the local ('tactical') level consent will be patchy while at the 'operational' or theatre level 'consent' will have been established by firm agreements with high authorities and is therefore easier to define.

At the 'tactical' level, the consent line is certainly wiggly. If a bunch of Serbs, Croats or Muslims opened fire on a UN military vehicle, or, later, an aid convoy, the British could – and often did – shoot back. On several occasions, one sniper shot was answered by scores of rounds of 'counter-fire'. In the course of the Bosnian war the British UN troops probably killed several hundred local fighters. The official figures are much lower, but they did not usually go to the sniper positions to count the bodies. However, this did not rupture the general consent. The senior local commanders usually blamed opposition to the UN forces on indiscipline and drunkenness, probably rightly. 'I've told those so-and-sos at that checkpoint not to shoot at the UN. Well done,' was a not uncommon response from them. On the ground where communications and discipline were not perfect, it was recognised that consent would be 'patchy'. But if that applies at the tactical level, why should it not apply equally at the operational?

The Bosnian war was, however, a special case, because the UN was, in effect, running two operations: one around the periphery between the Muslim-Croat Federation and the Serbs; and one inside, between the Muslims and Croats, preserving and developing the peace of February 1994. Having got its peacekeepers out of Bosnian Serb territory, the UN (and Nato) crossed the consent line and moved to peace enforcement against the Bosnian Serbs. By so doing, it actually regained and reinforced the very fragile consent it had from the mainly Muslim Bosnian government side and the Bosnian Croats. The UN was able to do this because, following the tidying of the map during the summer, it had a fairly consolidated position in central Bosnia, among the Muslims and Croats, and had withdrawn from Serb territory. Had the UN moved to 'enforcement' against the Croats and Muslims (as it might have done, for the Muslims also breached undertakings to the UN over the weapons exclusion zone around Sarajevo) it would have been in a very difficult position. The argument in the British manual still applied: it was vital to avoid inadvertent escalation.

Nevertheless, to deny the possibility of escalation runs counter to tried, classical military theory, which developed during the nuclear era, acknowledging and, indeed, exploiting the possibility of escalation at every level. If a spectrum of escalation was crucial to the way people thought about conflict between states, why should it not be so with intervention in conflict within states? In the end, it was escalation – crossing the consent line, with a move to air strikes at the operational level while refraining from all-out strategic attack on the Bosnian Serb command – which dealt a mortal blow to the Bosnian Serbs. The aim of peace enforcement is, after all, to restore consent, and that is what happened in Bosnia in September 1995.

In late 1993 senior US officers and officials started referring to 'Aggravated Peacekeeping', defined as

> military combat operations conducted by UN authorised forces and designed to monitor and facilitate an existing truce agreement; initially begun as non-combat operations (exclusive of self-defence) and with the consent of all major belligerents, but which subsequently, due to any number of reasons, become combat operations where UN forces are authorised to use force not only for self-defence but for defence of their assigned missions.[7]

So 'aggravated peacekeeping' was a traditional peacekeeping operation that had gone wrong. It was quite different, therefore, from the British concept of 'wider peacekeeping', and did not last long. By mid-1994, the term had disappeared from US drafts. The final version of *FM 100-23 Peace Operations* uses the term 'enforcement' to cover all the activities the British call 'wider peacekeeping' – tasks which require consent such as restoring law and order and protecting humanitarian aid, plus those which usually do not have consent, like enforcing sanctions, defending safe havens and forcible separation of warring factions. The only activities excluded are 'UN-sponsored wars', like Korea and the Gulf.

The British, meanwhile, were also working on their doctrine of peace support operations. In the end, when it was released in January 1995 it had just two divisions (peacekeeping and enforcement), rather than the three (peacekeeping, wider peacekeeping and peace enforcement) that might have been expected. That is probably right. If 'wider peacekeeping' is just a form of peacekeeping, why make it a category on its own?

The Missing Chapter in the UN Charter

Three categories – peacekeeping, wider peacekeeping and enforcement –
would have corresponded to the perceived divisions in the UN Charter:
Chapters six, seven, and something between which Dag Hammarskjöld
called 'chapter six-and-a-half'. In most of the specialist literature the
latter is written as an ungainly combination of a Roman numeral VI and
an imperfectly typeset Arabic fraction. I shall call it simply 6.5.

Chapter 6 operations are defined as those 'carried out with the *consent*
[my italics] of belligerent parties in support of efforts to achieve or
maintain peace, in order to promote security and sustain life in areas of
potential or actual conflict.' Chapter 7 operations are 'carried out to
restore peace between belligerent parties *who do not all consent to
intervention* [my italics] and may be engaged in combat activities.'[8] In
between lies a whole range of activity loosely referred to as 'Chapter 6.5'.
However, since the UN Charter contains no chapter 6.5, chapters 6 and 7
have been used, somewhat arbitrarily, to cover the ground between.
Between 1945 and 1989 the UN Security Council passed twelve Chapter
7 resolutions relating to five disputes – Palestine, the Congo, Southern
Rhodesia, South Africa and the Iran-Iraq conflict. In 1990–91 there were
twenty-three, of which all but two referred to Iraq and its invasion of
Kuwait. The other two referred to the former Yugoslavia. In 1992–93
there were thirty-six Chapter 7 resolutions – nineteen referring to ex-
Yugoslavia, six to Somalia, four to Haiti, three to Iraq and Kuwait, two to
Libya, one to Liberia and one to Angola. The worst example of the UN
being, as Richard Connaughton observed wryly, 'at sixes and sevens' was
in Rwanda, where the fact that the UN force had been deployed under
Chapter 6 severely inhibited its freedom of action.

Consent and Impartiality – Movable Goalposts

Peace eventually came to Bosnia after the UN and Nato went in for a
little peace enforcement, operating without the consent of the Bosnian
Serbs, and re-establishing consent by threat. Whereas the British manual
warned against such action, it was clearly possible to cross the 'line', zone
or threshold. What was clearly a single process straddled that divide.

It is important to be aware of the 'consent' boundary, but that is not
the same as saying you cannot cross it. You must, however, know what
you are doing. The zone or threshold of transition from operating with
consent to operating without it is of profound importance. Short of the

consent threshold you are there as the guest of the local factions. Cross into it, or beyond it, and you have to ask, 'By what right am I here?' The only answer can be 'as the authorised representative of an authority above the nation state' – of the UN, or the UN's appointed agent. The dilemma of shooting back takes on a new meaning. The scores of Croats and Serbs, and some Muslims, shot by UN peacekeepers in Bosnia, and thousands of people in Somalia, all had relatives to grieve for them. And it was 'their country'.

Stress on the importance of consent also presupposes the existence of a measure of order and government, and respect for the referee. Whether it is the state, a warring faction, or the local commander, *somebody* has some sort of authority. The British experience in Bosnia, part of a well-developed former Communist state where many people were well educated, familiar with world affairs and tended to do as they were told, was not necessarily typical. Although UN peacekeepers were occasionally killed, the Bosnian factions reserved their extreme brutality for each other. There were no atrocities against UN peacekeepers as there were in Rwanda, or even against the two French Nato pilots, shot down by the Serbs on 30 August and released unexpectedly before the signature on the peace deal in Paris. As I found, thankfully, certain standards were maintained when dealing with foreigners. After all, it was not our war. *Wider Peacekeeping* stressed the importance of consent because in that environment it meant something. The UN had a measure of authority, although it lost it progressively as the operation went on, and kept having to take measures to reimpose it. And two, if not three, of the factions had a good deal of respect for world opinion, if not always for the UN.

That leads to another problem. 'Consent' is not what the intervener decides. It is totally dependent on the parties intervened against. The warring parties can remove it totally, or make it meaningless, as would happen in an anarchic state with many factions, or, if they are well organised and clever, like the factions in Bosnia, they can move the consent line.

If an intervening party is unduly wary of crossing the magic line of consent, the local parties will exploit this, as they did in Bosnia. The consent line, or threshold, will move to the left, (see figure 6.3) and commanders will become more cautious and reactive.

It becomes obvious that consent is not a fixed feature of the landscape. Consent, or rather, *absence* of consent, is like Scotch mist or freezing fog or black ice. It appears suddenly round a bend in the road – like the Bosnian military police in the Prologue who, rather than politely kowtowing to a UN officer, told us to get our hands up. We then get a diagram something like figure 6.3.

Furthermore, the zone of consent is very wide. We are unlikely to see an operation where there is 100 per cent consent; or one where there is zero consent. Even in 'absolute' or 'total' war, there is a measure of consent – very little, it is true, but some. The British and Americans on one side, the Germans on the other, did not normally castrate each other's prisoners, or use poison gas. The conduct of war ultimately depended on there being someone on the other side who could be reasoned with. Even full-scale war, as Clausewitz observed, is an act of political intercourse.

Looked at in this way, 'traditional peacekeeping' appears as a rather specialised activity, to the left of the diagram. It depends on perhaps 90 per cent 'consent'. Far away lies general and total war – 5 per cent consent, or less. Between lies a wide border territory, the area of intervention. Lack of consent looms like a haze on the horizon. Like a cloud, it looks solid at a distance, but when you are in it, it is a fog. So it is represented here. The middle ground I shall call the zone of intervention.

The exaggerated emphasis on 'consent' as a solid line reflects another problem which has emerged in operations of this type over the last few years. It now looks as though anybody waging a civil war would be well-advised not to let the UN, or any other peacekeeping force, in at all. If they put up full-scale resistance, or even just turn the peacekeepers away when they arrive (like the Khmer Rouge in Cambodia), people will tend not to intervene. The intervening parties are then faced with the alternatives of doing nothing or upping the ante to full-scale invasion and enforcement. The latter happened in Haiti in 1995, and when Nato started attacking the Bosnian Serbs later the same year. If the intervening forces are very sensitive to casualties, it may still be possible to make them withdraw, even if they are immensely powerful – as happened with the United States in Lebanon in 1983 and in Somalia ten years later. This suggests that intervening parties either have to work entirely with the consent of the local authorities, if they are reasonably trustworthy, or they have to go in prepared for rapid escalation in response to changes over which they have no control. That explains why consent is so important, but suggests that the consent line, or zone, needs to be much further to the left on the diagram, and that most intervention operations must assume the line will be crossed.

'Impartiality' is an even more precarious reference point than consent. Even in the (relatively) well-ordered war in Bosnia, the three main

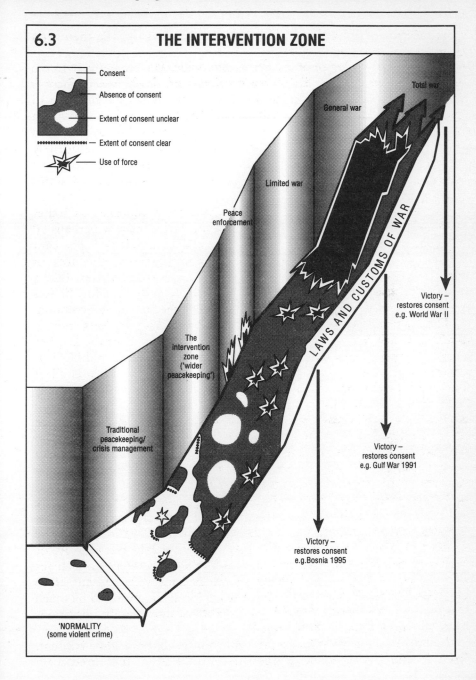

warring parties did not necessarily see that taking aid – food, water, fuel and electricity – to one of the others was 'impartial'. It was not. It was supplying their enemy with things he needed to stay alive and continue the war, the more so as the combatants and the civil populace were inextricably entwined. I remember our landlady in Vitez making sand- wiches for her husband before he headed for two days' duty as a platoon commander on the front line round the Vitez pocket in the winter of 1993. On the sideboard, she hacked away at a loaf of home-made bread, and big chunks of what would have been Parma ham had it been sliced much thinner. Outside, it was bitterly cold, and an east wind sent snowflakes spiralling down the Lasva valley. I left the candlelit table, and pulled a couple of bars of chocolate from my rucksack. I had brought it from Britain – a rare luxury. Should I give it to him? A Croat soldier? I pondered for a second in the darkness of my freezing room. Of course, I did. In a tiny way, I suppose I contributed to the Croat war effort. I had betrayed my impartiality as a foreign journalist, accredited to the UN. The sin was only excused by its scale.

It becomes clear that once one moves into the zone of intervention, anything can happen. It is therefore unrealistic and dangerous to make decisions about the nature of an operation and expect it to conform to one's wishes. It won't. Any intervening force needs to be able to up the ante quickly, in response to rapid and unpredictable action by the party intervened against. Success will be achieved by moving from a peacekeep- ing posture to a peace enforcing one and back again, creating new areas of consent in the fog. The success of a peace enforcement operation is measured by a return to peacekeeping.

The real decision is whether to start a risky operation of this kind in the first place. Once committed, you have to be prepared to run with it. Like the soldiers on the Somme, in 1916, you go over the top carrying all the kit you may need for weeks. They planned to keep going, right through the German lines. The tragedy was that most only made it a few hundred metres. In recent operations, the opposite has happened. Troops went in equipped, physically and mentally, for peacekeeping. And suddenly, in Somalia and Rwanda, they were, to all intents and purposes, at war. Bosnia was managed much better. The UN forces in the later stages, and the Nato forces which replaced them, deployed for 'wider peacekeeping' but were fully equipped and prepared to move to peace enforcement if necessary. It follows that governments should not be swayed into intervention operations by media pressure and dinner party chatter about the need 'to do something'. They must say 'no' if they believe the risks are too great.

The UN Charter, as written, does not fit this new reality. Because Chapter 6 does not give peacekeepers adequate teeth, such an operation would need to be mandated under Chapter 7, which was written with the prevention of conflict between states, not within states, in mind. The UN Charter is not Holy Writ. As the US Secretary of State John Foster Dulles once said, Article 2(7), which inhibits intervention in states' internal affairs,

> is an evolving concept. We don't know fifteen, twenty years from now what in fact is going to be within the domestic jurisdication of nations. International law is evolving, state practice is evolving. There's no way we can definitely define in 1945 what is within domestic jurisdiction. Let's just let things drift for a few years . . .'

After fifty years of drifting, the UN Charter needs to be rewritten.

Operating in the Zone of Intervention (ZI)

The principles of classical peacekeeping are derived from those issued to the UN Emergency Force which went into Sinai in the wake of the 1973 Yom Kippur war, sometimes known as 'UNEF 2 rules'. They specified: the need for support by the relevant international authority – the UN Security Council; the need for consent from the (former or potential) warring parties; the way the force was to be commanded and controlled, and its composition; the use of force only in self-defence; and the need for complete impartiality.

These principles apply to the two classic types of peacekeeping operation: UN observers, and 'interposition' operations, where the UN keeps former or potential enemies apart.

When it enters the zone of intervention, the intervening force, which may be a UN force or a UN-approved one, has several more jobs to do. Conflict has to be prevented between several factions – not just two – which may not have clearly defined frontiers and may not have agreed not to fight. Cease-fires may be ineffective, and troops may not obey the orders of the authorities (such as they are). Armed groups may need to be demobilised and disarmed. This normally falls into two stages: 'cantonment' (collecting the forces in a defined area) and disarming them and storing the weapons.

Law and order is likely to be precarious or to have broken down, and the infrastructure will be damaged if not totally destroyed. There are likely to be large numbers of refugees (who have moved from one country to another) or displaced persons (within a country). Humanitarian aid, its delivery and protection, is therefore likely to form an important part of any intervention operation. So is the guarantee and denial of movement: guaranteeing it to people who need to go about their daily business, and denying it, perhaps, to armed groups.

Obviously, prevention of conflict, in the first place, is the aim but if conflict is taking place an intervening force can make it less horrific by protecting civilians, trying to maintain law and order, facilitating exchanges of prisoners – or bodies – and acting as a bridge between the factions much as neutral states act to facilitate a dialogue during conventional war. Military assistance to the local authorities may help restore or maintain law and order, and can also help restore the infrastructure. The latter is an interesting reversal of traditional military ways. The British Army calls the activity G5 – the staff title which, in conventional operations, refers to liaison with the 'host nation', like the enormous support the Saudi government gave to the Allies before and during the Gulf War. In intervention operations, G5 does not usually mean the host country helping the intervening force, though it might in a base area – for example, Croatia as a base for operations in Bosnia. In the theatre of operations it means the intervening military helping the host nation.

Even before a decision is taken to intervene, the technology available to developed countries can be used to obtain the fullest possible picture of what is going on. Not only can satellites provide increasingly detailed surveillance, but the reports of aid workers and journalists can add vital 'human intelligence'. Local news broadcasts and official transmissions can be monitored without the parties in the area knowing.

Intervention in crisis areas has generally only taken place after conflict has broken out. This applies to the UN-sponsored wars in Korea and the Gulf, and to the traditional UN peacekeeping operations and new-style operations in the zone of intervention. In his 1992 pamphlet *Agenda for Peace*, the UN Secretary-General suggested there should be more preventive deployments and demilitarised zones: UN forces deployed along one or both sides of a boundary where conflict was likely, whether between states or between factions in a state. Such a force might be linked to a more formidable coalition force, as shown in figure 6.4. So far, the history of preventive deployments has not been illustrious. They might have worked in Rwanda and Bosnia if the UN had been blessed with

6.4 PREVENTIVE DEPLOYMENT

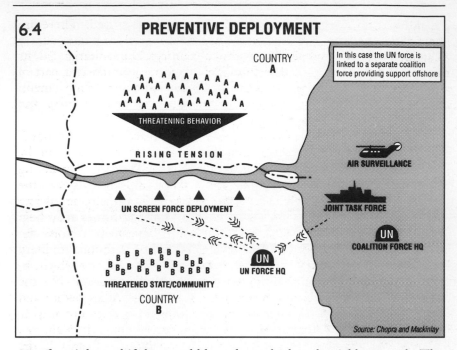

COUNTRY A

In this case the UN force is linked to a separate coalition force providing support offshore

THREATENING BEHAVIOR

RISING TENSION

AIR SURVEILLANCE

UN SCREEN FORCE DEPLOYMENT

JOINT TASK FORCE

UN
COALITION FORCE HQ

UN
UN FORCE HQ

THREATENED STATE/COMMUNITY

COUNTRY B

Source: Chopra and Mackinlay

some foresight and if they could have been deployed quickly enough. The UN guarantee to defend so-called 'safe areas' in Bosnia could have led to preventive deployments: UN troops to deter and, if necessary, fight off attack. In fact, the UN forces were too weak to do anything of the kind and just became hostages or acquiesced unwillingly in genocide, as at Srebrenica, where the Dutch troops stood by as Muslims were rounded up and taken off to be killed.[10]

The British Army Doctrine specifies conflict prevention, demobilisation, military assistance, humanitarian relief and the guarantee and denial of movement as the main operational tasks in what I have called the zone of intervention. A recent independent study of 'second generation' operations concurred. It listed preventive deployment, internal conflict resolution, assistance to the (interim) civil authority, protection of humanitarian relief and guarantee and denial of movement as the main tasks.[11] In carrying them out, the principles of impartiality, minimum force, the legitimacy conferred by an international authority, but according the local factions the respect they are due, all apply. However, the principle of minimum force is flexible. Faced with persistent violations of agreements by the Bosnian Serbs, the UN decided that it would respond 'proportionately', and proportionate did not mean equal. The Serbs fired artillery from areas from which it was supposed to be withdrawn. Guns are difficult targets to hit, so Nato hit the ammunition dumps supplying the guns instead. 'Minimum force' does not mean wimpishness. Most bullies are cowards, and, when faced with a perceptible escalation of the violence inflicted, preferably very precisely, they tend to back down.

'Peace building' – the restoration of the infrastructure – is an important area, identified in *Agenda for Peace*, and one which can proceed even before a general cessation of hostilities has occurred.[12] Cromwell's observation, 'though peace be made, yet it is interest that keeps peace', is as apposite now as it was 350 years ago. Indeed it is more so, as people are now dependent on standards of living and comfort, medical care and access to information which in Cromwell's time would have been unattainable, even for the very richest. Following the Muslim-Croat cease-fire, restoration of the infrastructure proceeded throughout large areas of central Bosnia, even though war with the Serbs continued and, indeed, intensified.

Every operation in the zone of intervention will be different. Rwanda was not Somalia, Somalia was not Bosnia. In ex-Yugoslavia, the war between the Muslims and the Serbs was quite different from the war-within-a-war waged by the Muslims against the Croats. The US, British and French manuals all enumerate the tasks to be performed, the principles to be applied and the techniques to be used. As noted, a 'doctrine' devised with one conflict in mind may prove inappropriate for wider application. Some of the total war theorists of the 1920s and '30s recommended, when examining the character of a future war, concentrating on the opening period because the character of the war would change as it progressed.[13] As Colonel Richard Connaughton, one of the leading authorities on this subject, has written, 'If the requirement for wide applicability results in the "*doctrine*" being reduced to a set of very broad brush principles, reinforced with [local guidelines] ... developed on the hoof, that may be no bad thing.'[14]

In Bosnia, it was recognised that local cooperation was essential to the success of the UN expedition. For the British, this was to be very much a young captains' war, whereas Northern Ireland had been a corporals' war. It was these young officers, bright and some with a gift for languages, who provided the liaison officers, to develop a 'framework of trust and confidence'. It was vital to establish working relationships with the leading civil and military personalities. The liaison officers took the lead, but the personality of the commanding officer was also cardinal. One problem, however, was that the battalions were replaced every six months, and to some extent the process of establishing personal relationships had to begin again. Each British battalion also had a different style, a different personality. In an operation of this kind, that probably helped. A vital role was also played by locally recruited interpreters. Those with the UN forces wore British uniform – at least one was killed by a stray bullet. But even braver were those who worked with the aid agencies and the press, who lacked the protection of a UN uniform, and had to interpret for people of a different ethnic group, carrying Kalashnikovs. I remember our vehicle being stopped and Muslim police scrutinising identification. The interpreter was a Croat. Seeing a Croat surname, they said something like, *'We're* a long way from home, aren't we, Mr . . .', and let us go.

Moving into a zone of intervention tallied with my image of what it must have been like to visit the Wild West in the 1870s. The UN – like the cavalry – provided military escorts, there were local people of different factions, and there were bandits and renegades. The normalities of civilisation did not end suddenly, but subsided gradually. From an airport, equipped with all the latest in modern technology, we moved inland. The towns became scruffier, and less well-appointed, the roads rougher. But there was always hard liquor to be found. Moving into Bosnia from Croatia, the Croatians would check us out but no one in Croat-held Bosnia would check us in. At first sight there were no perceptible differences between the countries. We passed through Tomislavgrad, the last big UN base, which was later connected to the Croatian telephone network. From now on, communication was by radio or satellite telephone only.

During the Muslim-Croat war, the Croats controlled movement on to the mountain road leading into central Bosnia through a checkpoint at Lipa, at the bottom. The UN demanded 'freedom of movement', but if they were taking supplies to the Muslims, the local authorities could be very difficult. From now on, every checkpoint became a test of coolness, good humour, and luck. Sometimes we were turned back for not having the right bits of paper from Croat authorities in Mostar – even though we had them from a joint Croatian and Bosnian-Croat bureau in Split, and our UN passes should have afforded us free movement. Sometimes we slipped in among UN trucks, or did a deal with the escorting Land-Rovers to help us. The writs of the UN and the local authorities overlapped and conflicted. Along the mountain road we encountered our first UN white armoured vehicles, the cavalry, there to escort aid. Twisting through spectacular scenery, the aid trucks looked like covered wagons. Fourteen kilometres up the mountain road, we suddenly encountered a Wild West fort – 'Redoubt'. Massive walls of steel baskets, lined with textile and filled with gravel, walls of logs, and prefabricated concrete towers. Wagon trains, moving between forts. That is my enduring memory of Bosnia.

The most worrying aspect of operating in such an area was not full-scale fighting between the factions, who tended to cordon off the 'war zones' with military police, but banditry. As unarmed civilians carrying a great deal of valuable equipment, we were soft targets. The most dangerous area was away from the front line, a steep, rocky valley, running north from Gornji Vakuf, which we called 'bandit gulley'. Halfway up the sinister canyon there was a deserted fish farm, and the bandits – Muslims – were known as the 'fish-head gang'. The UN forces often dismissed our concerns, because the bandits did not bother heavily armed British patrols. They did bother unescorted aid trucks and journalists, and invariably reappeared when people thought it was safe. One of my colleagues, driving alone, was held up at gunpoint, and was about to be taken off down a forest track when a UN Land-Rover appeared. The bandit thought better of it, and made off. On one occasion I stuck with a British Military Police vehicle. The soldiers told me they they were involved in 'anti-bandit patrols' with the local police – an example of 'military assistance'.

Protecting humanitarian aid against small-scale threats of this type is easy: a close escort, with armoured vehicles at each end and maybe in the middle, if it is a long convoy liable to be broken up, suffices. But taking aid convoys across front lines and through organised opposition is virtually impossible without local consent, unless a wide corridor is created. Sarajevo provides a very useful example. Aid can be brought in by air, but trucks can carry far more, and more economically. Any aid operation requires a secure mounting base, as shown in figure 6.5: in Sarajevo's case, it was the coast. Ideally, there should be unopposed access for most of the route. There were good, metalled roads into Sarajevo but for much of the war they were closed. The excellent Mostar road was closed by Croat hostility to the Bosnian government in Sarajevo, by fighting which raged across it and by the destruction of a key bridge over the Bijela river, one of the tribuatries leading into the fast-flowing, turquoise Neretva. We later learned that Serb special forces, working, at that time, with the Croats, were responsible. Therefore, aid came on a circuitous route over the mountain road described above.

Closer to Sarajevo, the Serbs controlled the main routes in, through well-organised checkpoints marked by red, white and blue bollards. When they were letting people through they required twenty-four hours' notice. So efficient were they that some of my colleagues reported being presented with faxes of articles they had written, and admonished. It was that kind of command and control which enabled the Bosnian Serbs to hold the more numerous Muslim troops at bay for so long, moving their own troops swiftly to respond to any threat. But, when Nato destroyed their command and control systems, they suddenly became vulnerable.

Another, far more difficult mountain track, over Mount Igman, remained in Bosnian government hands, even though the Serbs could rake it with fire from relatively short range. Following the withdrawal of its troops from Serb territory, the UN moved reinforcements, including artillery, on to Mount Igman, partly to help secure the mountain road in. Part of the UN Rapid Reaction Force (not to be confused with the Nato Rapid Reaction *Corps*, an altogether different formation ten times its size, which was deployed in December 1995), was formed to force a way

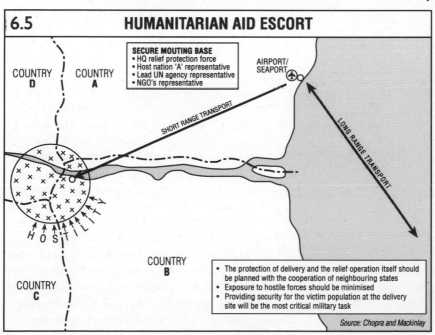

6.5 **HUMANITARIAN AID ESCORT**

COUNTRY D

COUNTRY A

SECURE MOUTING BASE
• HQ relief protection force
• Host nation 'A' representative
• Lead UN agency representative
• NGO's representative

AIRPORT/ SEAPORT

SHORT RANGE TRANSPORT

LONG RANGE TRANSPORT

HOSTILITY

COUNTRY C

COUNTRY B

• The protection of delivery and the relief operation itself should be planned with the cooperation of neighbouring states
• Exposure to hostile forces should be minimised
• Providing security for the victim population at the delivery site will be the most critical military task

Source: Chopra and Mackinlay

through to Sarajevo if necessary. In practice, it would not have been necessary for the UN to control all the territory in a corridor extending out to the maximum range of weapons likely to be used against convoys. The important things was to control key vantage points, on the assumption that, for most of the route, the authorities in the territory through which it passed were benign. Even if the target of aid is nearly surrounded by hostile factions, it only needs a secure corridor to get it in.

Delivering supplies by air has obvious attractions but the close proximity of warring factions tends to make life difficult. Pilots have developed procedures to evade anti-aircraft fire: they fly high, out of small arms range, and then dive suddenly into the airport, jettisoning flares to decoy heat-seeking missiles. Despite these precautions, if the Serbs had wanted to shoot down planes landing at Sarajevo, they could have, and in the less organised terrain around Tuzla the UN was unprepared to take the risk for most of the Bosnian war. As with land convoys, flights were, in practice, dependent on Serb consent. Aircraft can also only carry relatively light equipment: one Hercules carries about the same as one large road truck. People planning for the next fifty years of military operations need to devise an aircraft which carries more and can take off and land in a very short distance.

A cargo-carrying ballistic missile with enough fuel to get to the target and back would seem an ideal way of delivering aid to a besieged town. A typical ballistic missile can carry half a ton to a ton payload over a range of 100 kilometres to 300 kilometres, and will land within a few hundred metres, at most, of the aiming point. Those characteristics would have enabled missiles to be fired from safe mounting bases in Croatia into Sarajevo. The missile would land on its nose, retarded perhaps by a parachute; a ton of supplies would be withdrawn, and it would then be fired back, refuelled, and used again. Alternatively, solid fuelled, expendable missiles might be used for one-way trips. With all the spare missiles lying around, it should not be beyond the ingenuity of the United States and Russia to adapt existing short-range ballistic missiles which are now surplus to requirements and treaty obligations, or build new 'humanitarian missiles'.

Operations in the zone of intervention rely heavily on the same devices as colonial warfare: forts, magazines and convoy routes. Because the operation is about feeding the local population as well as the intervener's soldiers, aid workers and other hangers-on, like visiting politicians and media, logistics acquire a greatly enhanced importance. Whereas in conventional war commanders have sought to have as large a 'teeth to tail' ratio as possible, in the zone of intervention, a massive tail and relatively few teeth may be the optimum configuration. That is certainly the experience of intervention operations since 1991. It must also be remembered that soldiers in intervention operations are not, by and large, fighting for their lives or, indeed, for their countries' vital interests. They are there as volunteers – either as part of a volunteer system or as conscripts who have volunteered for peace operations – to help others. They expect and, indeed, deserve, a bit of comfort.

Those operations have also underlined the importance of 'safe areas' or 'safe havens', and how not to site them. The UN decision to establish 'safe areas' in Bosnia under UN Security Council resolution 824 of May 1993, taken in defiance of military advice, is a salutary lesson. The 'safe havens' in Kurdistan were, as we have seen, located right up against the Turkish border, and they could be supplied from Turkey, a well-organised, Nato country. In Rwanda, the French established a refuge in the Nyungwe forest, where there was a Tutsi enclave (inside a predominantly Hutu area), right up against the Zairean border south of Cyangugu (see figure 4.4).

Three of the six 'safe havens' in Bosnia – Zepa, Srebrenica and Gorazde – were an unbelievable piece of wishful thinking. Zepa and Srebrenica were overrun by the Bosnian Serbs with tragic consequences for thousands of people, and with dreadful consequences for the UN's reputation and authority. Zepa and Srebrenica had been isolated since the start of the Bosnian civil war. Access was in the gift of the Bosnian Serbs, and the journalists who got in, including my colleague, Robert Block, did so on foot. Gorazde survived, but could easily have fallen, too. The other three – Sarajevo, Tuzla and Bihac – were sufficiently robust to hold out, but with no thanks to the UN which had declared them 'safe'. Tuzla was the only one which was not, at that time, isolated.

Safe areas must be sustainable and defensible, as shown in figure 6.6. That will usually mean they have to back on to a neutral or friendly territory, through which supplies can pass and sick and wounded people be extracted. Otherwise they have to be sufficiently large and well defended to survive while isolated with a guarantee of whatever further support is necessary from the international community to ensure their survival, even in the face of mind-boggling incompetence by their own commanders. At the very least, there should be a good chance of air resupply. The half-hearted Bosnian Muslim defence of Gorazde in April 1994, which Lieutenant General Rose ridiculed in a private interview, disgracefully leaked, is an example.

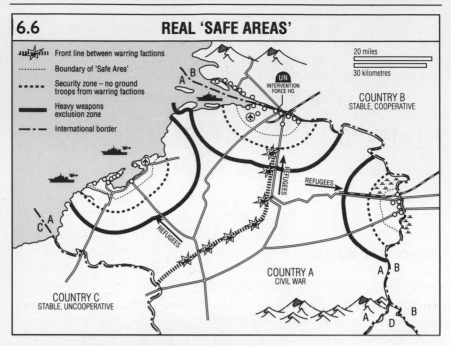

6.6 **REAL 'SAFE AREAS'**

A city like Dubrovnik, backing on to the sea, could be a 'safe area' with robust naval forces committed to its support, and so could a city on a broad river. But in many cases national boundaries, across which warring factions fear to tread, may be more secure than natural ones.

So, is this peacekeeping, war, or something else? The answer, like the problem, is fuzzy. It is, perhaps, a return to a form of warfare we knew before the nineteenth century, maybe even before the eighteenth. Wars in which pitched battles were rare, with small armies. Wars which resulted in misery for the population affected, and in which military commanders were as preoccupied with supplies and magazines as they were in securing any battlefield advantage. The movements of local forces were slow and depended on the weather, the seasons and, as ever, the terrain. Much of the fighting was for areas to be used as bargaining counters. Mercenaries – condottieri – did much of the fighting. The appearance of a talented commander and a disciplined force was as rare as it was devastating. Now the charismatic individual commander has, perhaps, returned as the arbiter.

CHAPTER SEVEN
PEACE ENFORCEMENT, LIMITED WAR AND NATIONAL DEFENCE

Genie in a Bottle

As we crested the hill, a scene of destruction unfolded. In one small area four Warrior Infantry Fighting Vehicles from the advancing battle group, their guns raised in submission, had been knocked out. Among the yellow grass, it looked like the Battle of Kursk – the biggest tank battle in history, in 1943. Armoured vehicles, killed in close combat, littered the golden plain. The infantry, luckily, had dismounted from the Warrior armoured fighting vehicles before they had fallen victim to a roving missile-armed tank.

But not quite. Flashing lights indicated their destruction. This was the British Army's training area at Suffield in Canada, and the tanks had been bombarded with gentle laser beams, which had set off the alarms. This was the new direct-fire weapons effect simulator, in use to simulate a battle between an armoured battle group – about 1,100 men – and an 'enemy', still using Soviet-style tactics. Only with such systems is it possible to come close to what it would really be like in a full-scale, 'high intensity' war, a 'first division' contest.

With the new simulator, lasers are fitted to every weapon in the opposing arsenals, simulating the trajectory, range and rate of fire of each one. The lasers are 'eye safe', except at very close range. Troops wear harnesses and helmets pockmarked with sensors like the suckers on an octopus's tentacles, and their vehicles are similarly equipped. It is not enough to see a fleeting target and claim a kill: the laser tells you whether you would have hit it, or whether it would have hit you. There is absolutely no argument. If struck by a laser, an alarm sounds and your rifle, weapon or vehicle stops working.

Further south we came on the 'tank' responsible for the destruction we had witnessed, which had itself been destroyed. 'We killed five Warriors and one Scimitar,' said its commander, a corporal from Orkney. 'Then we ran into *them*' – he pointed to a squadron of big Challenger tanks scattered across the opposite hillside. 'There were six of them, and some Milan anti-tank missile posts, so . . . it went wrong.'

Then he smiled, a giveaway. 'Brilliant fun.'

It would not have been 'brilliant fun' for real. This is the highest form of war. It is the most demanding on troops and on technology. The rival formations must be alert at all times, probing for the first contact. Yet we are not planning to fight tank battles against the Russians, nor is it really very likely we will again be fighting the Iraqis in the desert. So why practise it? *Because it is the highest form of war*: that, and that alone, was the point.

Only here, in the expanse of the prairie – selected, people joked, because of its resemblance to the Russian steppe – could these armoured formations spread out in the rarefied order they would adopt in a real, big war. Only here could the commander of the battle group cast his hand over a map and explain, in the elegant litany of such operations, that by drawing the enemy into this area he was 'fulfilling his commander's intent'. He was using *auftragstaktik* – the system of command where the senior commander outlines his broad aims and intent and lets his subordinates, who may not be able to contact him, then react to events with those in mind.

Whereas for the soldiers and junior commanders the battle is very much a test of their technical skills, for the battle group commanders, it is a test of will. 'It's a battle of wits, pitting your mind against the mind of the opposition,' said the opposition force commander, Lieutenant Colonel Nigel Aylwin-Foster. Both commanding officers had ordered their snipers (also equipped with laser simulators attached to their single-shot sniper rifles) to try to kill the other colonel.

Battle was joined at about seven the next morning, and one of the problems with the new system soon became apparent: the greater willingness of soldiers to risk being killed in a virtual war than in reality. Although the lasers accurately reflected whether a gun would have scored a complete kill, just immobilised the target, or missed, the human element still differed. Although no one wanted to be hit – it was humiliating – with no risk of blood, pain and mutilation, the soldiers were less cautious than they would have been for real. The result? Carnage.

Although the laser system to simulate engagements was the very latest, keeping track of the battle was still done in the traditional way, with wooden blocks on a vast map. Later that morning, the young major who had devised the system looked at the piles of 'kill cards', indicating vehicles which had been destroyed, and the pink and blue blocks, representing the two sides, intertwined in a deadly embrace. The 1st and 2nd Royal Tank Regiments had torn each other apart in a battle of unusual ferocity. In three hours, about half the forces had been destroyed – well over the critical level below which a unit cannot function effectively. There was something Wagnerian about it. 'Mutual annihilation,' he said. 'What you'd expect from a meeting engagement. Oh . . . and both commanding officers died.'

This battle was an abstraction, an exercise in the highest form of the art. That is why armies practise it. Any professional soldier will tell you that if you can do this, you could cope with Northern Ireland and Bosnia, and most certainly with an armoured battle against Iraq – which resembled it most closely. But you could not do it in reverse. The principle can be illustrated with a musical analogy. Grand opera is not everybody's cup of tea. More people go to rock concerts. An opera singer could probably, in extremis, do a rock concert. But not the other way round. If you lose the ability to stage and sing grand opera, or present a classical ballet, with its combination of orchestra, singing, dance and decor, you are unlikely to be able to resurrect it.

To practise the highest form of military art is equivalent to staging a dress rehearsal of an opera. It is also, on a less abstract level, like keeping a deadly virus, believed to be largely extinct, alive in a laboratory, in case the unthinkable happened, and an antidote was needed. A genie, kept in a bottle, to be magicked out in time of dire need.

Very Political Wars

The biggest kind of war we are likely to see again is a limited war on the Gulf War model. That was still a pretty big war, but astonishingly one-sided, thanks to western training, discipline and technology. Although western technology was not that far in advance of the Soviet technology used by the Iraqis in some areas, the Allies had a clear superiority in certain crucial sectors. Stealth aircraft, night vision equipment, satellite navigation and communications systems have been singled out as the war winners.[1]

Precision guidance was made for limited war. 'Total war' was, in part, a function of the imprecision of the means available. To use a medical analogy, we have moved from the amputation saw and bucket of tar, via the scalpel, to the body scanner and the laser. But surgery is still a bloody business.

The Nato air-strikes against the Bosnian Serbs in August and September 1995 marked the shift to 'peace enforcement', though they remained, in this author's view, in the zone of intervention. At the time of writing, the British are still working on their view of 'peace enforcement'. If you insist on maintaining the threshold of consent as the crucial divide, then it is very difficult to separate peace enforcement from limited war. The Serbs did not consent to being bombed. Enforcement, as we have seen, means becoming part of the conflict and, to some extent, taking sides. The Bosnian Serbs saw the incoming waves of bombers as part of the conflict, and the Muslims besieged in Sarajevo cheered. They saw them as being on their side.

The means employed for the two weeks of 'peace enforcement' were indistinguishable from those associated with a big but limited war.

The initial attacks followed the classic 1991 Gulf War pattern. The first targets were air defence missiles, guns and radars – the things most dangerous to the aircraft. Once they had knocked out the 'integrated' air defence network – the radars and missiles – they could operate safely at medium altitude (15,000 feet) and above, safely out of range of guns and hand-held missiles, which were more difficult, if not impossible, to find and destroy. The second wave concentrated on 'operational' level targets – factories, ammunition dumps and command centres. The third wave hit 'tactical' targets – artillery and mortar positions within the 20 kilometre exclusion zone around Sarajevo.

From warning against the dangers of escalation, the doctrine writers had to think again. Not only was this escalation, but it was carefully engineered to link the UN forces on the ground (who included the British and French artillery on Mount Igman) with the Nato planes in the air. The artillery engaged anti-aircraft missile and gun sites to stop them shooting at the Nato planes. It was an example of what, in the Cold War days, used to be called 'linkage'.

The attacks had continued for nearly two weeks when, on Sunday 10 September, thirteen cruise missiles – pilotless aircraft carrying half-ton explosive warheads, accurate to within six metres – were fired from the cruiser USS *Normandy*. They homed in on Serb anti-aircraft installations round Banja Luka. The target was relatively deep inside Serb-held territory, and Nato preferred not to risk pilots. American 'Stealth fighters', the strange angular planes virtually invisible to radar, and the only aircraft to operate over central Baghdad for most of the Gulf War, were placed on stand-by, but, as it turned out, were not needed.

Officially, the attacks had nothing to do with the collapse of Bosnian Serb fighting forces, especially around Banja Luka, in the second week of September. Nato said it had avoided hitting front-line Serb troops, partly because they were so difficult to find and partly to avoid accusations that they were helping the Muslims and Croats. However, they later said they knew the attacks would inevitably benefit the opposing armies. Knocking out somebody's air defence system means cutting the communications so that radars cannot alert missiles and guns further back. Aid workers confirmed that the Serb telephone network had also been wrecked. No more faxes of newspaper articles. Nato had punched out the Serbs' eyes: now, like the Croats and Muslims, they were groping in the dark – and, with less practice, they were not so good at it.[2] The command and control system was what strategists now call a *critical vulnerability*: the Nato air attacks led to systemic disruption.

There was a difference of scale from the air campaign in the Gulf War: 3,400 air sorties and 13 cruise missile attacks in the final Nato campaign over Bosnia as against 110,000 and 320, respectively, in the Gulf War.[3] There was also another, fundamental difference between the two campaigns. The Gulf campaign, like that against the Bosnian Serbs, began with attacks on anti-aircraft defences. Then it switched to the most dangerous things – nuclear, biological and chemical weapons facilities – and finally began to dismantle the Iraqi military system from the top down, from the rear forward. The campaign against the Bosnian Serbs was similar, so far, but the intention was not to knock out as much as possible as soon as possible. The air campaign proceeded slowly, deliberately. It was to persuade the Serbs to come to the negotiating table. It is possible that the Gulf air campaign could have persuaded Saddam Hussein to call a halt somewhere along the line, though unlikely. There was therefore a slight but very important difference in emphasis with the campaign against the Bosnian Serbs. Churchill's famous phrase, that 'jaw-jaw is better than war-war' comes to mind. War-war was pursued, tightly controlled, to encourage jaw-jaw. It was, as Clausewitz would have known, a 'very political war'.

Nato also had to be even more careful about avoiding civilian targets than the Allies had been in the Gulf. Out of thousands of possible targets, most were ruled out because of the risk of hitting civilians, and a list of 150 was compiled of which 56 were hit. The Serbs claimed there had been civilian deaths, but these reports were not substantiated. The carefully controlled use of force in this way has become possible because of the accuracy of modern weaponry and, even more importantly, the effectiveness of reconnaissance and surveillance. Nowadays, if I know where a target is I can hit it. The real problem lies in knowing exactly what it is. Is it a command bunker or a refugee shelter? I need to know who lives there. And, even more difficult, I need to know whether they are there when I try to hit the target, and whether someone else may be visiting at the time. Modern surveillance equipment, known euphemistically as 'national technical means', which usually refers to spy satellites (but also to interception of communications traffic), is superb at detecting whether something is there, and, because it operates in real time, can even keep track of moving targets. But surveillance may still be confused as to what is there. Nevertheless, it gives the most developed states an exponential advantage over most of their likely opponents, as modern surveillance methods enable a much smaller number of weapons to be focussed on the targets that matter. Had they been available, with the necessary intelligence, a few precision-guided bombs on the Berlin bunker would have been more valuable than the entire bombing campaign against Germany in the latter part of World War II – provided Hitler and his top advisers were there at the time.

Peace enforcement has given doctrine writers a problem. It may mean not actually using force, but deploying forces which are prepared and visibly ready to use it. As happened in Bosnia, intervention by a combatant force leads to the perception that the force is not impartial. The commitment to impartiality that underlines 'wider peacekeeping' operations cannot be maintained. However, the aim of peace enforcement is not to impose peace by any means, but to create conditions in which peace can take root. Therefore, it differs in some way from true war, in which victory is sought.

The Bosnian operation is, once again, instructive: the first of a new kind of operation on a spectrum in the zone of intervention. In peace enforcement it is more important than usual to avoid inflicting civilian casualties and destroying the national infrastructure. In a peace enforcement operation the subsequent peace has to be kept in mind. It may even be necessary to ensure the preservation of elements of the armed forces of the party being enforced, so as not to give rise to a destabilising imbalance. This was a difficult tightrope for the UN and Nato to walk in September 1995. They crippled the Serbs – so what incentive was there now for the Muslims and Croats, moving quite swiftly forward, to seek peace?

The endgame in Bosnia showed some sort of peace enforcement doctrine emerging. No longer able to rely on the 'impartial', third-party status of his troops as a guarantee of their security, General Smith pulled them out. There was an awkward gap in the spectrum of escalation between the lightly armed UN troops and Nato airpower. Artillery was brought in to fill that gap. In conventional war there is a maxim that 'the best form of defence is attack'. That usually means hitting the other side before he can hit you. It is here that the ultimate aim of a peace enforcement operation, to create the conditions for building peace, can interfere with traditional military logic. Operations have to be pursued with more restraint. The intervening force may be limited to responding to the other party's action. The most effective form of defence will be early warning and layers of concrete and armour. The intervening force cannot hit the party against which it is intervening with every means at its disposal; although, if it detects forces massing for an attack, it may take pre-emptive action (which would be very difficult in a 'wider peacekeeping' situation). That means a force engaged in intervention or peace enforcement has to be able to match anything the other party may throw at it.

The Gulf War, 1991 – the Paradigm of Limited War

On 5 August 1990 just after the invasion of Kuwait, General Colin Powell, the chairman of the US Joint Chiefs of Staff, set out his 'endgame' for dealing with Iraq. 'We can't leave them with nothing,' he said. 'We have to balance Iran. It would look best to me if we allowed them an army of about 100,000 with a thousand tanks.'[4]

The Allies did not quite achieve that during the 1991 Gulf war – immediately afterwards, Iraq had an army of about 350,000 and 2,000 tanks – but they had come close to one of the aims General Powell had selected. The stated aim of the Allied campaign against Iraq in 1991 was to ensure the Iraqi forces left Kuwait. A sub-plot was to destroy so many of them in the process that Iraq would not threaten other states in the region for a very long time. The Gulf War was limited by its political objectives, though not limited much in the means employed. In other words, it was a classic, Clausewitzian limited war. The moment the Allied command thought those objectives had been achieved, they switched off the action – some believe too soon.

Such a perfect opportunity to practise limited war and the 'AirLand Battle' doctrines developed for general war against the Soviet bloc is unlikely to recur. The open expanse of desert meant that the forces could manoeuvre relatively freely, and if the weather sometimes prevented aircraft from finding their targets, the weather problems were as nothing compared with those encountered in Europe, over Bosnia. Luckiest of all was the fact that in Saddam Hussein the Allies had an opponent of mind-boggling incompetence as a military commander, who laid his troops out in a fashion ideally suited to the Allied plan. Even so, at the tactical level, the Iraqis showed a good deal of skill at camouflage and digging in.

The air campaign was pursued with several, overlapping aims. Initially, it was to suppress air defences so that Allied planes could operate safely – a form of freedom of movement. Then came the strategic campaign against industry, command and leadership. The next stage was to isolate the chosen theatre for land operations – the 'Kuwait Theatre of Operations' or KTO. The final stage consisted of preparation and support for battlefield operations. The Scud hunt, which took up far more sorties than had been expected – 300 a day – was part of the 'strategic' campaign but could equally be numbered as a fifth phase. It was absolutely vital to devote – and to be seen to devote – substantial resources to this phase, as it was designed to keep the Israelis, who were being bombarded with Scuds, out of the war. If the Israelis had weighed in against the Iraqis, the fragile coalition, which relied on Arab support, would probably have cracked. The anti-Scud campaign was therefore, arguably, one with a 'grand strategic' rather than just a strategic role.

The way the air campaign proceeded showed that a land battle was always expected. Had it not been, the air attacks against Iraqi ground forces would have focused more on the Republican Guard, the better trained and equipped troops with the greatest loyalty to Saddam Hussein. As it was, the air attacks concentrated on the Iraqi troops guarding the front line on the southern edge of Iraq and Kuwait. General Schwarz-kopf, the US commander, made an announcement to this effect at a press briefing on the night of 27 February. This information came as a surprise to us: it was the opposite of what we had thought was happening. General Schwarzkopf explained that it was designed to minimise the risk of Allied ground troops getting 'hung up on the wire' and killed in large numbers. Instead – as happened – they were to break through swiftly and be able to exploit their advantages of manoeuvre, conferred by their equipment, communications and, above all, satellite navigation. They could then fight 'our kind of war'. Had the Iraqis been expected to withdraw as a result of the air attacks alone, a different approach would probably have been pursued. The Republican Guard, in relatively safe positions, would have been targeted more heavily, instead of the pathetic, starved, badly equipped infantry on the front line who surrendered in droves when the Allies moved in.

The destruction of the Iraqi command and control system actually made a ground war more certain because it broke the command links which would have enabled Iraq to withdraw its army. However, an Iraqi withdrawal from Kuwait under pressure of the air attacks remained on the cards, theoretically, until 23 February – the day before the ground attack began. On 22 February President George Bush of the United States gave the Iraqis until 23.00 on the following day to begin withdrawing from Kuwait or face ground attack. The statement gave Iraq a week to get out of all Kuwait, and forty-eight hours to get out of Kuwait city. That was probably just about feasible, but by this time the Iraqi command network was badly damaged, and even if President Saddam had given the order it is debatable whether those terms could have been met. Had he complied at that stage, however, it is likely that delays and hitches would have been tolerated, as long as the general principle was being observed. The principle which the UN and Nato used with Serbs in Bosnia. The air attacks would have been suspended, and the Alliance troops would have moved into Kuwait not as advancing combatants but as peacekeepers. Looked at like this, the difference between peace enforcement as applied in Bosnia and limited war as applied in the Gulf was not so great.

Saddam Hussein did not comply immediately, and on 24 February the ground offensive was launched. An order to withdraw from Kuwait was issued late on the 25th, an announcement which actually surprised the Allied commanders. By this time the Allied forces were committed to battle, and the extraction of the Iraqi forces became a rout.

On the evening of 27 February President Bush summoned his advisers. Most of the objectives of the limited war had been achieved, except for the destruction of the Republican Guard, which was the specific operational objective of the US VII corps, sweeping round to the west of Kuwait. Throughout military history, most casualties have occurred when an army breaks and flees, and this was now happening. The massacre of Iraqi troops at Mutla ridge, north of Kuwait, was a grisly warning. The

British, driving in from the west, came across a scene of scorched horror. The senior British and US generals were aware of the risk of being accused of butchery, of continuing operations against an enemy that was clearly defeated.[5]

Five years after the war, it has emerged that the US administration called a halt in anticipation of the effect the television pictures of Mutla ridge and other scenes of slaughter would have, even before the pictures were shown to the public. General Powell, who had been very reluctant to go to war in the first place, said, 'You don't do unnecessary killing if it can be avoided. At some point you decide you've accomplished your objectives and you stop. The question was, "How much additional destruction do we want to inflict upon the Iraqi army that was in the Kuwait theatre?" '[6]

General Powell said he then 'pointed out that we were starting to see some scenes that were unpleasant'. He explained that the objectives had largely been achieved, and that he would be recommending a cessation of hostilities within twenty-four hours – that is, by the evening of the 28th. President Bush then said, 'Well, if that's the case, we're within the window, why not end it now?' The Allies had been incredibly lucky. Throughout the build-up to the land war, many observers had warned of the risk of heavy Allied casualties. That they did not occur was a bonus, and a great relief. At any moment, a resolute stand by an Iraqi unit could have wiped out an advancing company which had become tired and careless. The British recommended continuing another twelve hours.

General Powell asked General Schwarzkopf if he could execute a cease-fire from midnight Washington time that night – 27 February. General Schwarzkopf said he 'could live with that'.

'Quite frankly, the driving force behind my saying that I could live with it was the fact that if we went on another day we were going to kill some more of our people and we had already won an overwhelming victory with a minimum of casualties and that was good enough for me.' He was glad, he said, to have a victory with minimum casualties, 'because that's a hell of a lot more than anybody's had in war in as long as I can remember.'[7]

The Americans called a halt right there. A cease-fire was declared from 08.00 Saudi time (midnight, Washington time) on 28 February.

The attitude to casualties, both 'enemy' and 'friendly' seems to mark a turning point in military history. The Iraqis, perhaps misguidedly, figured the Allies would have a very low tolerance of casualties and their strategy relied on inflicting quite a few, so that the 'soft' western democracies would recoil in horror. The Iraqi chief of intelligence, General Wafic Al Samarrai, later confirmed this when in exile. The Iraqis had launched a cross-border raid on Khafji in order to capture 4,000 to 5,000 British and American prisoners to use as 'human shields'. 'Saddam had always hoped casualties would undermine American resolve,' he said. He also confirmed that Saddam did not use his chemical weapons because he feared retaliation from the Israelis or the western Allies.[8]

The media bears much of the responsibility for 'hyping' the casualty issue. As General Schwarzkopf said, even one casualty was one too many. But, realistically, people get killed in wars. The Allied casualties were stupendously few, and many of them due to 'friendly fire'. That was nothing new either: it is probable that in earlier wars up to half the casualties in any battle were killed by their own side. Now every death was the subject of prolonged investigation. The nine British soldiers killed when the Americans attacked their Warrior by mistake, were the subject of endless hand-wringing. So, later, were two RAF Tornado crews, when it emerged that the RAF could have halted the costly low-level attacks a couple of days earlier.

By the standards of earlier wars, these incidents were minimal. However, democratic governments with electorates bombarded with information by the media will be very reluctant to embark on military operations where there is any risk of substantial casualties.

The Allied measures to cut off the theatre of operations, particularly the Iraqi armour, trapped by the rivers and marshes to the north, now impeded the Iraqi withdrawal – the original Allied objective. Yet the intermediate or 'operational' level of which isolating the theatre formed a part was a necessary stepping stone to the strategic aim, in this case the weakening of Iraqi military power and the ultimate withdrawal of Iraqi forces from Kuwait. The Allies were ill-equipped to pursue Iraqi forces which had escaped over the rivers, because they lacked the necessary bridging equipment. That was another reason for stopping.

One of the reasons why the Allies were able to stop so quickly was that they knew exactly where all their forces were. Satellite surveillance and navigation made it possible to 'turn off' the operation the moment the desired objective had been achieved. In an earlier era, it is probable the troops would have stumbled on, confusing and blurring the end of the operation. The Gulf War was a paradigm of limited war, thanks, in part, to very favourable conditions.

A Distinction Between Peace Enforcement and Limited War?

As related above, Allied attacks in the Gulf War had to be diverted from 'strategic' objectives in order to try to ensure the passage of Allied troops with as few casualties as possible. They were operational, contributing to the ultimate strategic success of the military operation.

In Bosnia, on the other hand, the Nato air attacks contributed more directly to a collapse of Serb will, and to a fundamental shift in the balance of forces. No Nato air attacks were mounted to make life easier or more certain for advancing Nato troops – because there were none.

This gives rise to a heretical explanation of the difference between the zone of intervention and peace enforcement, on the one hand, and limited war on the other. The 'operational level of war', it will be remembered, is defined as having objectives at one remove from a strategic (that is, political or economic) aim. In other words, it involves operations that are above the tactical or local level but still, in the end, mounted to help our own military campaign on its way. It emerged, as we have seen, in the context of vast military operations. Most people have assumed it applies to 'wider peacekeeping' and peace enforcement in the same measure as it does to war, limited or general. But why should it? Consent reached through theatre-wide agreements has been described as 'operational'. But surely such an agreement is strategic. An agreement that the Bosnian Serb government will abide by certain conditions and that UN troops will be permitted to oversee their implementation is surely a political agreement, a strategic agreement. In the zone of intervention, and peace enforcement, the gap between the local or tactical and the strategic is very narrow.

In limited war, however, the gap between tactics and strategy is wide, and the operational level is prominent. Military forces will do things which will, in the short term, contradict their strategic aims in order to ensure their fulfilment in the longer term. In intervention and peace enforcement, forces will move swiftly from tactics to strategy, with very little between. Heresy of heresies, perhaps, the 'operational level of war' does not apply in the zone of intervention, in 'wider peacekeeping', and peace enforcement, in the same way or to nearly the same extent as it does in true war. Perhaps the prominence of the operational level is the key factor determining what is, and what is not, a true war. The operational level has been likened to a series of stepping stones, towards a strategic aim. Is it peace enforcement or limited war? Count the stepping stones.

Surveillance

A force engaged in intervention or peace enforcement will probably enjoy its greatest advantage over the parties intervened against in the field of surveillance. In Bosnia, the British deployed teams using MSTAR (mobile surveillance and target acquisition radar) to keep an eye on the front line near Maglaj – the scene of the superb reconnaissance recounted in the last chapter.

In December 1994 I encountered some officers from the Royal Artillery at a party in Vitez. They had just come down from Maglaj. At that time, there were no guns in the theatre, so they were obviously doing artillery reconnaissance – plotting the positions of the local forces' guns. But the equipment could do much more than that.

'The locals call it black magic,' said one. 'It's streets ahead of anything they've seen.'

MSTAR could pick up individuals moving in the dark at several kilometres, and groups or vehicles much further away. With one of these sets, a small team was able to survey an area which would require an entire brigade of 5, 000 troops to hold it, or hundreds to man observation posts and sentry positions across it, merely to monitor movement. It was not their job to hold it, but merely to observe and report – for that is one of the most important aspects of peacekeeping and intervention operations. Sensors which can detect the heat of a human body or a vehicle enable areas to be guarded and surveyed by many fewer troops. Further radical advances in this area will work in favour of the intervener, since in this type of operation, more than any other, knowledge is power.

Air Power

During the Russian attack on Grozny, we went to see some Russian prisoners held by the Chechens. As we were leaving the cellar where they were held, a Russian aircraft appeared. There was panic, and people fell back down the stairs, very nearly killing more in the crush than the aircraft could have killed if it had dropped anything. On another occasion, a colleague of mine was in a car when an aircraft appeared. We always drove with the windows open, to hear them coming, and preferred four-door cars, to get out in a hurry. Everybody else dived for cover into the side of the road. He just looked up as it roared overhead.

'Weren't you frightened?'

'Oh, no. It wasn't carrying any bombs. I could see underneath ...'

Whilst I lacked the sang-froid of my colleague from *The Times*, I must confess I could not understand why any and every aircraft provoked such terror among the majority. I have an irrational fear of personal violence – the idiot in the black balaclava on the checkpoint – but I find the impersonality of a plane, whose pilot cannot see you, reassuring. However, it taught a lesson which senior RAF officers, pondering the role of air power in peace support operations, seemed not to understand. Why, they asked, is air power escalatory and artillery less so? 'Because people are shit scared of aeroplanes' was my considered response. Perceptions matter.

The Russian government also showed the importance of perception later the same year, when the US cruise missiles were launched against Banja Luka. They regarded their use by the Americans as an alarming form of escalation. Once again, it was not a question of what the things did, but of perception. To Nato, they were a logical means of hitting targets considered unduly risky for manned aircraft. To the Russians, they were cruise missiles – highly sophisticated, World War III weapons.

Unlike cruise missiles, manned aircraft can cruise the skies without bombing anything. They were used that way earlier in the Bosnian operation. When the Serbs were threatening Sarajevo and Gorazde in early 1994, Nato planes repeatedly buzzed Serb positions, to let them know they were there. The limited Nato air attacks of the time – before the big offensive of 30 August 1995 – were usually preceded by warning overflights. On some occasions, the media saw planes screaming in at low level, and reported 'air strikes', even though none had taken place. Aircraft, like ships, can provide a presence – reassuring or menacing – which is a potentially decisive weapon short of actually dropping bombs or firing missiles.

When it comes to bombing, the need to avoid civilian casualties and the loss of expensive aircraft and pilots, whose capture can be politically embarrassing, would seem to suggest Stealth-type aircraft with precision guided bombs as the dominant force. In the Gulf War the Stealth fighters, which made up only 2.5 per cent of the attack force, attacked 30 per cent of the strategic targets, including 80 per cent of those in Baghdad. Their laser guided bombs were usually accurate to within three metres, and the planes did not suffer a scratch. Although such technology is confined to the United States and, to a lesser extent, Russia, at the time of writing, other developed countries will undoubtedly follow. In the end, a very small force of very expensive aircraft may be more effective (and no more expensive overall) than the kind of air forces we have seen hitherto.

Sea Power

Navies are particularly good at deterring or coercing people without actually shooting them or occupying their towns and villages with soldiers. Navies can, as maritime strategists say, 'poise' offshore for a long time and provide 'leverage'. Being self-contained, with amphibious troops and aircraft, they can be used for keeping options open and signalling political resolve. In fact, they can match the pace and tone of diplomatic activity in a unique way. Besides providing visible signals, and, sometimes, neutral venues for talks, warships can also threaten to land troops anywhere along an extended shoreline. In that way, they can tie down disproportionate numbers of land-based troops.[9]

During the Cold War, the principal concern for European countries was a land-air battle in the central region of Europe. Navies were thus to some extent sidelined, used primarily to keep open the transatlantic sea lines of communication and protect the submarine-borne nuclear deterrent. Freed from the immediate threat of a massive land invasion, European countries with a maritime tradition (Britain, France, Spain and Italy, in particular), can and probably should put more emphasis back on the maritime forces. They are particularly useful in the confused situations now expected to arise in less easily accessible regions – as Mahan and Corbett envisage.

The cobbling together of the improvised UN 'Rapid Reaction Force' for Bosnia in summer 1995 was an example of a case where a maritime force – the 3rd Commando Brigade, completely self-contained – could have been used to good effect. The fact that most of the heavy equipment for the British deployments into Bosnia, first under the UN, later under Nato, had to come by sea (the railway tunnels were too narrow to bring Challenger tanks from Germany overland) strengthens the case for focusing on a maritime force which can be deployed swiftly anywhere. As most heavy cargoes still travel by sea, maritime forces are also important in embargo operations and to counter the resurgent threat of piracy around the world. It would not be surprising if, in the next fifty years, we saw an increase in seaborne strength relative to land-based strength.

'Non-lethal' Weapons

The need for restraint in operations in what I have called the zone of intervention, stretching into peace enforcement, makes this a logical point at which to examine a whole emerging area of technology which only the Americans, so far, have taken very seriously. This is the area of bloodless, 'less-than-lethal' or 'non-lethal' weapons. As the US Director of Non-Lethal Weapons at the Los Alamos laboratories said recently,

> The military only understand a weapon if it leaves a smoking hole in the ground. We can move beyond that era of warfare now.[10]

The 'smoking hole in the ground' definition of conventional weapons is perhaps more useful than defining them as 'lethal'. After all, the Allied air attacks on Iraq in 1991 and 1993 and the Nato attacks on *Republika Srpska* in Bosnia in 1995 did not primarily seek to kill people but to produce smoking holes in the ground, where radars and ammunition dumps had been. One 'non-lethal' – or 'non-smoking' – attack occurred in Iraq when the US launched cruise missiles trailing carbon-fire wires against an Iraqi power station. Rather than blowing up the power station, the trailing carbon fibre draped over the high-voltage power lines, and short-circuited them. It is in this area, between conventional 'hole in the ground' technology and the more fanciful ideas for glueing people or vehicles to the ground, trapping them in sticky nets, melting their tyres or suffocating their engines, that the most likely role for 'non-lethal', or non-smoking, weapons probably lies.

American interest in developing weapons that will immobilise and incapacitate rather than kill was stimulated by figures from Somalia indicating that thousands of civilians – estimates go as high as 10,000 – were killed in 'collateral damage' associated with peace-keeping and peace enforcement efforts.[11]

Although the ideal of 'war without killing' stems from the best of motives, one of the biggest obstacles to non-lethal, non-smoking weapons is a legal one. The conventions on war and the use of force specify that weapons have to be designed to kill – not to wound or incapacitate. If technology of this type is developed extensively, the laws of war will have to be amended.

In fact, non-lethal warfare has been around for a long time. The whole business of electronic warfare – jamming the other side's radars and radio transmissions – is, in itself, non-lethal. The dependence of modern institutions, including armed forces, on computers now makes them ideal targets for computer viruses and other interference. The increased use of fibre-optic cables means that it will be more difficult to introduce viruses to computer networks (there are fewer entry points) and they will probably need human agents to plant them, either before or during a conflict. However, there are simpler ways of interfering with computer systems. Most of us are familiar with the devastating effect of the computer 'crashing' on any sophisticated enterprise (particularly devastating when you are trying to produce a newspaper on a Friday night). Computers are vulnerable to sudden fluctuations in the power supply, for example. 'Pulse power' devices are now available, which can give out 100 megawatts in a single burst and can be attached to electric grids. Rather than blowing up the power station or substation, you can do better, and wreck all the important equipment attached to it.

If it is not possible to attach a device to a grid, it may still be possible to use a short burst of electromagnetic energy to induce a high-voltage pulse in any nearby antenna, power line or cable – an effect similar to the 'electromagnetic pulse' from a nuclear explosion, but without the associated damage. Cruise missiles seen with oddly shaped nose cones are believed to be equipped with such devices, which use a coil with a magnetic field compressed by an explosion to create an electromagnetic pulse.

Optical sensors are particularly important to modern military forces, and are becoming more so with the growth in night-vision equipment. Laser weapons to craze the prisms of optical sights on tanks and armoured vehicles can be as effective in disabling the vehicle as a hit from an anti-armour shell. However, the danger of causing blindness has already begun to inhibit development of these weapons. In October 1995 the inhumane weapons convention was amended to include a restriction on weapons deliberately designed to blind people. The US cancelled a laser weapon, the laser countermeasure system, which was designed to damage optical systems, because it might cause incidental damage to the human eye, although under the convention it would have been allowed.

All these devices can be regarded as an extension of electronic warfare, which has been around since the interception of telephone talk in the First World War, or of traditional military emphasis on attacking the enemy's command and control. Rather different are chemicals and microbes which react with vehicle tyres, accelerate rusting in metal, asphyxiate air breathing engines or transform roads into adhesive traps or skid-pans. Air breathing engines are very sensitive to any interference with their fuel or the fuel-air mixture – try starting a car on a cold day when the choke cable has snapped. And road surfaces are equally sensitive. Try braking on ice – or some chemical which has the same effect.

One promising area is that of sound – particularly low frequency sound. This can be directed to cause nausea, vomiting and bowel spasms, but not permanent damage. It is possible to construct barriers using sound but, as with many of the 'non-lethal' technologies being explored, the problem is one of cost versus benefit. You could build a sonic barrier around an installation but it would require a vast generator. A few coils of razor wire and a couple of armed sentries would be as effective, and far cheaper.

Finally, there are 'less than lethal' weapons which can replace the bayonet or the bullet. Again, the idea is not new: the rubber bullet, the water cannon and the stun grenade (the latter to give attacking troops a precious few seconds' advantage over terrorists without killing them or their hostages) have been used for years. In future, these can be supplemented by gluey nets, sticky foam dispensers and inflatable balls to impede movement across any confined space.

In many cases, such weapons would have few advantages over conventional methods. A prevailing view, still held by the British Defence Research Agency, is that if you use a non-lethal weapon on another party, they will quickly respond with a lethal one – the good old Kalashnikov, for example – and you will be back to square one. Another drawback is that it is difficult to predict the effect of non-lethal weapons: they might be lethal to someone with a medical condition, as trials by the Metropolition Police with CS gas have warned us, and even throwing jam at children could start a stampede in which people could be crushed to death. A great deal of scepticism still surrounds these technologies.

However, there are cases in the zone of intervention and in peace enforcement where a 'non-lethal option' might be useful. When UN soldiers were taken hostage by the Serbs on the outskirts of Gorazde, it happened because they knew the Serbs, and were reluctant to open fire, or believed the Serbs' intentions to be benign. There are many situations in such operations where young and nervous soldiers might encounter people of whose intentions they were unsure. The ability to immobilise a potential threat without doing serious damage could be handy. As one proponent of non-lethal weapons put it, 'just slime them . . .' Or, to emulate the popular TV series *Star Trek*, 'phasers on stun . . .'

The debate over 'non-smoking' weapons mirrors that over consent in peacekeeping and peace enforcement. Just as there appeared to be a clear divide between peacekeeping, with consent, and peace enforcement, without it, so there appeared to be a clear divide between the use of force, and not using force. Some see 'non-lethal weapons' as blurring the latter distinction, as recent experience has blurred the former. But in a peacekeeping or peace enforcement situation, the use of even a 'non-lethal' weapon would probably be perceived as the use of force.

The Shape of Future Armed Forces

It would be foolish for the world's great powers to forsake their ability to conduct a major operation on the scale of the Gulf War, in the event of a new actor emerging to challenge international security. It is most unlikely that any of them would have to do it alone. The genie in the bottle must be kept, even if it is not used, as the most exacting standard against which professional military forces can be measured periodically, between other tasks. The United States is being forced to rethink its 'bottom-up' strategy of being able to fight two major regional conflicts (Gulf Wars) simultaneously. One, plus a Bosnia-type operation – let us say 'one-and-a-half' – is likely to be the outcome. Many analysts believe, however, that the greatest threat the United States and western Europe face 'arises from the worldwide proliferation of local conflicts and their potential escalation into regional conflagrations.'[12] This will require armed forces to undertake a wide range of peacekeeping, intervention and crisis control activities. While less intense than major regional conflicts, they go on for a long time, and this can place a strain on even the most powerful military organisations. A marathon runner and a sprinter are not the same.

Short of another Gulf War, operations in the zone of intervention will be the most demanding undertaken by developed countries. The British Army has largely abandoned the use of the term 'low intensity' to describe operations other than war because it is quite inappropriate. The equipment of high intensity war is everywhere – it is best protection for peacekeepers, after all. And heavy engineering equipment is needed most in intervention operations – bridging rivers, hundreds of metres wide, swollen by sudden floods, for example.

At present, the biggest problem is the discrepancy between forces which can be deployed rapidly, and are relatively lightly equipped, and the heavy equipment needed for an effective intervention without placing the interveners' lives at risk. At present, it is possible to put firepower on lighter vehicles, but not protection. Hence the appearance of 60-ton tanks in Bosnia, not as offensive weapons of manoeuvre, but as mobile pill-boxes. In the short term, the UN adopted an age-old solution – fortifications. As equipment designers look to the next century, closing the gap between speed of deployment and weight on the ground must be their top priority.

Ballistic Missile Defence – the Ultimate Form of National Security

Freed from a one-dimensional 'threat', and given new security by what appears to be genuine and permanent groupings of the developed nations – Nato, G7, the EU – it would seem that 'national defence' is no longer the primary role of the armed forces of North American and west European states. They are primarily for use as instruments of the state's foreign policy.

The only real military threat to Britain, France and the United States is that of missile attack. All continue to maintain nuclear arsenals to deter attack by other powers with nuclear, biological or chemical weapons and the means to deliver them. At present, that could only be a resurgent Russia, or possibly China. But it is unlikely to stay that way.

The proliferation of nuclear, biological and chemical weapons and missiles to deliver them has generated huge concern. Investment has poured into studies on anti-missile systems: missiles to shoot down missiles, like the Patriots which intercepted incoming Scud missiles during the Gulf War. By 1990, US officials were reporting that 15 states already had ballistic missiles and that 20 were trying to acquire them. By 2000, they estimated, 24 countries would have them, including 6 countries with missiles able to fly 2,500 kilometres.[13]

The problem is that 'deterrence' may not work against a potentate who cares little for his own people and may not be 'rational', in the sense that nuclear deterrence theorists understand it, anyway. The combination of a nuclear-missile armed, third-world dictator may appear far-fetched, but Saddam Hussein was not far off getting nuclear weapons before the Gulf War. During that war, he also fired 38 improved Scud missiles at Israel, 41 at Saudi Arabia and 2 at Bahrain and Qatar.

There is validity in the argument that the potential threat of missile attack has been exaggerated to justify continued high military spending. After the Berlin Wall fell, there was a 'threat gap' which was quickly filled by the threat from 'rogue' or outlaw states, missile proliferation, and uncertainty in a world that was 'still a dangerous place'. The countries seeking to acquire ballistic missiles almost invariably see them as status symbols, giving leverage within their region of the globe, and probably have no intention of confronting the great powers. If a salvo of missiles were fired, it would certainly invite a swift response.

Nonetheless, an unexpected strike by a party insensitive to deterrence could wipe out a western city. The British Ministry of Defence has commissioned a £5 million study into the possible need for an anti-missile defence system. In discussion, the officials responsible said they expected a third-world country (in North Africa, presumably), to have missiles able to hit Britain within ten years. So many anti-missile defence studies were underway in the United States that by late 1995 the Pentagon had to admit that it would not be able to evaluate all the results.

The idea of shooting down incoming missiles has its origins in two places. First, there was the Strategic Defense Initiative – Star Wars – of 23 March 1983, which sought to examine building a shield of space-based interceptors which would block a missile attack on the United States. That proved impossibly expensive and could never guarantee to stop enough missiles to provide security anyway. However, after the Cold War ended, the idea of a more limited system to deal with a limited missile attack, either by a 'rogue' Russian general, a third-world dictator or an accident, gained some currency. This more limited idea was called 'Global Protection Against Limited Strikes'.

Meanwhile, an anti-aircraft missile, the Patriot, had been upgraded to intercept incoming ballistic missiles. Its first use, against Iraqi Scuds in the 1991 Gulf War, seemed spectacularly succesful. In fact, the initial reports of Patriot success were greatly exaggerated, and by breaking the missiles up the Patriots contributed to spreading the damage over a wider area. Nonetheless, as someone on the receiving end of the Scud attacks on Riyadh, all I can say is that whatever their inadequacies, the Patriots, at the time, were very good for morale.

The most effective way of countering missiles is to destroy them on the ground, before launch, and this was done with some success in Iraq by the US Air Force and the SAS. The next best solution is to destroy them soon after launch, in the 'boost phase'. Satellites and early warning aircraft already detect missile launches – the US did so successfully in the Gulf War – and some sort of screening force near potential launch sites should then be able to catch the missiles on their way up. Warships would be an important, probably the primary, component of such a system. Not only is three-quarters of the planet covered by sea, but the best place to destroy a missile with a nuclear, chemical or biological warhead would be over it. Warships could carry large and sophisticated anti-missile missiles and the associated sensors: it would be far more difficult to move them around on land. And most of the potential launch sites are separated from their potential targets by stretches of sea.

If we are looking at the future defence of nation states, some form of ballistic missile defence system to stop approaching missiles is the only one which has an obvious role. Small countries, like Britain, enjoy an advantage here over big ones, like the United States and Russia. American attention has shifted to defending US troops deployed abroad against missile attack – the origins of the term 'Theatre High Altitude Air Defence'. Such a system could defend an area a few hundred kilometres across, intercepting incoming missiles very high in the atmosphere. If we take Britain as an example, that would be quite adequate to cover the populated areas of England, with maybe another, overlapping system to cover the 'dumb-bell' of Glasgow and Edinburgh.

In the next half-century, the armed forces of the developed countries – the 'great powers', once again – will spend the overwhelming majority of their operational time in disaster relief, peacekeeping, intervention and occasional peace enforcement. They will be ambassadors and tools of foreign policy. They will not, in the main, be directly involved in 'national defence', except for low-level tasks, including the interception of increasingly organised drug cartels and criminal gangs.

However, the ability to conduct large-scale, high intensity operations as part of a multinational force must be maintained. It is quite likely that an emergency of this kind – a Gulf War – will occur about once every ten years.

Furthermore, it is not possible to hive off the specialised tasks connected with direct national defence, and to consider them completely separately, any more than it is possible for a javelin thrower to remain fit by exercising his right arm only. A submarine-launched nuclear deterrent does not just require submarines; it requires minesweepers and surface warships to protect the deterrent as it deploys, to resupply it, and so on. An anti-missile system could, in theory, be operated by a private contractor, with expertise in, for example, air traffic control. However, the author believes that unlikely, since it would need to be tied in with intelligence sources on the ground, with reconnaissance aircraft, with SAS teams who would try to disable missiles before launch, with naval missile cruisers near the potential launch sites, and with the nuclear deterrent force for possible reprisals. However, these activities – national defence in its traditional sense – are beginning to appear increasingly discrete from the work of the majority of the armed forces.

CHAPTER EIGHT

FUTURE WARRIORS

One minute, everything was fine. The hard, compacted gravel of the smooth track stretched ahead, between the pine forests tumbling down the mountain. This was route 'Triangle', the main route into, or, in this case, out of central Bosnia. The Royal Engineers had turned what had been a logging track over a high mountain into a fine, wide road. But it was still treacherous. Torrential rain had weakened the side of the road, and maybe I got too close to the edge. The next moment a tree was heading for the car in slow motion, and a giant spider cast a cracked web across the windscreen. The gear stick would not engage, knocked out of alignment. A write-off. Just one further problem. Bosnia is a war zone, and cars are uninsured.

'Never travel alone' was a good rule, and before too long my colleague in the car ahead, having realised I was no longer with him, returned. We were about four miles north of 'Redoubt', the familiar Wild West fort, and headed for it to get help. The priority was to get the car off the road, and to recover it before nightfall. The seemingly deserted forest would soon spawn pillagers, who would strip the car of everything of value.

At Redoubt, two soldiers were chatting with the sentry. They looked older than your normal private soldier, in their late twenties. I would have guessed they were sergeants, but they were wearing no rank insignia.

Earlier that day we had watched as the first British artillery – 105 mm Light Guns – had headed up the road towards the base at Gornji Vakuf. Armoured vehicles from the Devonshire and Dorset Regiment had been out picketing the route. The local parties had a habit of appropriating white painted equipment, and the Artillery were not going to lose their Regimental colours, which also had a range of 11 miles.

'Yeah, we'll have a go,' one of the soldiers said. They climbed into a Land-Rover with a winch, and followed us back to the sorry spectacle of the smashed car. They attached the winch and got it off the road, at least.

Before they did, my colleague had an idea.

'I'll just take a photograph,' he said, 'for insurance, or whatever . . .'

'For Christ's sake don't photograph *me*,' said one of the soldiers, and gestured with his hand to cover his face.

At the time, preoccupied with the likely cost of the day's proceedings, I just thought he was joking.

'Hire car, is it? Well, you could 'phone from Tomislavgrad. Once you've notified the hire company, it's up to them, in theory . . .' He chatted on, authoritatively.

We bade them farewell, and headed for the big base at Tomislavgrad, where we found the Reme (Royal Electrical and Mechanical Engineers), the Army's equivalent of the Automobile Association, and much more. They did not have to help, but they sent a big recovery truck to get the car, and by midnight it was back in the safety of Split in Croatia.

A few weeks later, back in London, my colleague telephoned. The conversation turned to the photograph.

'You realise they were SAS, don't you . . .'

Of course. 'Don't photograph *me*.' Joint Commission Observers – sometimes a euphemism for the SAS. They had been keeping an eye on the route, liaising with local commanders, watching over the progress of those guns.

And, like most of those people, they were pleasant, worldly, informal – and stupendously ordinary.

What type of soldier will be needed to practise the new art of war and peace? He or she may be called on to act as an ambassador, the lone representative of his or her country, or the UN, at a disputed barricade. To carry sacred artefacts from a church for safekeeping. To operate night vision equipment, laser rangefinders, and the 'battlenet' – a battlefield computer system similar to that in use in most big city offices – discarding irrelevant details as waves of information surge in over the equivalent of the Internet.[1]

Or to wait, unseen, unheard, unsmelt, in a blizzard, clothed in thermals but damp, imperfectly fed and uncomfortable, staring through a starlight scope sophisticated image intensifier to see in the dark in order to terminate a life by delivering a bullet with clinical precision, aiming at the 'centre of the mass', when the outline appears. That is why flak jackets cover the 'centre of the mass'. Or, as the caption to a painting in one of the SAS messes puts it, to move the last of a group of terrified hostages out as the last of the terrorists is 'dealt with'. Killed. Or to bring medical aid to malnourished children, screaming in a vile, sweating hell beneath a sun-roasted tin roof.

Clearly, future soldiers will have to be fit, bright, mentally and physically robust and incredibly adaptable. There are two apparently contradictory tendencies here. Soldiers, sailors and airmen will have to be very scientific, very technological. As General Rupert Smith put it,

> I was fighting my equipment, I was not equipping men. Men were an *embarrassment*. They had to be *fed*. They were *casualties waiting to happen*.[2]

The business of the armed forces has been very technical for a long time. Among the people who fly and service aircraft, who operate the sonar on ships, or operate fire control computers, the straightforward infantry soldier is in the minority. His or her trade will also became as technical as anyone else's. Yet in peace operations, you are often *equipping men* as well. It is the man or woman negotiating, acting as the intermediary, who matters. Ordinary soldiers, and certainly the most junior commanders, will need to understand their commanders' 'intent' very well, and apply it in their dealings with local parties who may be frightened, bitter – and very cunning.

Recruiting the right sort of people is already becoming a problem for volunteer armed forces. In 1995, the British Army found itself short of infantry for a variety of reasons. Half of those who applied were turned down on straightforward physical and medical grounds (a repetition of what happened with the volunteers for the Boer War of 1899–1902). They either had clinically detectable medical conditions, or were too fat – or too thin. Changes in the culture of western society were largely responsible: youngsters no longer kicked tin cans around the street or roamed far from home to climb trees. Instead, they spent much time watching television or playing computer games. And they wore trainers, not hard shoes, so their feet took weeks to get accustomed to army boots. However, when it came to manning the 'Battlenet' and other computer systems, this new generation were brilliant.

The Army and the Royal Marines had both adjusted their training procedures to cope with a generation which was physically 'less robust'. They did not make recruits run in boots until the tenth week of training, for example. But there was clearly a limit to what could be done in a given time. Either standards had to be lowered or training would have to be extended. The training of junior army officers was extended dramatically, from the six-month 'Standard Military Course' of the 1970s and even shorter courses for university graduates, to a fifteen-month course for everyone.

The problem of physical standards is exacerbated by the great expansion in education throughout the developed world. The British forces have always been stratified according to social class, which is still perceived as linked to education. Not so long ago, the fact that someone went to a university meant they were automatically considered 'officer material'. With a great expansion in access to university-level education, many of the young people on whom the services might have relied to provide good soldiers sailors, and airmen and women, who would progress through the non-commissioned ranks, are being tempted into higher education instead. The IQ and educational standards required for ordinary recruits into some of the more demanding branches of the armed forces are now the same as those required for entry to some of the newer universities.

The policy of encouraging service personnel to gain qualifications recognised in civilian life is also resulting in senior non-commissioned people acquiring degrees during their service. This is all to the good, but means the traditional divide between 'officer' and 'non-officer' in all countries may therefore be coming into question.

In the former Soviet bloc, the distinction was different. The officers, all of whom had university-level education, were the career professionals. The other ranks were conscripts. A conscript with a degree was likely to become a sergeant fairly quickly.

When, after the end of the Cold War, all-professional services met conscript-based services in the course of arms control inspections, the results were interesting. The Czechoslovak Army fielded inspectors who were all lieutenant colonels or majors: the British sent sergeants and staff sergeants. Under the terms of the Conventional Forces in Europe Treaty, all 'inspectors' enjoyed officer status anyway. 'There's no problem', said one of the British sergeants. 'They realise they don't have anything like us in their army.'

In time, the conscript army will probably disappear or be relegated to a form of extended social service, in Europe and North America if not elsewhere. The performance of conscripts, whether Russians in Grozny or some of the peacekeeping contingents in Bosnia, has been inadequate, to say the least. Smaller, all-volunteer, professional forces are the only ones which will be able to cope with the variety of tasks they may have to undertake.

The abolition of compulsory military service does have its disadvantages, which have become clear in Britain. Fewer and fewer people have any idea how the armed services work and what they are like. They become alienated, to some extent, from the rest of society. I recall the story of a defence industrialist's daughter, an intelligent young woman, who was taken to a military display one year. After a while she asked her father, 'Are *all* soldiers officers, or just some of them?' The debate about whether homosexuality should be permitted in the British services underway at the time of writing also betrays a lack of understanding of service conditions among some of the more 'liberal' minded commentators. 'What people do in the privacy of their own bedrooms is their business.' Absolutely. But in the forces you often do not have your own bedroom. That is the point. That said, this author is in favour of a relaxation, on the lines of the US policy of 'Don't ask, don't tell.' In this, as in all other areas, the armed forces must, and will, reflect trends in society as a whole, though a little delay in adapting may be no bad thing.

Even though professional armed forces may be distanced from the rest of society, they inevitably reflect its trends because people have grown up in normal society before they join. I spent a night with the Coldstream Guards at Gornji Vakuf, expecting the soldiers' accommodation to be a spartan and well-ordered barrack room. They had all built themselves little cubicles from packing cases, cardboard and blankets. We were fed on pie and chips. A colleague of mine asked if they had a vegetarian meal. 'Vegetarian meal? Certainly, sir.' A few minutes later a cook appeared. 'Vegetarian meal?' Chips. Well, it was Gornji Vakuf, on a front line. In some ways, the Army had changed a lot. But not, perhaps, in others.

The maintenance of reserve forces is one way that all professional armed services can stay in touch with society at large. However, the need for very rapid deployment is putting the role of reserves in some doubt. The calling up of reserves is an emotive issue. Before the Gulf War, General Colin Powell decided to present the President with proposals which would make him think twice about going to war. Most contentious of these was 'the political poison pill': the activation of National Guard and Army reserves.'

The whole system of calling up reserves harks back to the days of general or total war. There are two types of reserves: former members of the professional armed forces who may be recalled, and volunteer, 'weekend soldiers'. Reserves were designed to be used for home defence or in time of dire national emergency. The United States used reserve formations in the Gulf; the British only mobilised a few specialists. The difficulty was that the system of calling out reserves was designed solely for a World War III eventuality, and not for engagements in 'peacetime'. Yet, as we have seen, even these 'peacetime engagements' can put the armed forces of western powers under strain. Britain, for example, has a 120,000-strong army of whom 17,000 are in Ireland and 13,000 in Bosnia, but many of them need to be rotated every six months, so in the course of a year up to 60,000, or half the entire army, could pass through these two theatres.

In these circumstances, reservists could be used to provide back-up for the full-time armed services, but this can cause problems. If people are to leave their civilian jobs, they have to be guaranteed to get them back. Employers need to be compensated, but they may be reluctant to employ people who have a reserve obligation. In practice, the small number of reservists used in intervention operations tend to be people who are self-employed, or they may be casualties of economic recession, for whom six months on military pay is a welcome salvation. Few of the reserve officers I have encountered have been much good. If reserves are not going to be used in the type of operations which will be most prevalent in the next fifty years, or if they fail to match up to the necessary standards, then we do not need them. They become a waste of money.

The professional armed forces of the future, meanwhile, will need to be even better trained, and it will take longer. The individual soldier, sailor, airman or woman will probably be very well educated by past standards. The social structure is more likely to resemble that of the police, where individuals at the bottom of the rank structure are invested with a great deal of authority in their own right, and the sense of hierarchy is less dominant. All police are 'officers'. We may move closer to an 'all-officer' structure for the armed services.

Casualties

One of the most striking aspects of the Gulf War was the extraordinary concern about casualties, both coalition and Iraqi. Saddam Hussein believed that the western states, particularly the United States, would be intolerant of large casualty figures. The reaction of the media after the war suggests he was right. A collision between huge armies, one of which was known to have, and be prepared to use, chemical and biological weapons, was thought likely to lead to terrible losses. The enormous investment in medical facilities reflected a fear on the part of western governments that there would be many dead and wounded. In most wars, the rule-of-thumb is a ratio of one to three. In fact, the coalition lost 240 people, many of them to 'friendly fire'. The Iraqis probably lost 10,000 during the air campaign and another 10,000 in the ground war – far fewer than was thought at the time. Endless debate was sparked off by every incident which created casualties: the loss of US Marines and then nine British soldiers to 'friendly fire'; the destruction of the Iraqi al-Amariyah shelter with the loss of hundreds of civilian lives; the loss of a US barrack block to a Scud missile; the massacre of fleeing Iraqis at Mutla ridge.

The Gulf War was a conflict waged for important national interests – oil – and against an opponent who was perceived to be very dangerous, and evil. Public tolerance for casualties might therefore have been higher than expected. But if nations are going to intervene in 'other people's wars' out of 'conscience', the tolerance for casualties will be very low. One of the main lessons of the Gulf War was the need for greatly improved methods of 'identification – friend or foe?' to prevent aircraft attacking friendly vehicles on the ground, as well as each other, and vice versa. One of the interesting sartorial changes of recent decades has been that armed forces the world over look increasingly alike. In Bosnia all three local factions wore camouflage uniforms which closely resembled US or British uniforms. Identification has always been a prime require-ment – more important than concealment. For the British Army to go into action wearing red tunics was not so stupid. That way, through the smoke at several hundred metres, you might just know who was who. Even in the Second World War, soldiers were broadly differentiated: the Americans in olive green, the British and Russians in brown, the Germans in field grey. When there is a general similarity of uniforms and equipment, and numerous countries' forces are present on the same side, reliable electronic, acoustic or some other means of identification is vital.

Anyone considering an intervention operation must now take public tolerance of casualties into account and work out how to react to a number of contingencies. In spite of some press attempts to create a public demand for withdrawal from Bosnia, the casualties have not been sufficient for them to succeed. In conventional war, casualties are accepted as an unfortunate fact of life, and to be too squeamish may actually cost more lives. The famous Russian practice of ploughing ahead across minefields was rooted in cold calculations. Do you halt and let the Germans set up a machine gun on the other side? Or do you pursue them across the field, taking the odd casualty from mines? You will have fewer casualties with the latter. As Napoleon said, 'He who cannot look upon a battlefield dry-eyed will lose many men needlessly.'

However, that old rule of war is no longer applicable in such a callous, clinical way. Casualties *do* matter, and are part of the calculation. Any future operation by western forces is likely to have as its objective the achievement of the aim with minimum friendly casualties, minimum 'collateral damage' (the other side's casualties) and minimum environmental damage. These will be new, and welcome, limitations on the 'absolute' form of war.

The Commander

The experience of peace operations in the early 1990s has refocused attention on the senior commander as the prime mover in peace negotiations. His or her personality is absolutely crucial to the conduct of operations, the battle of wills with the other party and public perception. Even though some military figures exercised very strong leadership during the total war era, and deliberately cultivated a 'cult of personality' – Field Marshal Bernard Montgomery (1887–1976) and General Douglas MacArthur (1880–1964) spring to mind – no one military commander could exercise as much personal and rapid influence on events in the era of massed, impersonal destruction as they can now.

The media is assisting this process, partly because it can project an image with great power, and partly because it seeks to build up personalities since people find them interesting. The successive commanders of the UN forces in Bosnia are example enough. General Philippe Morillon, who appeared as something of a white knight, promising to save Sarajevo and Srebrenica. Sir Michael Rose, unusually urbane and charming, the quintessential Oxford-educated general, who courted the media. Sir Rupert Smith, who avoided obvious contact with the media but kept them well briefed, discreetly plotting his switch to peace enforcement, and impressing the warring factions with his quiet but unmistakeable toughness.

Leaders stand out by being different. In that sense, the people who rise to senior positions in the armed forces are much like the people in senior positions anywhere. The achievement of General Smith, who had a classic – and very narrow – military background, is perhaps the most remarkable. The career pattern of senior commanders in future will need to embrace other areas of human endeavour, and promising officers should be seconded to other organisations at a fairly senior level. One of the problems with a traditional military career is that you have to have done 'the right jobs'. With armed forces contracting, and an increasing variety of tasks, some very different from their traditional roles, this will become increasingly difficult. Why should an officer be disbarred from a very senior position – brigadier (general) and above – because they have not commanded a major unit? Running a similar-sized organisation in the cut-throat world of business should qualify them equally well, as long as they possess all the other military credentials. Before the Cold War ended, Richard Simpkin, one of the most talented thinkers on military affairs, suggested that business was probably the best training for commanders in real war. Whereas peacetime soldiering had innumerable safeguards built in, business was like a real battle, where risks were taken and results were quick, obvious and unambiguous. The 'bottom line' and the 'front line' have many similarities. Richard Simpkin was writing during the Cold War, when opportunities for real soldiering were few. But even today, a command appointment in a zone of real operations is coveted by any ambitious individual.

With the prominence of peace operations, attachment to an aid agency would also be a valid 'tour' for a promising officer, where the similarities between the work of military and civilian organisations in a crisis area would ensure that the arrangement was of mutual benefit. The Irish Army, heavily involved in UN operations, currently has such a scheme, and other states' armed forces will probably develop similar ideas.

Mercenaries

As armed forces' business becomes increasingly professional, it lends itself to experts who will sell their services to anyone for money. The phenomenon of the mercenary is as old as war, and even with the development of national armies in the seventeenth, eighteenth and early nineteenth centuries, most of the other ranks had enlisted out of desperation. The army of Frederick the Great of Prussia (1712–86), for example, contained many foreigners. Even Voltaire's Candide served a spell. It was only with the development of national, conscript armies in the nineteenth century that 'mercenaries' took a back seat: as we have seen, in World War I, that was the disparaging term used by the Germans about the professional British army. Clausewitz, a Prussian, and Jomini, a Swiss, two of our prominent military theorists, spent time in the service of the Russians. They, too, were mercenaries after a fashion.

There have been allegations, never proven, that US mercenaries fought with the Argentinian forces in the Falklands. They were at the centre of allegations that British paratroops had executed prisoners, but the charges were never pursued. It would not be surprising if small groups of mercenaries were found attached to national forces, although in a conventional war they would be unlikely to be of much value. A competent national army would have plenty of people of its own. However, if taking casualties were a particular problem for a government, the use of mercenaries could have its advantages – although the sort of governments who would be worried about public opinion would be the sort of governments for whom revelations about their use of mercenaries might cause a scandal.

'Mercenary', in the narrower sense, means small groups of individuals who undertake to fight for a party in a war, usually, by implication, a party of dubious morals or competence. Their employment has been limited because such parties tend not to have much cash. However, drug cartels would be the sort of organisation which would employ mercenaries, probably in fields where their expertise and qualifications could be checked easily. Possible candidates would be pilots, snipers, explosives experts, electronic warfare experts, computer hackers, people with counter-terrorist skills – gamekeepers turned poachers, rather than the opposite.

The contraction of armed forces, worldwide, in the wake of the end of the Cold War, and the expanding number of conflicts suggests there may be a bigger market for high-tech mercenaries. They will not, by and large, be attracted to national governments with their own armed forces, but to the people with whom those governments may be in conflict. However, the shortage of cash will probably keep the mercenary market limited. Oddly enough, there may be one very prestigious employer who will be on the lookout for mercenaries. The United Nations.

Genetic engineering and drugs

Western nations' professional armed forces of the future will not want supermen or psychopaths. They will want people who are, like the gentlemen I met on route 'Triangle', 'stupendously normal'. But that may not be the case worldwide. Although armies of ordinary people have tended to win, in the long term, over armies of fanatics, the fanatics can enjoy a short-term advantage, especially if they are unconcerned by death. The performance of certain élite groups – like the Waffen-SS and the

Japanese *kamikaze* pilots – had a certain edge over legions of 'normal' soldiers, although the 'normal' people won in the end.

The science of genetics and the possibility of genetic engineering are among the most exciting and challenging fields of study at the time of writing. If you wanted a particularly ruthless strike force, you could do worse than turn to a geneticist. It is known that the presence of a second male chromosome – the XYY combination – may dispose males to extra aggression, for example. But an unscrupulous dictator could do more than that.

What is the best size for a tank commander? Or a submariner? Or a pilot, come to that? About three feet high? It would not be impossible to breed dwarves to operate key items of military hardware, so they could be made smaller, or so there would be more space for other things: armour, armament and ammunition, and other supplies. Your combat infantry, on the other hand, would need to be large and athletic; your snipers, judging by Olympic shooting champions, perhaps rather well-built, for stability, and with exceptional eyesight. All these traits could, presumably, be genetically engineered.

Clearly, genetic engineering of certain traits would be risky – other traits might be lost. Exceptionally aggressive individuals would be useful for certain tasks but might also resist discipline. A safer bet is to alter the individual's performance on a temporary basis, using drugs. The use of anabolic steroids in athletic training, to improve muscle development, and to improve performance in events, has been commonplace.

Alcohol has always been widely used to give soldiers 'Dutch courage'. There were reports of the Russian troops in Grozny being given 'mind and body' injections, which might have explained their behaviour – especially when combined with alcohol, which they imbibed in large quantities. In battle, anabolic steroids would heighten aggression and tolerance of pain, but without slowing reaction times. Opiates would reduce fear, but would also cause troops to become 'spaced out', and probably reduce performance rather than improve it. Drugs can also be used to keep people awake – a very important part of any military operation.

Robots

Watch any military parade, and you will see that an important part of traditional military training was to make people into components of a machine. Modern drill has its origins in the Middle Ages (the salute is a lifting of the visor) but is largely based on eighteenth-century battlefield tactics. Inaccurate and short-ranged weapons had to be discharged en masse and reloaded quickly. The large formations needed to maximise their effect had to wheel quickly and precisely to deliver their fire where needed.

All those functions have now been taken over by machines. The commander of a tank or infantry fighting vehicle has, at his fingertips, in a modern 'chain gun', the same firepower as several battalions of eighteenth-century troops. In this sense, the idea of 'every soldier an officer' comes to life. But the replacement of troops by machines goes much further.

One of the first military thinkers to advocate the large-scale use of remotely controlled vehicles and robots was the Soviet Marshal Mikhail Tukhachevskiy (1893–1937). He envisaged using remotely controlled tanks to destroy enemy anti-aircraft guns, on the grounds that they could withstand far more hits than a manned vehicle before ceasing to function, and remotely controlled aircraft.[4] The use of remotely controlled vehicles in military operations has now become standard: to defuse bombs in Northern Ireland, for example, or the use of cruise missiles and unmanned drones in the Gulf and Bosnia.

The 1991 Gulf War was the first great conflict to see the widespread use of robot devices in place of manned vehicles. A typical combat aircraft would cost at least US $30 million, as against maybe $500,000 for an unmanned aircraft. The difference is mainly due to the need for self-defence measures, ejector seats and other devices designed to protect the pilot. In terms of effectiveness, sixty drones would be vastly superior to one manned aircraft.

During the Gulf War the US battleships *Wisconsin* and *Missouri* launched unmanned Pioneer drones to find Iraqi targets on the Kuwaiti coast. Because there was no great concern about losing them, these propeller-driven drones continued sending pictures back even when the battleships opened fire.[5] In any earlier war, highly trained special forces would have been needed ashore to provide the data for the battleship guns. Potential prisoners, potential hostages, potential casualties. The US commander of naval forces in the Gulf, Vice Admiral Stanley Arthur, was particularly struck by the events of 27 February 1991 – the last full day of the war. A group of Iraqi soldiers tried to surrender to a Pioneer: 'The first occasion in the history of warfare for human beings to capitulate to a robot.'

Since then, unmanned systems have improved. The US has been using

Gnat unmanned aircraft, operating from Albania, to scan the skies over Bosnia. With a range of 500 miles, they can transmit television and infrared pictures by satellite back to their operators.

There can be little doubt that unmanned systems will fulfil many of the roles performed until recently by people in conventional war. However, there are grave reservations about letting machines select targets, or kill people automatically. That is one reason why the systems described above have been limited, in the main, to surveillance. At present, the world's armed forces would prefer to use robotics to reduce the number of people needed to operate one piece of equipment – reducing a tank crew from four to one, for example – rather than let the machine take over completely.

That leads to another possibility. Rather than build single, large, omnicompetent robotic machines, similar to, and subconsciously striving to imitate human beings, it might be better to disperse the machines rather like ants. The individual ants would be small, and therefore difficult to find and destroy. But they could be linked on a sort of ant internet. No individual machine would be able to think for itself but, like an ant colony, they might be able to think together. Different 'ants' would have very different characteristics. Some would be optimised to cross obstacles, others to move very fast, others to take pictures, others to detect chemical agents, and others to attack any moving or stationary vehicle as kamikaze machines, laden with explosive.

Whereas robots will be able to undertake many of the functions associated with armed forces in conventional war – take out that machine-gun post, for example – they will not be able to supplant the human brain in negotiation, peacemaking and reassurance. The soldiers of the future will be responsible for that. 'Black magic', the MSTAR radar, will be able to detect movement across wide tracts of land. Unmanned drones will be able to fly in and have a closer look. But confronting the patrol in the kind of operation that is most likely in the next fifty years will require a human being. An intelligent, conscientious human being. Frederick the Great turned his soldiers into automatons. Technology has released us from that. An odd paradox. War has been taken *away from the people*. But command and control has been given *back to the individual*. The 'grunt' infantryman has been replaced by a machine, and very soon, the pilot of an aircraft will go the same way. In future operations, every soldier will be a commander and a diplomat. A challenging prospect.

CHAPTER NINE
LEGIO PATRIA NOSTRA:
A PERMANENT UN FORCE

A column of white armoured vehicles stretched past Victoria's guest house and all the way down the main street of Nova Bila, a hamlet outside Vitez, central Bosnia, to the British camp, encased in bomb-proof walling and razor wire. The vehicles were white painted, wheeled armoured reconnaissance troop carriers – French, VABs (*Véhicules de l'Avant Blindés*). The soldiers whose heads poked out of the top were wearing squarish helmets, a shade of duck-egg blue which differed subtly from those of other UN national contingents. They were on their way into Sarajevo through the Serb checkpoint at Sierra One, to the east, but dusk was falling. Lieutenant Colonel Alastair Duncan, the commander of the British battalion, the Prince of Wales's Own Regiment of Yorkshire, looked anxiously at the long column. He had not known they were coming.

'Is there an interpreter here? Where are you spending the night?'

'We'll spend the night 'ere, if it's all right with you, colonel.'

For a second, he was surprised at the gruff, broad north London accent. He should not have been. This was the French Foreign Legion. 'Brits, Poles, Germans ... we've got 'em all,' one of them said as we chatted and swapped cigarettes while they awaited orders to move.

The 8,500-strong French Foreign Legion is a unique organisation. It is recruited from foreigners, many of whom have served in other armies, but its officers are French – some of the very best. It is largely self-contained, with one light tank battalion, one parachute battalion, six infantry, and a regiment of engineers. It is admirably configured for rapid deployment anywhere in the world. And its soldiers, a hard bunch, some of the most professional in the world, come from every corner of the globe. They do not recruit criminals, and are very selective. Their motto – *Legio patria nostra* ('The Legion is our country') – tells of their identity, divorced from their parent states, and in the service of France.

Is this not a model the UN should follow?

The first requirement in intervention is speed. The story of the interventions in Chapter Four is one of delay, with disastrous consequences, especially in Rwanda. To date, it has taken between three and six months to assemble a UN peacekeeping operation. To be fair, there was a UN force already in Rwanda, but it was neither authorised nor equipped, technically or psychologically, to take on a new mission when the blood started flowing. Intervention in Somalia and Bosnia took too long. The delay with Somalia certainly created a larger problem, which, in turn, required a larger and more costly international response. The UN had to make resolutions; states had to offer forces; their offers had to be sifted and matched against the requirement. The tardiness is mainly the fault of UN member states, not the UN Secretariat. When mandates changed the response was too slow, again. The UN 'Rapid Reaction Force' which deployed in Bosnia in summer 1995 and the Nato 'Rapid Reaction Corps' which followed in December were not 'rapid' at all.

Furthermore, reliance on national contingents, reporting via 'dotted lines' to their own governments as well as to a UN or other multinational commander, compromises the UN's authority and the impartiality of the force. The most notorious example was the Italians in Somalia, who referred to Rome for orders rather than New York.[1] It can also result in a UN resolution being implemented in different ways, as happened in Mogadishu when the Americans and the Pakistanis interpreted the same Rules of Engagement quite differently.

Aside from these major problems, perceptions of different national UN contingents vary enormously in a theatre of intervention. We went into the Muslim enclave of east Mostar through Croat lines in February 1994 as guests of the Spaniards, and they were brilliant. But the inhabitants of east Mostar were unfairly critical. They had heard that the British, to the west, were much tougher on the Croats (which they were – they shot hundreds); so they wanted the British, not the Spaniards. The Pakistanis, who did a superb job and saved our skins at great risk to themselves, were the subject of the crudest and most despicable racial abuse from fellow Muslims who happened to be white and Slavic. A truly multinational UN force would have been largely immune to such partiality – or would, at least, have complicated the calculations of those seeking to deride it.

'Timely intervention' is recognised as vital by everyone who has

examined the problem of 'peace operations'. Article 45 of the UN
Charter says that

> In order to enable the UN to take urgent military measures, Members shall
> hold immediately available national contingents for combined international
> enforcement action. The strength and degree of readiness of these
> contingents and plans for their combined action shall be determined ... by
> the Security Council, with the assistance of the Military Staff Committee.[2]

No such force was ever established, and the Military Staff Committee of
the UN never acquired the role which had been envisaged in 1945. The
1945 Charter envisaged certain countries – probably the major powers –
holding forces ready, but the recent history of intervention operations
suggests that a permanent 'UN Legion' would be a better bet for a
spearhead force.

The present Military Staff Committee is an anachronism because its
core membership is restricted to the five permanent Security Council
members, with no assured role for the ten temporary members, never
mind anyone else. Clearly, if permanent membership of the Security
Council is to mean anything, then they should have extra weight in a
reconstituted MSC, but other expertise needs to be brought in. Current
and recent contributions to international peace operations should be
taken into account in establishing its membership.

Within the UN, responsibility for 'expanded' or 'wider peacekeeping'
still rests with the Department of Peacekeeping Operations (DPKO). In
May 1994 a reorganisation was announced, dividing the Department into
two sections: the Office of Planning and Support and the Office of
Operations, each headed by an Assistant Secretary-General. The Office
of Planning and Support is divided into a Planning Division and a Field
Division. It covers anti-mine operations, civilian police and back-up for
UN peacekeeping operations. The Office of Operations is divided into
three regional sections, plus a special electoral unit. The Military Adviser
comes under this organisation, but also reports to the UN Secretary-
General.

The problem is that the UN is no longer just involved in traditional
'peacekeeping'. Intervention operations and even peace enforcement are
now the day-to-day concern of forces not only authorised but actually
commanded by the UN. If you are going to have a dedicated UN force
which can – and must – operate anywhere on the spectrum between
intervention and peace enforcement, it needs to report directly to

someone higher up the chain than the Department of Peacekeeping Operations.

It is important to differentiate between traditional peacekeeping and intervention. The term peacekeeping is used, in the author's view wrongly, to embrace operations of greater scale, complexity and military risk than traditional peacekeeping, possibly crossing into the no-consent zone. Thus the legitimacy of traditional peacekeeping is undermined, and participants in a future civil war might reasonably be reluctant to let in a UN peacekeeping force. Any future UN organisation should therefore clearly differentiate between traditional peacekeeping and intervention operations, under the broad heading, perhaps, of 'peace operations'.

The UN has for some time had 'stand-by arrangements' for contingents from member states which are earmarked specially for UN duty. These units would be called in to serve in peacekeeping operations 'at short notice' – days or weeks. The aim is to reduce the time it takes to assemble a 'peacekeeping operation' or to reinforce one (Rwanda being the classic example of where the latter could have made a difference). At the time of writing, only two countries have signed a Memorandum of Understanding on 'stand-by arrangements' – Denmark and Jordan. Unfortunately, such an arrangement does not overcome the problem of persistent and pervasive national interest. Indeed, it might increase it, with these picked forces in the limelight as ambassadors for their countries on the world stage.

Furthermore, so-called 'stand-by arrangements' currently apply only to peacekeeping (which appears to include what I have called intervention), and not to peace enforcement. According to the UN Secretary-General in November 1995,

> The purpose of a stand-by arrangement is to have a precise understanding of the forces and other capabilities a Member State will have available at a given state of readiness, should it agree to contribute to a peacekeeping operation. Such an understanding facilitates the Organization's efforts to identify troops and equipment for new and ongoing operations, as well as to plan and budget for their deployment.[3]

By the end of October 1995 47 Member States had confirmed their willingness to provide stand-by forces totalling 55,000 personnel, and 30 had provided detailed information. But the forces identified lacked key specialists: communications, logistics, medical services, engineers and transport. And the proposals were lamentably deficient when it came to speed of reaction.

The UN defines 'response time' as the period between a request going out from the UN and the moment when the resources are ready to be lifted by sea or air into the theatre of operations – the 'mission area'. Response time includes time needed by governments for domestic political approval, administrative procedures (including calling up reserves) and military preparations.

Initially governments were given preferred response times of 7 days for key individuals, 14 days for troops needed for the reception phase (movements staff, reconnaissance parties and so on), and 30 days for other units. In 30 days at least 100,000 people were killed in Rwanda. Between half a million and a million were killed between April and July, and most were killed at the beginning, so the first 30 days might have seen nearer a quarter of a million dead. Yet, unsurprisingly, even these modest UN targets were very difficult to meet.

> It was found that there were considerable differences in the response times for various categories of personnel eg standing professional armies, call-up mechanisms (reservists) and/or conscript forces, the last of which require a longer period of preparation ... the response times given for confirmed stand-by resources vary from 7 days to over 90 days, with many governments needing over 60 days to prepare for deployment.[4]

Another factor is the time taken to deploy once the force gets to its theatre of operations. The Secretary-General made a special plea for sea and air transport from 'Member States having that capacity'. Finally, although states were willing to declare forces as available, the principle of 'voluntary' contributions to peacekeeping meant they were still under no obligation to send them if and when the UN asked.

None of these problems would exist if the UN had its own force. If the aim is to get there fastest, with the mostest[5], to be impartial, and to be untrammelled by the particular national interests of contributing nations, there is no substitute for a standing UN force.

Such a Legion could not undertake all UN-commanded, never mind UN-mandated, intervention operations alone. Some operations would, as now, be UN-authorised but delegated to regional alliances such as Nato or the Commonwealth of Independent States. The UN standing force would act as the vanguard, and as the core or backbone of certain operations, providing the first troops in, available very quickly, and a ready-made multinational command structure. Its existence would be connected with, and further influence, the development of an internationally recognised doctrine for the use of force in internal conflict.

Such a truly stateless force would be of particular value where other potential interveners might be perceived as being too closely allied with one of the parties, or where historical association would raise unfortunate memories. The UN Legion would also be a true rapid reaction force. Once in, it would need to be augmented by other forces, and possibly replaced by them, before too long.

The idea of a permanent UN force has many adherents. In September 1994 the Dutch Minister of Foreign Affairs, Hans van Mierlo, reacted to a UN official's assessment that a single mechanised brigade deployed to Rwanda could have pre-empted the bloodbath there.

If the deployment of a brigade could have prevented the indiscriminate slaughter of many hundreds of thousands, what then prevented us from doing so? The reason was that under the circumstances no government was prepared to risk the lives of its citizens ... If member states are not in a position to provide the necessary personnel, will it then not become unavoidable for us to consider the establishment of a full-time, professional, at all times available and rapidly deployable UN Brigade for this purpose, a UN Legion at the disposal of the Security Council?[6]

One proponent of such a Legion, the 'Project for Defense Alternatives', wrote

Based on an analysis of the 1988–1995 high-tide period for peace operations, we calculate that a UN capability to deploy and continuously maintain 15,000 troops in the field could meet these goals. Had such a UN capability existed in the period 1988–1995 it would have substantially facilitated the achievement of UN mandated goals in Cambodia, Mozambique, Namibia, Angola, Somalia, Rwanda and the republics of the former Yugoslavia.[7]

To maintain '15,000 troops' in the field, bearing in mind the need to replace the troops every six months, plus bases, headquarters and a UN general staff would require a total force of about 44,000, the report's writers calculate.[8] It would have four brigade headquarters, able to pick and mix mechanised infantry, light armour, engineers and helicopters. They calculated such a force, which would be slightly larger than the armed forces of Denmark and smaller than those of Belgium, once established, would cost $2.6 billion a year to maintain, plus $900 million a year of additional costs directly attributable to operations by a 15,000-strong contingent.

An alternative proposal, devised by a group of US officers in 1993 and called *A Blue Helmet Combat Force*, was for a contingent modelled on a US corps – 55,000 troops – comprising troops from no more than five nations of which one should not be a permanent member of the Security Council. The corps headquarters and key elements would be provided by one Security Council member on a rotation basis. The proposal is therefore for dedicated national contingents, similar to the Nato Rapid Reaction Corps, and does not obviate the possibility of national interest interfering with the force's international mission, and of nations getting jumpy when their contingent heads into a dangerous and difficult situation.

'If you want something done, do it yourself' is a good maxim. It suggests the UN Secretary-General should have his own military force, loyal to no one else and commanded by a highly qualified officer reporting to him, either through a revived Military Staff Committee or some other powerful body below the Secretary-General. The UN Legion – call them the White Knights if you want – would deploy on the Secretary-General's orders.

The creation of such a force would be dependent on resolving the UN's current financial crisis. Member states would then contribute to its creation and upkeep and would, in time, be able to reduce their own defence budgets correspondingly. Such a permanent force would probably be smaller than the *Blue Helmet* proposal, and in line with that for a Legion-sized force of 10,000 or 15,000, plus supporting elements and could not therefore be responsible for all the intervention operations necessary or undertake them for very long. Keeping the UN permanent force that small would therefore depend on member states undertaking binding commitments to make further rapid contributions of their own.

With Britain and France's position as permanent members of the Security Council in some doubt, the position of powers at the 'top table' could be used to ensure that the Legion was not left in the lurch – although, in fact, Britain and France have done more than their fair share of international peacekeeping and enforcement. At the time of writing, Japan is a possible candidate for Security Council permanent membership, on the grounds of its economic strength and influence, and is keen to expand its peacekeeping contributions as a ticket.

One way of ensuring the necessary back-up for a UN Legion would be to make further contributions mandatory for all permanent members of the Security Council, and perhaps to make lesser commitments mandatory conditions of temporary membership. Ideally, all competent UN member states would offer resources in the event of an emergency of sufficient magnitude to invoke the deployment of the UN Legion.

However, if sufficient back-up was not forthcoming immediately, the permanent members would underwrite the UN Legion, undertaking, collectively, to provide supporting forces within, say, two weeks of the Legion's deployment up to a maximum between them of, say, five times the strength of the Legion force.

That way, the Secretary-General could order immediate deployment of one brigade of the Legion – 5,000 troops. Within two weeks, the permanent members (currently the United States, Russia, Britain, France and China) would be obliged, between them, to ensure that another 25,000 troops were en route for the theatre of operations. Those failing to contribute would lose their seats on the Security Council. Other contributions would also be expected. For example, the United States would provide strategic air lift in the form of planes like the Galaxy C-5, large enough to carry full-size tanks and guns. It would not be permissible to discount these further contributions against the need to underwrite the deployment of the UN's own ground troops.

The prospect of a genuinely super-national force, able to call on the best quality personnel and equipment, worldwide, is inspiring; although some people might find it rather frightening. The UN Legion, untrammelled by national procurement policies, would be able to choose the best or most suitable equipment. At the time of writing, this would be South African long-range artillery, Israeli mine-proof light armoured vehicles, US sniper rifles, British Warrior Fighting Vehicles, which have proved resilient to everything that anybody, other than the Americans, can throw at them, and so on. However, the need to deploy the force very quickly – by air – must be paramount.

The French Foreign Legion provides a good model for such a force. Its tanks are relatively light, wheeled machines, and it is predominantly a mixture of highly trained infantry and engineers – exactly the type of force most useful in intervention operations. In addition, powerful logistical support would be necessary to make the UN Legion able to operate, self-contained, in the most demanding climatic conditions. Like the French Foreign Legion and current Nato multinational forces, it would specialise in operating in conditions from the Arctic to the desert.

The idea of a dedicated UN force has not made much progress in New York, primarily because of political reservations by the member states. 'Member states are not willing to give up their control,' said Hiro Ueki, a UN spokesman, at the turn of 1995. 'I don't recall any debate in the UN on that question [the formation of a UN Legion].' Exactly how such a force should be paid for is another problem.

A revived Military Staff Committee with a dedicated planning team would be of value, with or without a UN Legion. It would give unity and direction to UN military efforts, whether or not the UN had its own force, in the most possessive sense, or was reliant on contributions from certain members, trained and placed on short notice to fulfil UN missions.

Nation states, in particular the great powers and the permanent members of the Security Council, fear the idea of an international army of this type, minuscule though it would be in global terms, because it threatens their 350-year monopoly on the conduct of international affairs. But why? A UN Legion would merely be a tangible recognition of the UN's authority, the only authority under which armed force can now be exercised legitimately in international relations. In any big operation, it would be in the lead, prominent, symbolic, and disproportionately effective, but not alone. It would require – and need to be guaranteed – back-up from the great powers. And commitment to give it that back-up would be a necessary qualification for great powerdom.

A true UN force, working under an international UN staff, would also enjoy advantages dealing with the other UN and non-governmental agencies needed in a war zone – particularly the UNHCR and Red Cross. Liaison with regional security and national organisations would also be eased by the UN Legion's unchallenged authority. This has proved to be a particular problem in the plan to rebuild Bosnia, where a very coherent and well-integrated military force, Nato, is now working alongside a shambolic patchwork of civilian organisations from the Organisation for Security and Cooperation (OSCE) in Europe, the European Union and the UN.

Whilst the UN Legion's UN-ness should be its greatest advantage, it could also be its biggest problem in dealing with the United States. The US has made no secret of its dislike of the UN in Bosnia. The United States embarked on what one commentator called a 'vindictive sidelining campaign' against the UN.[9] The current reconstruction arrangements in Bosnia cast some light on the American attitude. Nato, led by the United States, provides a centralised and coherent military task force, but the complementary and vital task of civil reconstruction – 'peace building' – has been left, some argue deliberately, to a disparate collection of organisations, with the EU and OSCE vying with the UN with a former Swedish Prime Minister, Carl Bildt, in an ill-defined coordinating role. If the UN is to be effective in maintaining world peace the United States will have to treat it with some respect rather than using it both for its own purposes and as a scapegoat for American politicians to criticise during Presidential election campaigns. If the United States could be made to recognise the value and importance of the UN, that would pave the way for a permanent UN force to undertake certain missions, without threatening the dominant position of the United States in the world. If a highly professional UN Legion were established which could undertake some of the tasks which might otherwise have to be undertaken by the US military, it is hardly likely that anyone in the United States would then object.

What sort of Legion?

The first UN Secretary-General, Trygve Lie of Norway, proposed a 'UN Guard' of brigade strength – 5,000 strong – but the Cold War got in the way.[10] A similar force was proposed by the British diplomat Sir Brian Urquhart in 1993.[11] In my view it should be larger, with maybe 10,000 to 15,000 troops, and very much on the French Foreign Legion model, but it should also have its own air transport and possibly its own assault ship, able to carry one marine battalion. Although most of the proposals for such a 'fire brigade' or 'rapid intervention force' stress the need for light infantry and wheeled vehicles, in my opinion a heavily armoured component would be essential. Light armour and mechanised infantry are the most commonly available troops from contributing nations. A UN Legion might more profitably focus on specialised troops of a type which are *not* commonly available: very heavy armour, very skilled combat engineers, amphibious forces, and so on.

In order to guarantee entry to a crisis area, a parachute battalion, at least, would be needed. As the commander of the British 5th Airborne Brigade, Brigadier John Holmes, explained, 'We don't parachute for the sake of it. You can't guarantee you will be able to use the airfield at the other end.' In order to seize and defend an airfield you need a battalion (600 troops, plus support), at least. Military parachuting normally takes place from 800 feet; to avoid radar, aircraft carrying the paratroops may have to fly lower, at about 300 feet, and then suddenly climb to reach a safe height from which to drop them. The British have developed a low-level parachute, which can be used from 300 feet, thus making life safer for the dropping aircraft and the soldier. The UN Legion must be at the cutting edge of all such developments.

Once an airborne battalion has landed to secure an airfield, reinforcements can be flown in by conventional aircraft. The battalion would also need to be trained in 'tactical air landing operations.' This means 'crashing' an airfield as uninvited guests might 'crash' a party – landing by surprise and driving out of the transport aircraft in light armoured vehicles, as the Israelis did at Entebbe in 1976 and the Russians at Kabul in 1979.

As noted, engineers are enormously important in peacekeeping and intervention operations to create and repair routes, to build fortifications and to clear mines. The first three casualties of the Nato peace implementation force in Bosnia, it will be remembered, were to mines.

Helicopters are an exceptionally good way of getting around, and also a powerful attack weapon in their own right. The use of 101st Airborne Division in the Gulf War, sweeping rapidly up the right (western) flank of the Iraqis, establishing a new airbase in the desert, and then moving on to maul the withdrawing Iraqi forces with maximum savagery, is an example of what 'airmobile' or 'AirLand' forces can do. Although most of its complement would be expert at deploying by air, the UN Legion would require perhaps one very heavily armoured battalion – tanks and armoured infantry – to punch through a corridor with guns to the right and guns to the left, into a city like Sarajevo, for example. Armoured reconnaissance – fast, light tanks – has also proved exceptionally useful in intervention operations. In Bosnia they could get up roads where the heavy (30-ton) Warrior infantry fighting vehicles could not. These would also provide the armour for the air-landing operations.

A marine battalion, also trained in the use of small craft, would be essential to control a port or monitor waterways (for example, in Cambodia), and to monitor refugees and 'boat people'. The Gulf War also showed the exceptional power of multiple launch rocket systems, able to deluge a target with deadly fire at ranges beyond that of conventional artillery. The Legion would therefore have an artillery regiment concentrating on multiple rocket launchers, surface-to-surface missiles (to carry supplies as well as for aggressive use), reconnaissance and target acquisition.

The UN Legion would comprise a main headquarters, which would liaise directly with the Secretary-General and be responsible for day-to-day running of the Legion, equipment and training, and two or three brigade headquarters, each able to control most of the Legion in the field. That would enable the Legion to deploy in up to three places at once.

The brigade headquarters would also be able to command national units attached to the UN Legion. They would each include intelligence, signals and electronic warfare specialists, including people expert in the skills associated with special forces: long-range reconnaissance, signals and counter-terrorism. The Legion would also have its own unmanned reconnaissance aircraft – 'remotely piloted vehicles' or 'drones' – to carry out reconnaissance while employing a relatively small number of people to monitor the results. Because of its high profile, the force would need exceptionally competent officers to handle the media (no more 'Fancy a ride in a helicopter?').

The brigade headquarters would then be able to pick from the following main ingredients: two helicopter regiments; two engineer regiments; a heavy armoured regiment, designed to drive through a rain of shells with virtual impunity; an armoured reconnaissance regiment; an airborne (parachute) battalion; a marine battalion; two mechanised infantry battalions; an artillery and missile regiment, which might also control air defence missiles; a signals and electronic warfare regiment to reinforce the brigade headquarters as necessary; and a full, extremely well-equipped field hospital, with a disproportionate number of specialist staff. The latter would be very important not only to ensure the Legion could operate anywhere in the world, but also to give instant aid of the highest quality to local civilians, displaced by war or struck by natural disaster, in the area where intervention occurred.

If the composition of such a force sounds unduly aggressive for one to be engaged in 'peace operations', it must be remembered that it has to go into the unknown prepared for anything. Because it has multiple launch rocket systems and ballistic missiles does not mean it has to use them. The UN Legion would be a visible expression of the emerging principle of war and peace in the new world order: walk softly, and carry a big stick.

The UN Legion's main language would probably be English, since it is the current lingua franca worldwide, but insistence on a second language – probably French or Spanish – would greatly expand the area where it could operate easily, giving greater access throughout Africa, South-East Asia and South America. A fourth language, maybe Russian, should be compulsory for all those in senior posts. At first, the UN Legion would need to recruit its officers and non-commissioned officers from national armed forces. In time, it would develop its own career structure. Selection would be rigorous and it should be common knowledge that UN Legion personnel were better qualified than anyone of a similar rank in a national army, navy or air force. It would be an élite of élites: a modern-day Knights Templar.

Although it is clear that no expense should be spared to ensure the UN Legion has the best people and equipment, its size, measured on a global scale, and therefore its cost, would be minuscule. To be fully independent of nation states, the UN Legion or UN Guard would need bases away from the national territory of any significant world power, the military equivalent of tax-havens, which would also permit it to practise operations at sea and in the air as well as on land, and in arctic, desert and jungle conditions. There are still plenty of suitable places. The UN Legion would also need to maintain huge stocks of aid supplies – food, water, clothing, medical supplies and shelter – which it should be able to deliver very quickly to cope with disasters, natural or man-made, on a huge scale, until the other aid agencies could be deployed. Amongst those supplies, large quantities of blood or blood substitutes would be needed. As this is being written, human trials are to begin with a new blood substitute which can be freeze-dried and given to anybody, whatever their blood group. That would make the UN Legion doctors' lives a lot easier. Realistically, the Legion needs to be able to cope with the biggest imaginable disaster, alone, for at least a week – and with plenty to spare in case another disaster strikes.

At the main UN Legion base, there would be a training school for new recruits which would gradually expand to develop careers within the Legion. Right from the start, there would be a high-level academy to develop senior officers and to act as a think-tank to develop doctrine and procedures for peace operations. Certain specialised training might be contracted out to nation states, such as parachute and amphibious warfare training, and survival. UN Legion officers would attend national staff colleges, and certain officers from the United States, Russia, Britain and France, for example, might also attend the UN staff college. But each nation state's military training reflects its own ethos and idiosyncrasies. The UN Legion should, wherever possible, develop its own.

The UN Legion academy would also provide a valuable international forum for examining issues like those examined in this book, free from the pressures of national domestic politics which impose limitations on the study of security issues by the very people who are best qualified to study them – soldiers, sailors and airmen. In the field of security the government of the day exercises a veil of control over freedom of thought and expression which is unthinkable in any other scientific or practical field. If I want to know how a surgical operation is performed, I ask a surgeon. I do not have to ask permission from the Department of Health. If I want to know about a police matter, in Britain, I can talk to a Chief Constable or the Police Federation. I do not have to ask permission from the Home Office. But if I want to talk to anybody above the rank of colonel about a military question, in theory, I need permission from a minister. That is ridiculous, but it is unlikely to change. As a result, publicly expressed opinions on these questions come only from so-called academics, most of whom know nothing of the practicalities of war, or from retired senior officers whose knowledge is often out of date.

The UN Legion academy would be able to pursue these profoundly important issues in a rarefied and free atmosphere. Sir Basil Liddell Hart (1895–1970), a well-known military theorist and fellow defence correspondent, saw the need for such a body in 1937.

> The War Office has organs for research into weapons etc., but not into the conditions of future warfare ... There are no means for the comprehensive analysis of past experience, and thus no synthesis of adequately expressed data to serve as a guide in framing policy. At present the investigation of problems is pushed to officers who are occupied with current military business. The task ought to be given to a body of officers who can devote their whole time to exploring the data on record, collecting it from outside, and working out the conclusions in a free atmosphere ... They should be supplemented by a permanent nucleus consisting of some first-rate university men who have been trained in scientific enquiry.[12]

No one has quite managed to achieve this model. The Russians have a formidably scientific approach to military problems, but the experts have always been servicemen. Recent attempts to cultivate 'civilian experts' in defence and related fields – disarmament and 'soft security' issues – have been frustrated because the 'civilian experts' do not know enough. The same has happened in Britain and the United States, where the people in a position to think are too preoccupied with 'current military business'. They also, inevitably, have a national perspective and are dependent on their domestic political masters for funds, which may not help in considering problems which are increasingly global. Maybe the proposed UN military structure could at last achieve what Liddell Hart proposed sixty years ago. And it would have a very short line of communication to someone who was in a position to implement its proposals. The UN Secretary-General.

Backing up the UN Legion

The UN Legion will be distinguished by its supernatural speed of reaction, demonstrable impartiality, a fearsome reputation for utter fairness and formidable hitting power if abused, and very specialised skills.

In any large operation, the UN Legion would need rapid support from national or Alliance forces, as discussed. In Bosnia and Somalia, UN-assigned troops in the theatre were supported by other organisations who provided forces 'offshore' – the Nato air forces and navies over and off Bosnia, and US forces off Somalia, where, at one stage, US and UN troops were operating side by side. That could pose a problem. Although the UN Legion would be demonstrably impartial and immune to distraction by any national objectives, the same would not be true with elements of the 'offshore' forces, or with those forces working alongside the UN Legion.

However, the existence of a UN Legion respected for its armaments and expertise would, in time, modify national attitudes. The reason why the UN has appeared so weak is precisely that it has had no real fighting forces of its own. It has been utterly dependent on begging favours from national governments. To use an analogy from my own experience in a war zone, it is the difference between paying through the nose to use someone else's satellite telephone or having your own – and charging other people. Instead of conforming to their agenda you can set your own – and often other people follow you. Because the UN would have its own fighting forces – its own troops and helicopters and possibly ships and aircraft – it could place the supporting national or Alliance forces in a very different position. If the UN decided to bomb or shell one of the parties in a civil war, the supporting forces would have to go along with it. Finally, the UN Legion, as proposed, would have its own headquarters staff, and would also attach members of its own staff to other organisations.

A UN Legion would not be a purely 'military' force in the traditional sense. This is one of its great advantages. One of the lessons of Bosnia was the awkward nature of the relationship between the UN Protection Force and the UN High Commissioner for Refugees' organisation, which it was there to protect. In many operations, the role of the UN military planners and UNHCR officials became almost indistinguishable. It has been suggested that there should have been a single chain of command for both the military operations of UNPROFOR and the interlinked aid operations of the UNHCR.[13] The UN Legion could be designed with such a joint chain of command built in.

In summary, there are two ways of looking at the future role of the UN. The first is that the UN must make an absolute distinction between its role as a source of legitimacy for intervention and its role as a controller of operations. The UN was not designed to 'make war on war'.[14] It has been very successful in traditional peacekeeping – an innovation developed by accident. Many people believe it is unlikely to have more than a marginal military role in the future, and that large operations which may breach the consent barrier should be conducted by organisations like Nato, acting on the UN's behalf.

The creation of a UN Legion would not confuse this essential distinction between the UN's roles. If the UN is to have a command role of any kind – even in traditional peacekeeping, or in new areas of endeavour such as conflict prevention and peace-building after a conflict – then recent experience suggests it must have its own force. The UN Legion proposed is not intended to take on a huge conventional military operation alone, and its existence does not imply the UN should necessarily control such operations. It is designed to get to a trouble spot quickly, save lives and hold the line until something else is devised. Put another way, not to create a UN Legion would confine the UN to acting solely as a source of legitimacy.

The second approach is less intellectually rigorous but perhaps more realistic.

The idea of a UN Legion is compatible with the way the nation state has begun to face challenges to its position as the supreme authority in the world. It would be odd if the emergence of supra-national organisations like the European Union and their increased authority over national governments were not matched by the emergence of some sort of international armed forces. This is happening with the creation of organisations like the Nato Allied Rapid Reaction Corps which has now taken the field in Bosnia, and multinational formations like the 'Euro-corps'. The UN stresses it is not a world government but an association of sovereign states. Fine. But if the collective will of those sovereign states is being expressed increasingly by action for which the UN is the only legitimate authority, then the UN needs its own executive body. A UN Legion would be a logical next step. Furthermore, its formation would reflect the changed composition of the UN. In 1945, the UN consisted, in effect, of the victorious powers in World War II. Now, it comprises some 185 states. The more members you have, the more you have to take direct action away from them and place it in the hands of special committees and professional bodies. Even the permanent membership of the Security Council may be ripe for change. No civilised country will now take any form of military action without a supporting UN mandate. The number of peacekeeping and intervention operations has increased dramatically, as have expectations of what the UN might do.

Rather than trawling around for troops, the UN should establish a body that can lead by example. A formidably professional force, transcending national interests. A little monastic, perhaps, tending the sick and conducting diplomacy as well as being fearsome in battle. First on the scene, respected and feared the world over. Knights, in White Armour.

CHAPTER TEN
CONCLUSION: REVISED PRINCIPLES OF WAR AND PEACE

'The centuries-old doctrine of absolute and exclusive sovereignty no longer stands, and was in fact never so absolute as it was conceived to be in theory' wrote the UN Secretary-General in 1992.[1] The previous year, just after the decision to intervene to help the Iraqi Kurds, Javier Perez de Cuellar said something similar. 'We are clearly witnessing what is probably an irresistible shift in public attitudes towards the belief that the defence of the oppressed in the name of morality should prevail over frontiers and legal documents.'[2]

At the time, 20,000 troops were moving into northern Iraq without the consent of the Iraqi government. Just two months earlier, the US-led coalition had taken quite a different view of events in southern Iraq. As rebellion flared in the wake of the Allied victory, General Colin Powell refused to get involved in Iraq's internal affairs. 'This did not seem to me an operation that we needed to get involved in because I couldn't figure out who was doing what to whom.'[3] It would not, however, be possible to plot the paradigm change between early March and early April 1991: the reasons for non-intervention in the south were pragmatic. Had the coalition gone into southern Iraq, they would probably still have been there five years later, and bearing responsibility for the reconstruction of the country. They wanted to avoid that at all costs.

After nearly 350 years of reluctance to intervene in the internal affairs of people we regard as our equals, we are now more willing to do so, although only in 'weak' or 'failed' states like Somalia or former Yugoslavia – not in big, powerful states, like Russia. The change in our attitude to statehood, after 350 years, means a change in our attitude to conflict. Clausewitz's view of war, which he began to formulate 200 years ago, centred on conflict between states, not within them, though his description of the nature of war could apply to either. But where we are trying to calm things down, and are not quite sure why we are there, then the nature of military operations is altered, too. Clausewitz described the 'duel', the essence of war, 'as a pair of wrestlers. Each tries through physical force to compel the other to do his will.'

In a peace operation, we try not to wrestle. One of the parties has a problem. I tell him I understand his problem, and offer to buy him a drink, while, at the same time, anxiously checking out my exit route and gaining the sympathy and eliciting the support of the assembled onlookers. If there is a fight, I need witnesses. Otherwise the international policeman will throw us both in jail.

Throughout the history of war, experts have endeavoured to distil principles for the successful conduct of campaigns. For easy reference, these are shown in Table 10.1. The first are the 'five fundamental factors' enunciated by Sun Tzu: moral influence, weather, terrain, 'command' and 'doctrine'. By 'moral influence', Sun Tzu said, he meant 'that which causes the people to be in harmony with their leaders'. Terrain included not just the sinuosities of the ground, but distance as well. 'Command' meant what we would call leadership, and 'doctrine' meant organisation and administration.[4]

Historically, the experts' approach to the 'art' or 'science' of warfare reflected the scientific thinking of their time. Clausewitz and Jomini both thought in terms of Newtonian physics. Clausewitz enunciated four principles: to employ all available forces with the utmost energy; to concentrate at the point where the decisive blow is to be struck; to lose no time and surprise the enemy; and to follow up success with the utmost energy. Jomini enunciated but two: to use freedom of manoeuvre to bring masses of one's own troops against fractions of the enemy's, and to strike in the most decisive direction.[5]

Whether waging conventional war or 'peace operations', it seems to me the 'master principle' of the current British list remains valid, if not dominant: 'Selection and maintenance of the aim' or, as the Americans say, the 'objective'. In war the aim is to break the will of the enemy to continue fighting. In 'preventive diplomacy' and peacekeeping it is to break the will to initiate or recommence war, respectively. In an intervention operation, the aim will, again, be to persuade the warring factions, or potential warring factions, that to pursue war is not in their

10.1. Principles of war and peace through the ages

	Sun Tzu, 400–320 B.C.¹	Clausewitz, early C19	Jomini, early C19	Fuller, 1920s	Soviet/Warsaw Pact, 1950s–80s	British, 1995	US, 1995	New art of war and peace
1.	Moral influence	Employ all available forces with utmost energy	Use freedom of manoeuvre to bring masses against fractions	Direction	Mobility and high tempo of combat operations	Selection and maintenance of the aim	Objective	Objective
2.	Weather	Concentrate where the decisive blow is to be struck	Decisive direction	Concentration	Concentration of main efforts at the decisive place and time	Maintenance of morale	Offensive	Moral influence (including appearances, legitimacy and fulfilling your word)
3.	Terrain	Lose no time and surprise the enemy		Distribution	Surprise	Offensive action	Mass	Speed
4.	Command			Determination	Constant energy (aktivnost')	Surprise	Economy of force	Maximum strength, minimum force
5.	Doctrine			Surprise	Preservation of own troops' effectiveness	Security	Manoeuvre	Go with the flow
6.	Deception			Endurance	Adjust the end to the means	Concentration of force	Unity of command	Freedom of movement
7.	Supernatural speed			Mobility	Cooperation	Economy of effort	Security	Interest keeps peace
8.	Know your enemy and know yourself			Offensive action		Flexibility	Surprise	Give him, and yourself, a way out
9.	To win without fighting is the acme of skill			Security		Cooperation	Simplicity	Ample moral and material support
10.						Administration		(includes logistics and media)

¹ Sun Tzu lists the first five as 'factors'. The other principles are enumerated elsewhere in *The Art of War*

interest. That might be by the provision of amenities, or by threatening to bomb the hell out of them if they move forces in an aggressive fashion.

In a modern peace operation it is as important as ever to select the aim and to keep one's eye on it – as a senior UN official commended Rupert Smith for doing in Sarajevo. Connected with choosing the aim is a constant awareness of the time and resources available to be expended on it. 'Open-ended' commitments will be unpopular, and heavy casualties will not be tolerated. These considerations need to be 'factored in' to the aim.

This principle may also lead us not to intervene at all. One of the strongest conclusions from a high-level seminar conducted at Chantilly in summer 1995 was that it might be appropriate in some circumstances to do nothing. Not to intervene. To resist the 'tyranny' of the media.

In some cases, military action will not be the right thing. Military forces will be, in the Russian phrase, unusable. Unfit. *Negodnye*. Yet, so far, the Russians seem blissfully unaware of the principle they enunciated. What other great power would send in tanks and commandos to blast its own parliament building, or inflict savage destruction and a medieval reign of terror on a province where a rebel leader led a secession movement, without giving sanctions and other political remedies time to work?

The second principle of war on the current British list, maintenance of morale, is also clearly applicable to peace operations. The maintenance of morale depends on a shared sense of purpose, clear understanding of the aim, self-respect, and confidence in the equipment available and in the leadership, political and military. In a modern peace operation that would include the UN as well as national leadership. Morale begins to sound very like Sun Tzu's 'moral influence'.

The increased role of the media is also cardinal to morale. As the Royal Air Force's Air Power Doctrine says, 'A war effort by a democratic state cannot be maintained in the face of public hostility or indifference.'[6] The media will be crucial to maintaining that interest 'back home', and also to maintaining the morale of peacekeeping or intervention troops in the theatre. There is nothing more demoralising for a soldier, or, for that matter, an aid worker or a journalist than thinking 'no one cares'. From then on, perhaps, the classic principles of war and those of war and peace in the new world order may diverge, though they are seldom totally contradictory. 'Offensive action' might at first seem ill-suited to peace operations. When it is interpreted more widely – as seizing and holding the initiative – it is still relevant, though interpreted more as a state of mind.

Richard Connaughton has recently formulated thirteen suggested principles of intervention.[7] The first is, once again, selection and maintenance of the aim. The second is to 'operate under the auspices and coordination of a valid and supportive international organisation'. In other words, you need legitimacy – conferred by the UN and maybe delegated to another, regional organisation. Next, establish a 'simple and agreed unified command, control, communications and intelligence organisation'. That is clearly right, although it is perhaps a bit of a mouthful for a principle. Furthermore, in recent UN and UN-blessed interventions it has not been followed. The UN has traditionally shied away from establishing an intelligence organisation – except in the Congo – and the UN chain of command in Bosnia was a complicated, convoluted disaster. Starting in December 1995, Nato sorted out the military chain of command, but the organization for rebuilding the country was a baroque doodle if ever there was one, with a disembodied Swedish Prime Minister floating around trying to coordinate it. Richard Connaughton's next two principles are thoroughly sensible. Maintain a *cordon sanitaire* around the target area and plan the force extraction concurrently with the planning of force insertion. Both principles were followed in Bosnia. A *cordon sanitaire* was established and although not perfect, it undoubtedly kept the fighting at a lower temperature than would have been the case if more petrol had been thrown on the fire.

The initial plunge into Bosnia was taken with little regard for the 'extraction'. The UN forces rapidly dug in with huge resources invested in bunkers and a great deal of heavy equipment which it would be difficult to withdraw in the face of opposition – particularly when women and children started blocking the roads. The importance of being able to withdraw equipment was twofold. First, no cost-conscious government wants to lose loads of expensive military hardware. Secondly, they did not wish it to fall into the hands of the warring parties and further fuel the fighting.

By summer 1995, extraction was being taken very seriously, even though all the UN contingents seemed determined to stay. Route 'Diamond', one of only two routes available for 'extraction', was being resurfaced and repaired, and it was commonly thought the need to withdraw UN troops was the main reason. The UN 'Rapid Reaction Force' was formed, allegedly to make the UN more robust and therefore extend its stay, but it could equally have acted as a withdrawal force. The presence of large UN contingents at Ploce, on the Croatian coast, which never went very far inland, also suggested they were there for a Crimea 1920-style withdrawal of 'white' forces (white in this case meaning UN), from its ample port. Never get into anything you can't get out of seems like a good principle in life. It is certainly a good principle for peace operations.

Connaughton's last principles are: maintain consensus; agree and adhere to national contributions; operate within the law; remember that military action is the last resort of a collective security machine; utilise the UN's legal mechanism; restructure the UN's military organisation; design a strategy and allocate resources. All are valid, although some are perhaps more like proposals for reorganisation than principles. No matter: his was the first attempt to devise a new set of principles for the new world order.

The British manual *Wider Peacekeeping* focuses on maintaining the consent divide within what I have called intervention operations. Therefore, it stresses impartiality, minimum force, legitimacy, credibility, mutual respect and 'transparency' – letting other people know what you are doing.[8] Among the principles of conventional war, security and surprise feature strongly. General Smith's switch to peace enforcement in Bosnia in summer 1995 was kept pretty secret, it must be said. But, by and large, the military preoccupation with secrecy and 'need to know' is one that will be heavily modified in peace operations. In many cases it is necessary to let the other party or parties know *exactly* what your intentions are. Then, having given the indication, you have to fulfil your word.

The British stress on the one-way traffic across the zone between consent and lack of consent appears to be slightly exaggerated to make a particular point. But it is a useful idea. The analogy that comes to mind is that of rape in law. The distinction between an act of love and the most horrible of crimes may lie, in some cases, in the perception of one party – in the presence or absence of 'consent'. In many cases, rape accompanies assault by a stranger, and the facts appear fairly clear. In other cases, the 'perpetrator' and the 'victim' may know each other well, and the truth may be more difficult to discern. And in others still, the most problematical of all, the 'victim' may have changed his or her mind after the event. Significantly, these cases tend to occur when one party is invited in by the other. The similarities with the presence of a peacekeeping force, invited in by one or more of the parties, are obvious. And ideas like 'mutual respect' are closely linked with consent.

What then are the principles that have emerged in this book?

The first has to remain selection and maintenance of the aim. Decide what you want to do, and keep at it, without distraction. In order to achieve that aim, military forces may not be the answer. Sun Tzu understood this. 'Weapons are tools of ill omen. War is a grave matter; one is apprehensive lest men embark on it without due reflection.'[9] Before the Gulf War, Colin Powell wanted to give sanctions another two years to work against Iraq. People could not wait that long and, with hindsight, sanctions probably would not have worked. Boris Yeltsin might have thought the same about Chechnya, which had, after all, declared independence in 1991. But the Russians' use of military power was crude and counter-productive. The United States wanted Saddam Hussein out of Kuwait: the Russians wanted to retain control of the oil pipelines through Grozny and to terrify other republics within the Russian Federation into obedience. Both succeeded. The Americans practised the new art of war and peace in its most aggressive form. The Russians practised the old. It was Stalingrad, but without the skill.

Short of limited war, a vast spectrum of intervention operations has opened up. In Bosnia, the aim of the UN, which was predominantly the aim of the great powers, enjoying a new, amicable relationship, was to keep atrocities and casualties to a minimum, and to bring about a negotiated peace. It was a long, hard road, but they succeeded.

Having decided you want to act, the second principle has to be moral influence – indeed, it might be the first principle. To act in somebody else's war you need the unchallenged authority of a global body: the United Nations is the representative of the will of the international community. Nothing else will do. And that authority – moral influence – has to be maintained and reinforced right through the operation. In recent times, the 'international community' has, on occasion, meant the western powers, which is not good enough. Every effort must be made to maintain 'moral influence' – to hold the moral high ground, if you will, throughout any operation. As General Philippe Morillon, one of the UN commanders in Bosnia, said, 'I repeated it every day. We must be respected. If not, we have to withdraw.'[10]

Appearances are an important part of moral influence. They matter. As the earlier account of the UN's arrival in Cambodia and the US posture when the Americans finally arrived in Bosnia showed, a robust attitude from the start and a formidable appearance can make all the difference. People are generally frightened of the unknown, and this should be exploited. Peace forces do not only need to be exceptionally competent. They need to look the part.

The third principle, particularly in forestalling conflict, has to be speed. Get there fastest, with the mostest. Or, as Sun Tzu put it, 'While we have heard of blundering swiftness in war, we have not yet seen a clever operation that was prolonged.' And, citing another adept, 'An attack may lack ingenuity but it must be delivered with supernatural speed.'[11] Closer to our own time, General George Patton (1885–1945) said that a good plan now was better than a perfect plan next week. Speed would have saved hundreds of thousands in Rwanda, and might have forestalled the Bosnian conflict altogether. From this principle, recommendations for the organisation of peace support forces follow. The UN needs its own rapid reaction force, and reliance on cumbersome reserves that are dependent on more political sanction should be minimised, if not totally excluded.

Fourth, walk softly but carry a big stick, or, to put it another way, maximum strength, minimum force.[12] When you enter the zone of intervention you do not know what dragons lurk there. Forces committed for peacekeeping may find themselves suddenly catapulted into peace enforcement. The fact they are there means they will have to cope and not, as in Rwanda, pull out. Any forces committed to a zone of intervention must be robustly equipped and able to be reinforced very rapidly.

Fifth, go with the flow. This is perhaps the most subtle and difficult – and probably contentious – principle. It is an adaptation of the western democracies' traditional approach to war. Confident of their economic strength, the western democracies, particularly the United States, formulated an approach to war which endeavoured to bring their nascent strength to bear. A combination of the strength of the industrial base, the technological expertise and resources of the population would be utilised to create an 'overwhelming mass of military and national force'.[13]

In intervention operations this option does not arise. The innate strength of the intervener's military power cannot be applied. Instead, the intervener draws strength from the other forces in the area. The Bosnian example is a classic case, so far. It was well known that the Bosnian government enjoyed superior manpower and interior lines of communication, and that in combination with the Croats, it could defeat the Serbs. During 1994 and 1995, the Muslim-Croat federation appeared to gain strength, but it took Nato air-strikes to break the will and crack the 'key vulnerability' of the Serbs – their command, control and communications. Earlier in this book, we used the analogy of a rowing eight. The strength and fitness of the rowers – the engine – are important, but a skilful coxswain will find the fast-running stream and use the flow of the water to maximise their potential. Rowing against the tide is a bad bet. As noted, peace in Bosnia eventually came because of a military victory. In most peace operations, the interveners will not be able to stand against and reverse the tide of history. That is one of the reasons for the debacle in Russia in 1918–19. What they can do is mitigate suffering and ease the progress of the inevitable. There is a clear analogy with medicine, and in particular with homeopathic medicine which, rather than directly confronting the disease itself tries to stimulate the body's own defences.

The principle of going with the flow also applies at a more mundane level, in the organisation of supply routes and so on. The UN decision at the start of the Bosnian operation to 'go with the ethnic grain' was a manifestation of the same idea, and worked well until the grain changed with the outbreak of war between the Muslims and Croats.

The sixth principle is probably freedom of movement, in every sense. Freedom of movement over sea and through the air, exploiting the freedom which the intervener, confident in superior technology, will almost certainly enjoy. That means dismantling or destroying air defences as the first priority, for example. Among the classic principles of war, 'freedom of manoeuvre' and 'freedom of action' – which equates with initiative – feature prominently. And then there is freedom of movement within the country. Resistance to the checkpoints beloved of the local jobsworths. UN peacekeeping forces, constrained by the doctrinal insistence on maintaining 'consent', were increasingly hampered by restrictions on movement in their various theatres of operations. In Bosnia, Nato took a different view. 'We're going to take a very robust line on that,' said Major-General Mike Jackson, commanding the British division. They did. Serb checkpoints, which had locked tight the siege of Sarajevo, gave way. But 'freedom of movement' does not come naturally to some people. Even after the various peace accords were signed in Bosnia, banning unauthorised checkpoints, they still sprang up. At the risk of compromising the principle of respect, we shouted at Bosnian children who annoyed us. 'Yes, and when you grow up, you can run your *own checkpoint.*'

Seventh, 'though peace be made, yet it is interest that keeps peace'. One of the reasons for the prevalence of internecine warfare in 'weak' or 'failed' states is not only that the local leaders feel it is in their interest to wage war, but that the threshold for it being in their interest is much lower. That is probably why wars do not happen in well-developed states with fair legal systems and a reasonable standard of living. When peace is achieved, it is vital to pour in resources to achieve a perceptible rise in the standard of living. Respect for local authorities is part of this process. A former brigade commander will not take kindly to being insulted when he asks for your bus ticket. He might prefer to go back to war than to do a less prestigious job, unless the material rewards of peace are very obvious. People are not only acquisitive and greedy, they are also proud.

Eighth, give the parties intervened against, and yourself, a way out. This is, again, a variant of a classic military principle. In conventional warfare, the aim has often been to trap the enemy. To destroy him. But everyone knows a cornered rat fights hard. An alternative is to provide a bridge so that the opposing party can retire along it. This device has been called the 'golden bridge'. It is probable that generals Schwarzkopf and Powell gave the Iraqis a 'golden bridge' in the closing stages of the 1991 Gulf War, though they never admitted it. Had the Republican Guard really been trapped, they might have inflicted significant casualties on the Allies, which would have struck at the heart of western nations now mesmerised by the prospect of war without significant casualties. Instead, the Iraqis had a controlled opportunity to escape. This is a principle which clearly applies to the 'very political wars' higher up the spectrum of violence, and even more so to peace operations where the application of force is more circumscribed. Again, Bosnia provides a good example. If the defeated Bosnian Serbs were to retire rather than fight to the end, they had to be allowed to do so with some dignity. Large areas of territory were returned to them, and a key corridor linking the territory they controlled guaranteed. It is like tackling the drunken lout in the bar, again. Don't corner him. Give him a way out. And give him space.

But in giving the other party or parties a way out, do not neglect yourself. As Connaughton rightly says, consider the extraction of any force concurrently with its insertion. Don't trap the other guy in an alley. And don't lay yourself open to being trapped.

Ninth, ample moral and material support. Logistics – the supply of ammunition, medicine, fuel, food and other comforts, and the maintenance of morale and public support. I have grouped these ideas together because they all refer to essential support, whether material or mental. During the Cold War, we admired the minimalist approach of the Soviet forces, which was still evident in Grozny, in supplying the bare essentials to large numbers of fighting troops. But, just as modern surveillance methods permit the focus of fewer weapons to achieve maximum effect, so can logistics. And many intervention operations centre on the supply of these items anyway. Traditionally, military thinkers have thought in terms of logistics as an undesirable but essential means of keeping soldiers in the field and fit to fight. Meeting the requirements of the soldiers at Verdun in 1916 or Stalingrad in 1942–43 was not simple. But those requirements were at least basic. The less ferocious the fighting, the more, paradoxically, the troops require in relative terms. In an intervention operation, logistics are the heart of the matter, and fighting troops are only there to protect the logistics. In this respect, as in many others, the conduct of war and peace has returned to a pre-Napoleonic model.

The maintenance of public interest and support is cardinal to any military or aid effort by a democracy. There is a clear parallel with material support. The less obviously evil and formidable the enemy, the more complex the task, the greater the need for moral support and encouragement. And the more complex and information-centred the society, the greater still the need for intelligent and genuine media coverage. On numerous occasions, service personnel have told me they heard of events of operational significance through the broadcasting media before they heard of them through their own chain of command. There is nothing wrong with that. The media are professionals, and, if the armed forces of a democratic state get into a fight or into competition with the media, they will lose. Public information is no longer an adjunct to the conduct of operations. It is an integral part of it.

As we approach the third millennium, the most visible trends in the evolution of conventional armed forces are the end of the mass army, and probably a reduction in the importance of armies vis-à-vis navies and other types of force, plus the increasing irrelevance of nuclear weapons and nuclear deterrents, combined with the need to be able to deal with a wider variety of problems by responding at more or less the same level of violence, without having to 'up the ante' because you have nothing more suitable available. At the beginning of 1996, France, where conscription began in 1793, announced an end to compulsory military service after two centuries, a reflection of the end of the era of total war which this book has documented.[14] At the same time, it became clear that Russia, also long committed to the unrealisable aim of a mass army of high quality, began to create a new, rapid-reaction force based on the 50,000 or so members of the airborne forces – the only troops who had performed with much credit in Afghanistan and Chechnya – and to assign artillery and tank units to provide them with additional firepower.[15] Two of the states most committed to the idea of a 'nation in arms' had realised, nearly 100 years after H. G. Wells first wrote it, that large masses of men are more an encumbrance than a power.

The smaller armed forces which will supersede the mass armies of the past increasingly will take on some of the characteristics of 'special forces', although I would counsel against running an entire military establishment on those lines. Training will have to be longer in order to ensure consistent and universal high standards. But true 'special forces' should remain very small in number, distinguished by specialist expertise and secrecy. You cannot have an entire army of SAS men and women, nor would it be desirable.

Inevitably, the new millennium will see the revival of the mercenary. Not only the individual, but also, perhaps, the mercenary state. States which have particularly good armed forces, but, perhaps, a relatively weak economy, will be able and prepared to place their private armies at the service of others, in return for financial gain or maybe just for recognition and status. Britain is one such country. Although the idea will be sharply criticised on moral or sentimental grounds, a highly professional armed force is one of a country's greatest assets.

Armed forces will be used in all kinds of operations, from traditional peacekeeping and humanitarian aid, through what I have called intervention, up to limited war. The United States will probably need forces designed to cope with one-and-a-half major conflicts: a Gulf war and a Bosnia, perhaps. A country like Britain should probably plan for two Bosnias.

The use of nuclear weapons for any purpose whatever, save as a symbolic weapon of last resort, is looking increasingly unlikely. The US Navy is considering the idea of a 'very heavy conventional deterrent', to bridge the gap between a response to a crisis like the Gulf War and the use of nuclear weapons. In a seventeen-page report published recently, entitled *2020 Vision*, the Navy outlined plans for a conventional striking force able to intimidate a power ashore with scores of long-range missiles and aircraft carrying precision-guided weapons.[16] Such a force could immobilise an adversary or merely threaten to do so. The Royal Navy's recent acquisition of conventionally-armed cruise missiles is another example of employing a highly accurate sea-based weapon as a deterrent rather than relying on nuclear weapons which it would be almost impossible to justify using.

As the new century approaches, navies are beginning to look increasingly attractive. Many of the new technologies which are likely to evolve – lasers and beam weapons, for example, require enormous power which is more easily generated and transported on a ship than any other way. Navies possess unique freedom of movement, and operate at a unique state of readiness. As Mahan explained, they bridge the gap between peace and war – the very dilemma which modern strategists face. They can 'poise', threaten and, if necessary, attack targets increasingly far inland and put highly trained forces ashore. And they take all their supplies with them. Our preoccupation with large land armies has been very much a function of the particular problems of European security over the last two centuries, although maritime nations have never lost sight of the particular nature of maritime power. The new century is likely to see a revival of maritime forces and of maritime strategy.

It is becoming clear that the word 'defence' is a rather inappropriate term. So far, we have discussed the use of military power as a tool of national policy and, increasingly, the policy of multinational groups or alliances. The ultimate form of defence will probably be some form of anti-missile system, but such a system is only needed when every other aspect of security policy (from diplomacy through arms control, and activities to prevent the proliferation of weapons of mass destruction, to intelligence) has failed. The attacker may be doing you a favour by using a ballistic missile which you can shoot down. A biological warfare agent in a suitcase may be far more dangerous.

Struggles of greater importance, touching the survival of nation states and civilisations, will lie increasingly outside the immediate area of military responsibility, although military personnel will work with other agencies to ensure national survival (or the survival of our increasingly international civilisation) is not threatened. To some extent this was always the case. The formidable British code-breaking effort at Bletchley Park during World War II and its successor organisation, the Government Communications Headquarters at Cheltenham were subordinate to the Government of the day, not to the services. The Joint Intelligence Committee is not a military body: military intelligence is just one of the inputs to its assessments. Tracking a biological bomb before it is delivered to a major city is not a military responsibility. It is one for intelligence services, police, and customs.

The information revolution of the last quarter of the twentieth century has opened up a vast area of potential threat and conflict, which will also lie largely outside the military's area of responsibility. An information war, between or against information-based societies, would be a struggle at strategic or grand strategic level. It will be remembered that strategic aims can be couched in political or economic terms. Information war would have profound political and economic consequences. In World War II the secret war waged by the code-breakers was of strategic importance, but so was the physical destruction of cities and industrial capacity – a military task. The strategic aspects of struggle between or against modern, information-based societies utterly dependent on computers would probably have no direct military involvement at all.

An attack on the information base would have catastrophic consequences. Aircraft and trains could not be controlled and would crash. Business would cease to function. Trillions of pounds' or dollars' worth of stocks and shares would be wiped out, not to mention personal wealth which now only exists in the memory of the bank's computer. And because communications would be disrupted, nobody would know what was happening. That is a gaping, strategic vulnerability which hardly existed thirty years ago, when records were kept on paper. And whereas, a few years ago, such an attack might have been directed primarily at one country in Europe, today it would inevitably engulf the entire European Union.

It would be difficult physically to disable a significant proportion of the millions of computers and the hundreds, thousands of miles of fibre-optic cable linking individuals in a developed country. Indeed, the resilience shown by the computer systems in the City of London, after the Stock Exchange and Canary Wharf bombs, shows that modern computer networks are quite robust in the face of conventional, high-explosive attack. An information war would be waged within the network, not against it. An attacker would gain access to the net – which is easy from anywhere in the world, and spread destruction from within. Military and civilian organisations are aware of the threat posed by 'hackers' already, and there are obvious precautions. Newspapers, for example, severely restrict their staff's access to the internet because someone has only to leave the gate open for a rival to gain access to everything in an organisation's system.

Such an attack on a western state or the European Union would be a 'strategic offensive' comparable to a nuclear attack. Mercifully, it would not kill millions of people – just those in aircraft which happened to crash. Thousands of people would not be frozen or drowned as they were in the strategic attacks on ocean convoys in World War II. Cities would not be levelled by firestorms. Telephone exchanges and radars would not be blown to pieces. But such an offensive, infiltrating the information base, would isolate everybody. Sitting by candle-light, listening to reports on the radio or terrestrial television, the population would then be unable to react to other kinds of attack.

If the internet is the critical innovation many people believe it is, then it will acquire strategic significance as surely as the railways and telegraph lines did in the nineteenth century. The latter inaugurated the era of total war. The information revolution and the internet could bring about a new form of 'total war', but a war not fought with military means.

An attack on the information base of our civilisation would take place in what we call 'peacetime', as could a terrorist attack with nuclear, biological or chemical weapons. The struggle against such threats goes on all the time, in the design of computer systems, surveillance, and the work of numerous agencies which are not part of the armed forces. Meanwhile, the armed forces of Britain and France, to name just two countries with similar histories and interests, are now fully stretched to meet the demands of real operations, not exercises, round the world. Therefore the higher forms of conflict are increasingly taken out of the hands of the armed forces who become ever more preoccupied with conflict lower down the scale.

During the Cold War, both sides adopted an interesting approach to deterring the other. The shop window approach. Both sides – Nato and the Warsaw Pact – had impressive arsenals ranged against each other. But when a real emergency arose, in the Gulf in 1990, the British found that only a fifth of their tanks actually worked. When the mighty Russian army faced a relatively minor war in Chechnya, it blundered terribly. In the coming century, armed forces are going to be used for real with increasing regularity. There is no time to switch from 'peace' to 'war'. Indeed, the distinction between the two has largely dissolved. This book has focussed on the rise and fall of total war, and the types of military operations we are most likely to see in future. One thing has been overwhelmingly apparent. Like warships at sea, we need to be on something close to a 'war footing' all the time. More than ever before, strategy evolves constantly in 'peacetime'. And the role of military personnel overlaps increasingly with that of other professionals, from aid workers to computer engineers.

We have probably seen the last of the kind of 'total war' fought twice in this bloody century. Any future struggle of 'total war' intensity will be fought primarily with non-military means. But that has brought about a world full of challenge, risk, and continuous engagement in military operations. The end of 'war' and 'peace'.

NOTES

Chapter 1

1. Epigram of 23 February 1882, inscribed on Sherman's statue in Washington DC.

2. Tacitus, *Annals*, iii, c. 110.

3. 'Pentagon forced to Rethink its World Strategy', *Independent* 20 September 1995, citing *Aviation Week and Space Technology* of the previous week.

4. Maj. Gen. Mike Willcocks, 'Future Conflict and Military Doctrine' (lecture of 2 February 1994), *RUSI Journal*, vol. 139, no. 3, pp. 6–10, this p. 7.

5. C. van Vollenhoven, *The Framework of Grotius' Book De Iure Belli ac pacis, 1625*, Noord Hollandische Uitvermaatschappij, Amsterdam, 1931, p. 8; *De Iure Belli ac Pacis*, 303. II, 15, 8; Edward Dumbauld, *The Life and Legal Writings of Hugo Grotius*, University of Oklahoma, 1969, pp. 33–34.

6. Van Vollenhoven, op. cit., p. 10.

7. James Mayall, 'Ideological Sources of Conflict: the Principle of Self-determination, Religion and the Legitimacy of the State', *Future Sources of Global Conflict*, eds. Trevor Taylor and Seizaburo Sato, (Royal Institute for International affairs, London, 1995), p. 1.

8. *Charter of the United Nations and Statute of the International Court of Justice* UN department of Public Information, New York, March 1994, pp. 5, 22.

9. See Roger Parkinson, *Clausewitz: a Biography*, Wayland, London, 1970.

10. Carl von Clausewitz, *Vom Kriege*, translated as *On War* by Michael Howard and Peter Paret, Princeton University Press, Princeton NJ, 1976, bk 1, ch. 1, section 2, p. 75. This is by far the best edition, superior to the earlier English translations by Graham (1874) and Jolles (1943) and contains excellent introductory essays and commentary by Howard, Paret and Bernard Brodie.

11. Ibid.

12. Ibid., sections 6–11 (pp. 78–81), sections 23–24 (pp. 86–87); bk 1, ch. 7 (pp. 119–121).

13. Ibid., p. 69. Note of 10 July 1827.

14. Julian S. Corbett, *Some Principles of Maritime Strategy*, Conway Maritime Press, London, 1972, p. 52. See also pp. 38–48. *Some Principles of Maritime Strategy* was first published in 1911, based on lectures given to the Royal Naval War College subsequent to its foundation in 1900.

15. Ibid., p. 53.

16. Captain Alfred Thayer Mahan, USN, *Naval Strategy Compared and Contrasted with the Principles and Practice of Military Operations on Land*. Lectures delivered at the US Naval War College, Newport, RI, between the years 1887 and 1911, Simpson Low, Marston, London, 1911, p. 122. Mahan is more famous for *The Influence of Seapower on History 1660–1783*, though this is a historical work.

17. Clausewitz, *On War*, op. cit., bk. 1, ch. 1, section 25 (p. 88).

18. Erich von Ludendorff, *Der Totale Krieg*, Munich, 1935, translated as *The Nation at War* by Dr A. S. Rappoport, Hutchinson, 1936, p. 14; Liddell Hart in *The Ghost of Napoleon*.

19. Antoine Jomini, *Précis de l'Art de la Guerre*, 2nd ed., Librairie pour L'Art Militaire, les Arts et les Sciences, Paris 1855, translated as *The Art of War* by Capts. G. H. Mendell and W. P. Craighill, Lippincott, Philadelphia and Trubner, London, 1879. Quotation on p. 26.

20. *On the Greatness of Kingdoms and Estates*, 1595, cited in Corbett, op. cit., p. 55.

21. Michael Ignatieff, 'The Seductiveness of Moral Disgust', *Index on Censorship*, 5/1995, pp. 22–38.

22. Comfort Ero and Suzanne Long, 'Humanitarian Intervention: a New Role for the United Nations?', *International Peacekeeping*, vol. 2, no. 2, Summer 1995, pp. 140–56.

23. Compilation Group for 'History of Modern China', *The Taiping Revolution*, Foreign Languages Press, Peking, 1976, pp. 99, 131.

24. Ero and Long, op. cit., p. 133.

25. 'War Crimes and Crimes against Humanity, Including Genocide', *Human Rights. A Compilation of International Instruments*, UN, New York and Geneva, 1994, vol. 1, second part, pp. 673–77.

26. Ero and Long, op. cit., p. 153.

27. Willem van Eekelen, *The Security Agenda for 1996: Background and Proposals*, Centre for European Policy Studies, paper 64, Brussels, 1995, pp. 7–8.

28. Joseph Conrad, *Heart of Darkness*, Penguin, London, 1995, pp. 83–84.

29. Ignatieff, op. cit., pp. 23–24.

30. Cited in Ian Williams, *The UN for Beginners*, Writers and Readers Publishing, New York, 1995, p. 92.

31. *Independent on Sunday*, 5 November 1995, p. 5.

32. G. D. Kaye, D. A. Grant and E. J. Edmond, *Major Armed Conflict. A Compendium of Interstate and Intrastate Conflict, 1720 to 1985 (R95)*, Operational Research and Analysis Establishment, Ottawa, November 1985, pp. 1–3.

33. Clement Adibe, *Managing Arms in Peace Processes: Somalia*, (UNIDIR 95/30), UN Institute for Disarmament Research, Geneva, 1995, p. 3; Robert Jackson, 'Why Africa's Weak States Persist: the Empirical and Juridicial in Statehood', *World Politics*, vol. 35, no. 1, 1988; Gerald B. Helma and Steven R. Ratner, 'Saving Failed States', *Foreign Policy*, no. 89, Winter 1992/93.

34. Thomas S. Kuhn, *The Structure of Scientific Revolutions*, 2nd ed., enlarged, Foundations of the History of Science, vol. II, no. 2, University of Chicago Press, 1970. (1st ed. was 1962.)

35. Ibid., p. 99.

36. Sun Tzu, *The Art of War*, edited and translated by Samuel B. Griffith, with an Introduction by Sir Basil Liddell Hart, Oxford University Press, 1963, pp. x, 12.

37. Ibid., pp. 63–64.

38. Ibid., p. 101.

39. Jomini, *Art of War*, op. cit., pp. 48–49.

40. Mahan, *Naval Strategy*, op. cit., p. 114.

41. Ibid., p. 122.

42. Ibid., p. 20.

43. Sun Tzu, *Art of War*, op. cit., VII, Manoeuvre, p. 106.

44. WO 32/13087 *Report of Committee on the Lessons of the Great War* (A 3629), October 1932, p. 29.

45. See Peter Coveney and Roger Highfield, *Frontiers of Complexity*, Faber, London, 1995.

Chapter 2

1. Clausewitz, *Uber das Leben und den Charakter von Scharnhorst*, Historische-Poliitische Zeitschrift, i, Berlin, 1832, pp. 196–97, cited in Parkinson, *Clausewitz*, p. 228.

2. Engels to Marx, 23 May 1862, in *Karl Marx and Friedrich Engels Correspondence 1846–95*, translated and edited by Dona Torr, Martin Lawrence, London, 1934, pp. 243–45.

3. Ludendorff, *The Nation at War*, op. cit., pp. 13–14.

4. Parkinson, *Clausewitz*, op. cit., p. 243.

5. Edwin A. Pratt, *The Rise of Rail Power in War and Conquest, 1833–1914*, P. S. King and Son, London, 1915, pp. 1, 6–7.

6. Ibid., pp. 9, 27.

7. Fyodor Gershel'man, *'Zadachi kavalerii'* (*'The Tasks of Cavalry'*), *Voyenny Sbornik* (Military Collection), 7/1898, p. 79.

8. 'The Siege of Sevastopol', *New York Tribune*, 15 November 1854, in

Aveling and Aveling, *The Eastern Question*, pp. 493–94. Marx is believed to have been the author: the *Tribune* used many of his letters as anonymous leaders.

9. Captain E. A. Martynov, *Strategiya v epokhu Napoleona I i v nashe vremya* (*Strategy in the Age of Napoleon I and in our Time*), General Staff Press, St Petersburg, 1894, p. 297.

10. Martynov, '*Neskol'ko slov . . .*' ('A Few Words in Explanation of [my] Work, *Strategy* . . .) *Voyenny Sbornik* 8/1894, p. 236.

11. Gen. Nikolay Mikhnevich (1849–1927, Chief of the General Staff 1911–1917), '*Poyavyatsa-li . . .*' ('*Will Million-strong Armies Appear in a Future Major European War*'), *Voyenny Sbornik*, 2/1898, p. 264.

12. H. G. Wells, *War and Common Sense*. Reprinted from the *Daily Mail*, April 7, 8, 9, 1913, pp. 7–9.

13. H. G. Wells, *The War that will End War*, Frank and Cecil Palmer, London, September 1914, pp. 66–67.

14. Philip Thornthwaite, *Nelson's Navy*, Osprey, London, 1993, p. 3.

15. Rhodri Williams, *Defending the Empire: the Conservative Party and British Defence Policy 1899–1915*, Yale, New Haven and London, 1991, pp. 8–9, 11.

16. Ibid., p. 219.

17. Ross Davies and Graham Madocks, 'An Army that Died without Glory', *Independent on Sunday*, 12 November 1995, p. 6.

18. Ludendorff, *The Nation at War*, op. cit., pp. 14–15.

19. Leader, *New York Tribune*, 31 October 1854, in Aveling and Aveling, op. cit., p. 490.

20. Ivan S. Bliokh (Jan Bloch), *Budushchaya voyna v tekhnicheskom, ekonomicheskom i politicheskom otnosheniyakh* (5 vols, plus Atlas of diagrams), Tipografiya A. I. Yefrona, St Petersburg, 1898; *Is War Now Impossible, Being an Abridgement of the 'War of the Future in its Technical, Economic and Political Relations' by I. S. Bloch* . . ., Grant Richards, London, 1899.

21. The bibliography in the Polish edition of Bloch, *Wnioski Ogolne . . .*, Gebethner and Wolff, Warsaw, 1899, pp. 342–56; General Conclusions of the Russian edition, pp. 49–59.

22. *Budushchaya voyna*, op. cit., vol. 4, pp. 153–279, with Atlas.

23. Ibid.

24. Norman Angell, *Europe's Optical Illusion*, Simpkin, Marshall, Hamilton, Kent, London, 1909, reprinted as *The Great Illusion: a Study of the Relation of Military Power to National Advantage*, Heinemann, London, 1910, 1913, and many subsequent editions between the two world wars.

25. Clausewitz, *On War*, op. cit., Bk 2, ch. 1, p. 128.

26. G. A. B. Dewar and Lt Col J. H. Boraston, *Sir Douglas Haig's Command December 19, 1915 to November 11, 1918* (2 vols.), Constable, London, 1922, vol. 2, pp. 354–6; Gen. Dr Baron Hugo von Freytag-Loringhoven, *Generalship in the World War*, translated from the German of 1920, US Army War College, Washington, 1934, p. 34.

27. Generalleutnant H. von Sandrart, '*Operativeführung uber die Gefechtstaktik hinaus*' ('*Operational Command Goes Beyond Combat Tactics*'), *Europäische Wehrkunde* 9/1987, p. 504 citing Moltke's *Essays for the Years 1857–1871*; Fuller, *The Foundations of the Science of War*, Hutchinson, London, 1926, pp. 88–89.

28. Sun Tzu, *Art of War*, op. cit., III, p. 77.

29. A. V. Golubev, *M. V. Frunze o kharaktere budushchey voyny* (*M. V. Frunze* [early Soviet war commissar and military thinker] (*on the Character of Future War*), Voyenizdat, Moscow, 1931, p. 8.

30. Gen André Beaufre, *Introduction to Strategy*, London 1965, cited in *Makers of Modern Strategy from Machiavelli to the Nuclear Age*, ed. Peter Paret, Oxford University Press, 1986, p. 788.

31. *Soviet Military Encyclopedia*, vol. 6 (1979), p. 55.

32. Brigadier Richard Simpkin, *Race to the Swift. Thoughts on Twenty-First Century Warfare*, Brassey's, London, 1985, p. 24.

33. Ellsworth L. Raymond, *Soviet Preparations for Total War, 1925–51*, PhD, University of Michigan, 1952.

34. Alexander I. Svechin, *Strategiya*, 2nd ed., Voyenny Vestnik Press, Moscow, 1927 (Preface to 1st ed. was written in 1925), pp. 46–48.

35. Tukhachevskiy's introduction to the Russian translation of John

Fuller's *The Reformation of War* (1923), in the former's *Collected Works*, Voyenizdat, Moscow, 1964, pp. 147–56. The chief exponent of 'armoured knights' in Russia was A. I. Verkhovskiy – see '*Voyna zavtrashnego . . .*' ('War of the Future'), *Red Star*, 18 October 1925.

36. R. Eydeman, 'On the Character of the Opening Period of a War', *Voyna i Revolyutsiya* (War and Revolution), 3/1931, p. 17.

37. Vladimir Triandafillov, *Kharakter operatsii . . . (The Character of the Operations of Modern Armies)*, 3rd ed., Gosvoyenizdat, Moscow, 1936, p. 41.

38. Air Chief Marshal Sir Arthur T. Harris, *Despatch on War Operations 23 February 1942 to 8 May 1945*, with an introduction by Sebastian Cox and a German view by Horst Boog, published Frank Cass, London, 1995, p. 7.

39. Robin Cross, *The Bombers. The Illustrated Story of Offensive Strategy and Tactics in the Twentieth Century*, Transworld, London, 1987, pp. 49, 58.

40. Harris, *Despatch*, op. cit., p. 7.

41. Ibid., p. 19.

42. John Erickson and David Dilks, *Barbarossa: the Axis and the Allies*, Edinburgh University Press, 1994, pp. 255–77.

43. Public Record Office (PRO), *PREM 3/89*, Prime Minister to Ismay D 217/4, 6 July 1944; 'Military Considerations Affecting the Initiation of Chemical and other Special Forms of Warfare', 1944, pp. 1–4.

44. David Holloway, *Stalin and the Bomb*, Yale University Press, New Haven and London, 1994, p. 227.

45. PRO Defe II 1252, *Examination of the Possible Development of Weapons and Methods of War*, TWC(46)3 (Revise), 30 January 1946, Part II 'Effects on Warfare', p. 8.

46. Ibid., Part I, 'Matters of Fact Relating to Atomic Energy, section B(e) 'Effect on Army Targets'; Holloway, p. 228.

47. Maj. Gen. of Aviation E. Tatarchenko, '*Nekotorye problemy razvitii vozdushnoy moshchi*' ('*Certain Questions of the Development of Air*

Power'), *Vestnik Vozdushnogo flota (Air Force Herald)*, 5–6, 1946, pp. 60–63, this p. 61.

48. Holloway, op. cit., pp. 226–27.

49. Ibid.

50. Lawrence Freedman, 'Nuclear Strategists', in Paret, *Makers of Modern Strategy*, op. cit., p. 740.

51. John Foster Dulles, 'The Evolution of Foreign Policy', *Department of State Bulletin*, vol. 30, 25 January 1954.

52. Freedman, op. cit., p. 739.

53. Alfred Goldberg, article in *International Affairs*, October 1964, cited in Humphrey Wynn, *RAF Nuclear Deterrent Forces*, HMSO, London, 1994, p. 86.

54. Ibid., p. x.

55. Albert Wohlstetter, 'The Delicate Balance of Terror', *Foreign Affairs*, 37, no.2, January 1959.

56. Freedman, op. cit., p. 757.

57. *Pravda*, 26 February 1986, p. 8.

58. Freeman Dyson, *Weapons and Hope*, New York, 1984, p. 55, cited in Paret, *Makers of Modern Strategy*, p. 868.

Chapter 3

1. Louis L'Amour, *Shalako* [a western, later made into a film], Bantam, London, 1962, p. 18.

2. Sir Charles Callwell, *Small Wars: Their Principles and Practice*, War Office, Intelligence Division, published by HMSO, London, 1896, revised version 1899, pp. 1, 62.

3. Ibid., 1899, pp. 4, 51.

4. Ibid., pp. 63–66.

5. Ibid., p. 31.

6. Interview with General Vitaliy Shabanov, Soviet Minister for Armaments, on ministerial flight from Leningrad to Moscow, 18 May 1990.

7. See T. F. Lawrence, *Seven Pillars of Wisdom*, Penguin, Harmondsworth, 1962.

8. See John Shy and Thomas W. Collier, 'Revolutionary War' in Paret, *Makers of Modern Strategy*, p. 815.

9. *Charter of the UN*, p. 23. See Richard Connaughton, *Military Intervention in the 1990s. A New Logic of War*, Routledge, London, 1992, pp. 6–9.

10. *Charter*, p. 25.

11. *Yearbook of the United Nations*, 1947–48, p. 495.

12. *The Fundamentals of British Maritime Doctrine, BR1806*, HMSO, London, 1995, pp. 43, 216.

13. Michael Howard, 'War and Technology' (lecture of 18 February 1986), *RUSI Journal*, December 1987, p. 19.

14. Lt Col Scott McMichael, *Stumbling Bear: Soviet Military Performance in Afghanistan*, Brassey's, London, 1991, p. 66.

15. Clausewitz, *On War*, op. cit., bk. 6, ch. 26, p. 479.

16. Samuel B. Griffith, *Mao Tse-tung on Guerrilla Warfare*, Praeger, New York and Washington, 1961, p. 65.

17. Richard Clutterbuck, *Riot and Revolution in Singapore and Malaya 1945–1963*, Faber and Faber, London, 1973, p. 17; Frank Kitson, *Low Intensity Operations: Subversion, Insurgency Peace-keeping*, Faber and Faber, London, 1971, p. 3.

18. Kitson, op. cit., pp. 4–5, 25–26.

19. Ibid., pp. 25–26.

20. Foreword to Frank Kitson, *Gangs and Counter-Gangs*, Barrie and Rockliff, London, 1960, p. xi.

21. Anthony Parsons, *From Cold War to Hot Peace: UN Interventions 1947–1994*, Michael Joseph, London, 1995, pp. 13–14; Marrack Goulding, 'The Evolution of United Nations Peacekeeping', in *International Affairs*, vol. 69, no. 3, July 1993, pp. 451–464.

22. Goulding in *International Affairs*, July 1993, pp. 452–56; quote from Boutros Boutros-Ghali, *An Agenda for Peace: Preventive Diplomacy, Peacemaking and Peace-keeping. Report of the Secretary-General Pursuant*

to the Statement Adopted by the Summit Meeting of the Security Council on 31 January 1992, UN, New York, 1992, p. 17.

Chapter 4

1. John Silverlight, *The Victors' Dilemma. Allied Intervention in the Russian Civil War*, Barrie and Jenkins, London, 1970, p. ix.

2. Ibid., p. 44.

3. Ibid., p. 7.

4. Ibid., pp. 261–63, 367–68. On 5 July 1919 the *Manchester Guardian* published a long statement by a group of leading writers, including E. M. Forster, protesting against British action in Russia.

5. Parsons, *From Cold War*, op. cit. pp. 77–93; A. Walter Dorn and David H. Bell, 'Intelligence and Peacekeeping: the UN Operation in the Congo 1960–64', in *International Peacekeeping*, vol. 2, no. 1, Spring 1995, pp. 11–33.

6. Dorn and Bell, op. cit., pp. 11–12.

7. Ibid., p. 14; Parsons, op. cit., p. 87.

8. Dorn and Bell, op. cit., pp. 18–23.

9. I am grateful to Tom Hardie-Forsyth, then the British Army's only Kurdish speaker, for sharing his experiences with me. The rest of this account is based on my experience and reporting from Kurdistan in April 1991.

10. Parsons, op. cit., p. 200.

11. This account is based on contemporary newspaper reports and on the Annex 'UNOSOM', which stresses the UN and military elements, in the British Army Field Manual *Wider Peacekeeping*, HMSO, London, 1995; Digest, in *International Peacekeeping*, vol. 2, no. 2, Summer 1995, p. 251.

12. African Rights, *Rwanda: Death, Despair, Defiance*, African Rights, London, 1995, p. 1065.

13. Richard Connaughton, 'Wider Peacekeeping – How Wide of the Mark', in *British Army Review*, no. 111, December 1995, pp. 55–64, 61–62.

14. Ibid., p. 63.

15. African Rights, op. cit., p. 1070.

16. Ibid., p. 1115.

17. Ibid., p. 1118.

18. Interviewed by the American Broadcasting Corporation (ABC) radio, 24 July 1995.

19. Richard Dowden, 'Paris Ready to Send Troops to Rwanda', *Independent*, 20 June 1994.

20. Testimony of a French Marine, cited in Robert Block, 'Pattern of Slaughter Confounds French', *Independent on Sunday*, 3 July 1994.

21. This account is based on Annex UNAMIC/UNTAC, in *Wider Peacekeeping*, and on conversation with Colonel John Mackinlay.

22. Parsons, op. cit., p. 166.

23. The preceding account is derived from the author's coverage in the *Independent*, October 1992–December 1995. On Gen. Smith's remodelling of his forces and movement with the flow of events, Kurt Schork of Reuter, despatch of 19 December 1995, and *Independent*, 21 December 1995, p. 8.

24. Larry Minear et al., 'Caught in a vice' in Ben Cohen and George Stamkoski, ed., *With no Peace to Keep. United Nations peacekeeping and the war in the former Yugoslavia*, Grainpress, London, 1995, p. 87.

25. *Independent*, 22 January 1996, p. 8.

Chapter 5

1. Geoffrey Lean and Don Hinrichsen, *Atlas of the Environment*, Helicon, London, 1992, p. 17.

2. 'Al-Qaddafi lectures university students', Tripoli TV, 21 June 1987, cited in Rosemary Durward, *Arms Control, Disarmament and the New World Order*, Strategic and Combat Studies Institute (SCSI) Paper No. 13, HMSO for Staff College, Camberley, 1995, p. 7.

3. Samuel P. Huntington, 'The Clash of Civilisations?', *Foreign Affairs*, vol. 72, no. 3, Summer 1993, pp. 22–49.

4. Alexander Yanov, *The Origins of Autocracy. Ivan the Terrible and Russian History*, California University Press, 1981.

5. Radovan Pavic, ed., *Zivot i Djelo Jurja Krizanica (The Life and Work of Yuri Krizanic)* [1618–83, generally acknowledged to have been the founder of the Panslav movement], Biblioteka politicka misao, Zagreb, 1974.

6. Frank Barnaby, introduction to *Global Security: the View from China*, Report no. 16, Oxford Research Group, December 1995, pp. 4–5.

7. 'How the Croats Armed and Trained for Victory', *Independent*, August 1995, p. 7.

8. Kurt Gastgeyer, 'Sources of Future Conflict: a Global Overview', lecture to Tri-Service Seminar, *British Defence in 2010*, Church House, London, 16 November, 1995.

9. Michael Portillo, to the same seminar. *Independent*, 17 November.

10. Robert Kaplan, 'The Coming Anarchy: how Scarcity, Crime, Over-population, Tribalism and Disease are Destroying the Social Fabric of our Planet', *The Atlantic Monthly*, February 1994, cited in UN High Commissioner for Refugees, *The State of the World's Refugees: in Search of Solutions*, UNHCR/Oxford University Press, 1995, p. 23.

11. *The State of the World's Refugees*, op. cit., p. 233.

12. Lean and Hinrichsen, op. cit., pp. 17, 19; G. W. (Bill) Hopkinson, *Changing Options: British Defence and Global Security*, Occasional Paper, University of Cambridge, 1992, p. 5.

13. Hopkinson, op. cit., p. 4.

14. *The State of the World's Refugees*, op. cit., pp. 12–13, 104–09, 229.

15. E. Bos, T. My, E. Massiah and R. Bulatao, *World Population Projections, 1994–95 Edition*, John Hopkins University Press, Baltimore and London, 1994, pp. 18–29; World Bank, *Population and Development: Implications for the World Bank*, Washington, 1994, p. 22, cited in George Joffe, 'The Impact on Security of Demographic and Environmental Change', paper to Tri-Service seminar, 16 November 1994.

16. Joffe, op. cit., p. 5.

17. Lean and Hinrichsen, op. cit., p. 23.

18. Ibid., p. 93.

19. John Bulloch and Adel Darwish, *Water Wars: Coming Conflicts in the Middle East*, Gollancz, London, 1993, p. 16.

20. The following account is based mainly on Darwish and Bulloch, and also on information in Joffe.

21. Author's reporting from Riyadh during the Gulf War.

22. Michael Harbottle, *New Roles for the Military: Humanitarian and Environmental Security*, Conflict Studies 285, Research Institute for the Study of Conflict and Terrorism, London, 1995, p. 1. An earlier study, *What is Proper Soldiering?* was published in 1992.

23. International Institute for Strategic Studies (IISS), *The Military Balance, 1995–96*, Oxford University Press, 1995, pp. 23, 113, 157, 176.

24. Harbottle, op. cit., pp. 14–22.

Chapter 6

1. Brigadier Ian Durie, '1st Armoured Division Artillery in Operation Granby', *Journal of the Royal Artillery*, vol. CXVIII, no. 2, September 1991, pp. 19–21; on the operation, the author's *Expert Witness: a Defence Correspondent's Gulf War*, Brassey's, London 1993, pp. xxvii, 118–126.

2. Richard Connaughton, 'Wider Peacekeeping – How Wide of the Mark?', *BAR*, no. 111, p. 57, citing Uppsala Conflict Data Project and University of Cambridge Global Security Programme Analysis.

3. *Wider Peacekeeping*, HMSO, 1994, p. 1.2.

4. Ibid., p. 1.3.

5. Ibid., p. 1.2.

6. Department of the Army, *FM 100–23: Peace Operations*, Washington DC, 1994, p. 12; discussion of changing doctrine in Theo Farrell, 'The Somalia Imbroglio', *International Peacekeeping*, vol. 2, no. 2, Summer 1995, pp. 208–211.

7. Dennis J. Quinn, 'Peace Support Operations: Definitions and Implications', in Quinn, ed., *Peace Support Operations and the US*

Military, National Defense University Press, Washington DC, 1994, pp. 20–21, cited in Farrell, 'The Somalia Imbroglio', op. cit., p. 209.

8. *Wider Peacekeeping*, op. cit., pp. 2–5, paras 8a, 8c.

9. Cited in Connaughton, 'Wider Peacekeeping', op. cit., p. 56.

10. *Agenda for Peace*, UN, 1992, pp. 16–18; on the fall of Srebrenica, see my colleague Robert Block's reports in the *Independent*, December 1995.

11. John Mackinlay and Jarat Chopra, *A Draft Concept of Second Generation Multinational Operations 1993*, Brown University, Providence RI, 1993, pp. 12–21.

12. *Agenda for Peace*, op. cit., pp. 32–34.

13. Mikhail Tukhachevskiy, *Voprosy sovremennoy strategii (Questions of Contemporary strategy)*, pamphlet, Voyenny Vestnik Press, Moscow, 1926, in *Collected Works*, Moscow, Voyenizdat, 1964, vol. 1, p. 252.

14. Connaughton, 'Wider Peacekeeping', op. cit., p. 63.

Chapter 7

1. Maj. Gen. Rupert Smith, lecture to RUSI, 7 November 1991, listed Global Positioning Systems (GPS); the ability to fight at night, automatic encoding and decoding devices attached to radios, which obviated the need for complex codes; and the killing power and accuracy of modern artillery systems. Stealth technology was 'worth every penny': Lt Gen Chuck Horner [US air commander during the Gulf War], 'The Air Campaign', *Military Review*, September 1991, p. 26.

2. 'How Nato Paralysed Serb Command', *Independent on Sunday*, 17 September 1995, p. 15.

3. David Gates, *Airpower: The Future?*, Centre for Defence and International Security Studies, Lancaster University, 1995, pp. 14–15.

4. John Bulloch, 'How Bush lost the Gulf War', *Independent on Sunday*, Sunday Review, 8 December 1991, citing Gen. Tom Kelly, the US Director of Operations during the war.

5. Brigadier Patrick Cordingley [who commanded the 7th British

Armoured Brigade], 'The Gulf War – a Personal Account', *Seaford House Papers*, Royal College of Defence Studies, London, 1991, p. 22.

6. Gen. Powell interviewed in BBC documentary *The Gulf War*, BBC/ Fine Art Productions, January 1996, episode four 'The Ragged End', 12.40–14.41.

7. Ibid., Gen. Schwarzkopf interview, 15.32–16.02, 18.31.

8. Ibid., episode two, 'Thunder and Lightning', 23.30, 43.42.

9. *BR 1806 British Maritime Doctrine*, 1995, p. 60.

10. BBC interview, 28 March 1993, cited in David Shukman, *The Sorcerer's Challenge: Fears and Hopes for the Weapons of the next Millennium*, Coronet, London, 1995, p. 203.

11. 'Less than Lethal', *International Defense Review*, 7/1994, pp. 29–39.

12. Michael Klare, *Rogue States and Nuclear Outlaws: America's Search for a New Foreign Policy*, Hill and Wang, New York, 1995.

13. Martian Navias, *Going Ballistic: The Build-Up of Missiles in the Middle East*, Brassey's, London, 1993, p. 3; the chapter on missile prolifera- tion in the International Institute for Strategic Studies, *The Military Balance 1995/6*, IISS/Oxford University Press, London 1995, pp. 281–84.

Chapter 8

1. 'Cautious Britain Goes Tactical on the "Battlenet"', *Independent*, 28 October 1995.

2. Maj. Gen. Rupert Smith to RUSI, 7 November 1991.

3. BBC, *The Gulf War*, episode one, 'Invasion', 46.08.

4. Mikhail Tukhachevskiy, *'Novye voprosy voyny'* ('*New Questions of War*'), *Military Historical Journal*, 2/1962, pp. 68–69. '*Teleupravlyayemye tanki.*'

5. Shukman, *The Sorcerer's Challenge*, op. cit., pp. 182–192.

Chapter 9

1. Parsons, *From Cold War*, op. cit., p. 204.

2. UN Charter, p. 25.

3. UN Security Council, S/1995/943, *Report of the Secretary-General on Standby Arrangements for Peace-Keeping*, 10 November, 1995, p. 2.

4. Ibid., p. 4. See also S/1994/777, 30 June 1994.

5. Attributed to Maj. Gen. Nathan Bedford Forrest, 1821–1877, American Civil War commander. He probably said, 'I always make it a rule to get there first with the most men,' but 'I git thar fustest with the mostest men' is a common interpretation.

6. Press release from Netherlands' Ministries of Foreign Affairs and Defence, January 1995.

7. Carl Conetta and Charles Knight, *Vital Force. A proposal for the Overhaul of the UN Peace Operations System and for the Creation of a UN Legion*, Project on Defense Alternatives, Commonwealth Institute, Cambridge, Ma, 1995, p. xiv.

8. Ibid., p. 93.

9. 'UN Flounders over Plan to Rebuild Bosnia', the *Independent*, Friday 5 January 1996, p. 9.

10. Lukas Haynes and Timothy W. Stanley, 'To Create a United Nations Fire Brigade', *Comparative Strategy*, vol. 14, no. 1, p. 9.

11. Sir Brian Urquhart, 'For a UN Volunteer Military Force', *New York Review of Books*, 10 June 1993, p. 4.

12. Sir Basil Liddell Hart, *Thoughts on War*, Faber, London, 1964, p. 125.

13. Mark Prutsalis, 'Too little, too late', in Cohen and Stamkoski, op. cit., p. 78.

14. Rosemary Righter, 'A marriage made in Hell', Cohen and Stamkoski, op. cit., p. 28.

Chapter 10

1. Boutros Boutros-Ghali, 'Empowering the United Nations', *Foreign Affairs*, winter, 1992–93, pp. 98–99.

2. Speech to the University of Bordeaux, 24 April 1991.

3. Powell interview, BBC, *The Gulf War*, episode 4, 'The Ragged End', 33.24.

4. Sun Tzu, *Art of War*, op. cit., I, 'Estimates', pp. 62–65.

5. Julian Lider, *Military Theory: Concept, Structure, Problems*, Swedish Studies in International Relations, Gower Press, Aldershot, 1983, pp. 221–23; John F. C. Fuller, *Foundations of the Science of War*, Hutchinson, London, 1925; Bruce Keenan, 'The Principles of War: a Thesis for Change', US Naval Institute Proceedings, November 1967; Don H. Starry, 'Principles of War', Military Review 9/1981; V. Ye Savkin, *Basic Principles of Operational Art and Tactics*, (translated from the Russian of 1972), US Government Printing Office, Washington, 1982; *BR 1806, British Maritime Doctrine*, HMSO, 1995, Annex A pp. 185–88.

6. *Air Power Doctrine: AP 3000*, published under the direction of the Chief of the Air Staff, 1991, p. 1.

7. Richard Connaughton, *Military Intervention in the 1990s*, p. 17.

8. *Wider Peacekeeping*, op. cit., pp. 2.8, 4.1.

9. Sun Tzu, *Art of War*, op. cit., I, 'Estimates', p. 63.

10. Ed Vulliamy, 'Only passivity is dishonourable', *Guardian*, 12 January 1996, p. 10.

11. Sun Tzu, op. cit., II, 'Waging War', p. 73.

12. Richard Smith, *The Requirement for the United Nations to Develop an Internationally Recognized Doctrine for the Use of Force in Intra-state Conflict*, occasional paper no. 10, Strategic and Combat Studies Institute, Camberley, 1994, p. 13.

13. Gen. Donn A. Starry, 'A Perspective on American Military Thought', *Military Review*, July 1989, pp. 4–6, cited in Smith, ibid., p. 18.

14. *Independent*, 22 February, 1996, p. 10, 24 February pp. 1, 14.

15. 'Kremlin scraps massive army for elite force', *Independent* 19 February 1996, p. 11.

16. 'Navy vision sees greater role in "conventional deterrence".' *Defense Daily*, 28 February 1996.

GLOSSARY

Centre of Gravity A critical position, asset or characteristic from which
  a force or country derives freedom of action, physical strength or
  will to fight.
Collateral Damage Damage which, though caused by military action, is
  incidental to its purpose.
Conflict Prevention Diplomatic, economic and, occasionally, military
  measures to anticipate and prevent conflict. The military means
  include early warning measures, surveillance, stabilising measures
  and *preventive deployment*.
Containment Military containment centres on restricting enemy forces'
  freedom of movement: crisis containment involves limiting the
  geographical spread of a crisis.
Critical vulnerability The Achilles' heel of a fighting force or a country
  which, if destroyed, will lead to systemic disruption, with his whole
  fighting effort falling apart.
Decisive point An important, geographical position, possession of which
  may confer a marked advantage. Decisive points are distinct from
  the *centre of gravity*, but may provide an avenue to it.
Fog of War Uncertainty and confusion caused by lack of information,
  deliberate deception and the generally chaotic nature of combat.
Friction In military operations, as in life generally, if anything can
  possibly go wrong, it will. Enemy action, weather, terrain and
  equipment failure combine so that even the simplest thing becomes
  very difficult. The more complex the machine, the more moving
  parts there are, the more friction there will be.
Interior lines These are advantageous because the party on the 'inside',
  with shorter lines of communication can move more swiftly and
  easily to counter an attack mounted by the party operating on

exterior lines, and can therefore offset superior numbers. The wars of Frederick the Great of Prussia in the eighteenth century are a good example. However, at some point, the advantage of interior lines become the disadvantage of being encircled. See also *Lines of communication*.

Intervention A campaign with limited objectives involving the entry of military forces into the territory or territorial seas of another nation, with or without invitation. Also preferred by some to cover the spectrum of military operations between *peacekeeping* and *limited war*.

General War War involving all the resources of a nation.

Grand Strategic The application of all the resources and talents of a nation (diplomatic, political, military, economic, media and technology), and, usually, a coalition of nations, to achieve overriding national objectives which can often be measured on a global scale. The defeat of fascism in World War II and the collapse of communism in eastern Europe were grand strategic objectives.

Limited war War waged to achieve limited aims, short of the complete overthrow of the enemy, and which does not utilise the full resources of the nation. The 1991 Gulf War is probably the most perfect example.

Lines of communication The arteries – land, sea and air – along which logistics flow, from the the grand strategic level – the transatlantic convoys in World War II – to the tactical.

Lines of operations 1. Lines between a force and its objective and between that force and its base.

2. The direction of application of military force through *decisive points* towards the opponent's *centre of gravity*.

Logistics The supply of everything a force needs to operate efficiently: ammunition, fuel, food, building materials, warm clothing, mail, beer . . .

Minimum force The application of the minimum level of violence or coercion, sufficient to achieve the desired end, which is proportionate and reasonable and confined solely to the intended target. Non-lethal weapons may, in future, further reduce the amount of force needed.

NATO (North Atlantic Treaty Organisation) a military alliance created in 1949. Currently has 16 members. Following the break up of the Warsaw Pact and the Soviet Union, many east European nations would like to join.

Operational 1. A military system or organisation which is up and
   running.
              2. (Loosely used) Relating to military operations.
              3. Relating to the Operational level of war. The level
   between *tactics* and *strategy*, Operational objectives are military
   objectives lying at one remove from those which can be couched in
   political or economic terms and which are therefore *strategic*. But
   they are nevertheless focused on *decisive points* and *centres of gravity*.
Peace building Action to build trust and confidence between former
   warring factions and to restore normality, thus preventing a relapse
   into conflict.
Peace enforcement Forcible action to separate warring factions and to
   restore peace, with or without their consent. More loosely, to use
   force to compel compliance with internationally agreed norms of
   behaviour.
Peacekeeping Operations by a third party to the peace between two
   other parties with their consent.
Peacemaking Diplomatic efforts to maintain peace through diplomacy,
   persuasion, mediation and negotiation.
Peace support operations The full spectrum of operations covering the
   four categories above.
Preventive deployment Putting a third armed force in the way of one
   party which might attack another.
Preventive diplomacy Action to prevent disputes arising between parties,
   to prevent existing disputes from growing into conflict, and to limit
   the spread of the latter when they occur.
Proliferation The spread of new weapons.
Poise What a maritime force does when it remains in international
   waters for a long period, able to influence and, if necessary,
   become involved in events ashore.
Strategic The level of command at which military resources are
   applied to achieve political and economic objectives; attack on an
   enemy's centres of gravity (especially using nuclear weapons).
Strategic deterrent Nuclear weapons which are held ready to be fired at
   an assailant inflicting unacceptable damage, thus deterring him
   from action he might otherwise be tempted to take.
Sub-strategic deterrent Small, highly accurate nuclear weapons which
   could be used as a warning shot to deter an adversary without
   totally destroying him. The British Trident missiles, originally
   acquired to be a strategic nuclear deterrent, may also be used, with

single warheads, as a sub-strategic deterrent. Highly accurate conventional weapons, able to hit enemy *centres of gravity*, could in future also provide a sub-strategic deterrent.

Strategy The use of the results of battles to achieve a political objective.

Tactics How battles are fought.

Total War General war waged towards unlimited objectives.

War An act of violence to compel another party to do your will, usually in the form of continuous hostilities on a large scale. For a country to declare a state of war has legal and social implications, which is why hostilities are often referred to as 'armed conflict' instead.

Western European Union (WEU) The European states within Nato – currently ten in number. Some would like to see the WEU take responsibility for European defence matters in which the United States and Canada would not wish to be involved. Others would like to see the European Union take on that role.

Wider peacekeeping British official term for the spectrum of operations between traditional peacekeeping and limited war, carried out with the broad consent of belligerent parties but in an environment which may be volatile and where consent is fragile. It includes conflict prevention, the disarmament of warring factions, military assistance, humanitarian relief and the guarantee and denial of movement.

SELECTED FURTHER READING: BOOKS AND ARTICLES

The Classics

ANGELL, SIR NORMAN, *Europe's Optical Illusion*, Simpkin, Marshall, Hamilton, Kent, London, 1909, reprinted as *The Great Illusion: a Study of the Relation of Military Power to National Advantage*, Heinemann, London, 1910, 1913, and many subsequent editions.

BLOCH (BLIOKH), IVAN S, *Is War Now Impossible?*, Grant Richards, London, 1899, an abridgement of the *General Conclusions* of *Budushchaya voyna v tekhnicheskom, ekonomisheskom i poiticheskom otnosheniyakh*, 5 Vols., plus Atlas of Diagrams, A. I. Yefron, St. Petersburg, 1898.

CALLWELL, MAJOR (later Major General Sir) CHARLES, *Small Wars, Their Principles and Practice*, Intelligence Division, War Office, 1896, revised and expanded 1899.

CLAUSEWITZ, CARL VON, *On War* (*Vom Kreige*, 1832), trans. Michael Howard and Peter Paret, Princeton University Press, 1976.

———— see Parkinson, Roger, *Clausewitz. A Biography*, Wayland, London, 1970.

CORBETT, JULIAN, *Some Principles of Maritime Strategy*, Conway Maritime Press, London, 1972, another edition with Introduction and Notes by Eric Grove, Brassey's, London, 1988.

DE GAULLE, CHARLES, *Vers l'Armée de Méteir (Towards the Professional Army)* (Berger-Levrault, Paris, 1934), Livres de poche, Plon, Paris, 1973.

EARLE, EDWARD MEADE, ed., *Makers of Modern Strategy. Military Thought from Machiavelli to Hitler*, Princeton University Press, 1943.

GROTIUS, HUGO (Huig de Groot), *The Law of War and Peace: selections from de Iure Belli act Pacis*, *1625*, trans. W. S. M. Knight, Peace Book Company, 1939.

———— see Van Vollenhoven, C, *The Framework of Grotius' Book de Iure Belli ac Pacis*, Noord Hollandische Uitgermaatschappij, Amersterdam, 1931.

———— see Dumbauld, Edward, *The Life and Legal Writings of Hugo Grotius*, University of Oklahoma Press, 1969.

JOMINI, ANTOINE HENRI, *Précis de l'Art de la Guerre*, (1838). 2nd ed., Librairie pour les arts et les Sciences, Paris, 1855, trans, as *The Art of War* by Capts. G. H. Mendell and W. F. Craighill, Lippincott, Philadelphia and Trubner, London, 1879. Also translated in Phillips, *Roots of Strategy*, Vol. 2.

KITSON, MAJOR GENERAL FRANK, *Low Intensity Operations. Subversion, Insurgency, Peacekeeping*, Faber and Faber, London, 1971.

KUHN, THOMAS S, *The Structure of Scientific Revolutions* (1962) 2nd ed., enlarged Foundations of the History of Science, Vol. II, No. 2, University of Chicago press, 1970

LAWRENCE, TERENCE E, ('Of Arabia') *Seven Pillars of Wisdom*, (1927), Penguin, Harmondsworth, 1962.

LIDDELL HART, SIR BASIL, *The Ghost of Napoleon. A History of Military thought from the Eighteenth to the Twentieth Century*, Faber and Faber, London, 1933.

————, *Strategy: the Indirect Approach*, Faber and Faber, London, 1967.

LUDENDORFF, ERICH VON, *The Nation at War*, trans. from *Der totale Krieg*, Munich, 1935, by Dr. A. S. Rappoport, Hutchinson, London, 1936.

MAHAN, ALFRED THAYER, *Naval Strategy Compared and Contrasted with Principles and Practice of Military Operations on Land*, Simpson, Low, Marston, London, 1911.

MIKSCHE, FERDINAND OTTO, *Atomic Weapons and Armies*, Faber and Faber, London, 1955.

PARET, PETER, ed., *Makers of Modern Strategy. From Machiavelli to the Nuclear Age*, Princeton University Press, 1986; Oxford University Press 1994, a development of Earle's earlier work.

PHILLIPS, BRIG. GEN. T R, ed. *Roots of Strategy. The Five greatest military classics of all time. Sun Tzu, Vegetius, de Saxe, Frederick, Napoleon*, Stackpole, Harrisburg, Pa., 1985.

———— *Roots of Strategy. Book 2. Du Picq's Battle Studies, Clausewitz, Principles of war, Jomini's Art of War*, Harrisburg, Pa., 1987.

PRATT, EDWIN A, *The Rise of Rail Power in War and Conquest*, P.
S. King, London, 1915.

SIMPKIN, BRIG RICHARD, *Race to the Swift. Thoughts on Twenty-
First Century Warfare*, Brassey's, London, 1985.

SUN TZU, *The Art of War*, (400–320 BC), trans. and ed. Samuel B
Griffith, Oxford University Press 1963; Oxford University
Paperback 1971.

SVECHIN, ALEXANDER A, *Strategiya (Strategy)* (1926), 2nd ed.
Voyenny Vestnik press, Moscow, 1927.

WELLS, HERBERT GEORGE, *The War that will end War*, Frank
and Cecil Palmer, London, 1914.

UN, Peacekeeping and Intervention

————— BR 1806, *The Fundamentals of British Maritime Doctrine*,
HMSO, London, 1995.

————— *Wider Peacekeeping*, HMSO, London, 1995.

————— *FM 100–23: Peace Operations*, Department of the Army,
Washington D.C., 1994.

————— *Bosnia. Country Handbook*, DOD–1540–16–96, Department of
Defense, Washington D.C., December 1995

AFRICAN RIGHTS, *Rwanda: Death, Despair, Defiance*, African Rights,
London, 1995.

BOUTROS–GHALI, BOUTROS, *An Agenda for Peace: Preventive
Diplomacy, Peacemaking and Peacekeeping. Report of the Secretary-
General pursuant to the Statement adopted by the Summit Meeting of
Security Council on 31 January 1992*, UN, New York, 1992.

————— *Confronting New Challenges. Annual report on the Work of the
[UN] Organization, 1995*, U.N., New York, 1995.

COHEN, BEN & STAMKOSKI, GEORGE, ed., *With no Peace to
Keep. United Nations Peacekeeping and the war in the former
Yugoslavia*, Grainpress, London, 1995.

CONNAUGHTON, COLONEL RICHARD, *Military Intervention in
the 1990s. A New Logic of War*, Routledge, London, 1992.

————— 'Wider Peacekeeping – How Wide of the Mark?', *British
Army Review*, No. 111, December 1995, pp. 55–64.

————— *Military Support and Protection for Humanitarian Assistance,
Rwanda, April–December, 1994*, The Occasional, number 18,
Strategic and Combat Studies Institute/HMSO, London, 1996.

CONNETTA, CARL & KNIGHT, CHARLES, *Vital Force. A Proposal for the Overhaul of the UN Peace Operations System and for the Creation of a UN Legion*, Commonwealth Institute, Cambridge, MA, 1995.

CONRAD, JOSEPH, *Heart of Darkness* (1898), Penguin, London, 1995.

DORN, WALTER A & BELL, DAVID H, 'Intelligence and Peacekeeping: the UN Operation in the Congo, 1960–64', *International Peacekeeping*, Vol. 2, No. 1, Spring, 1995, pp. 11–33.

ERO, COMFORT & LONG, SUZANNE, 'Humanitarian intervention: a New Role for the United Nations?', *International Peacekeeping*, Vol. 2, No. 2, Summer 1995, pp. 140–56.

DURWARD, ROSEMARY, *Arms Control, Disarmament and the New World Order*, The Occasional, number 7, Strategic and Combat Studies Institute/HMSO, London, 1995.

FARRELL, THEO, 'Sliding into War. The Somalia Imbroglio and US Army Peace Operations Doctrine', *International Peacekeeping*, Vol. 2, No. 2, Summer 1995, pp. 194–214.

FONDATION POUR LES ÉTUDES DE DÉFENSE, *Opérations des Nations Unies. Leçons de Terrain. Cambodge, Somalie, Rwanda, ex-Yougoslavie*, Proceedings of a symposium organised by the FED, Chantilly, 16 and 17 June 1995, (Documentation française, Paris, 1995)

HARBOTTLE, MICHAEL, *New Roles for the Military: Humanitarian and Environmental Security*, Conflict Studies 285, Research Institute for the Study of Conflict and Terrorism, London, 1995.

HOPKINSON, G W, *Changing Options: British Defence and Global Security*, Occasional Paper, University of Cambridge, 1992.

IGNATIEFF, MICHAEL, 'The seductiveness of moral disgust', *Index on Censorship*, 5/1995, pp. 22–38.

MACKINLAY, JOHN & CHOPRA, JANET, *A Draft Concept of Second Generation Multinational Operations*, Brown University, 1993.

McMICHAEL, SCOTT, *Stumbling Bear. Soviet Military Performance in Afghanistan*, Brassey's, London, 1991, p. 66.

PARSONS, ANTHONY, *From Cold War to Hot Peace. UN Interventions 1947–1994*, Michael Joseph, London, 1995.

QUINN, DENNIS J, ed., *Peace Support Operations and the U.S. Military*, National Defense University, Washington D.C., 1994.

SMITH, RICHARD, *The requirement for the United Nations to develop an internationally recognized doctrine for the use of force in intra-state conflict*, The occasional, number 10, Strategic and Combat studies Institute/HMSO, London 1994.

TAYLOR, TREVOR & SATO, SEIZABURO, ed., *Future Sources of Global Conflict*, RIIA/Redwood Books, London 1995.

UN HIGH COMMISSIONER FOR REFUGEES, *The State of the World's Refugees: in Search of Solutions*, UNHCR/Oxford University Press, 1995.

WILLCOCKS, MAJ-GEN MIKE, "Future Conflict and Military Doctrine", lecture of 2 February 1994, *RUSI Journal*, Vol. 139, No. 3, pp. 6–10.

WILLIAMS, IAN, *The UN for Beginners*, Writers and Readers Publishing, New York, 1995.

Military History, Recent and Future War

BELLAMY, CHRISTOPHER, *The Future of Land Warfare*, Croom Helm, London and St Martin's Press, New York, 1987.

———— *Expert Witness. A Defence Correspondent's Gulf War*, Brassey's, London, 1993.

BULLOCH, JOHN & DARWISH, ADEL, *Water Wars: Coming Conflicts in the Middle East*, Gollancz, London, 1993.

DUFFY, CHRISTOPHER, *Frederick the Great. A Military Life*, Routledge, London, 1985.

ERICKSON, JOHN & DILKS, DAVID, ed., *Barbarossa. The Axis and the Allies*, Edinburgh University Press, 1994.

GAREYEV, GENERAL MAKHMUT A, *Esli zavtra voyna? . . . (Chto izmenitsya v kharaktere vooruzhennoy bor'by v blizhayshiye 20–25 let)*, *(If there is war tomorrow? What will change in the character of armed struggle in the next 20–25 years)*, Vladar, Moscow, 1995, distributed by Eastview Publications.

GROVE, ERIC, *The Future of Seapower*, Routledge, London, 1990.

HARRIS, SIR ARTHUR, *Despatch on War Operations*. With an Introduction by Sebastian Cox and a German View by Horst Boog, Frank Cass, London, 1995.

HUNTINGTON, SAMUEL P, 'The Clash of Civilisations?', *Foreign Affairs*, Vol. 72, No. 3, Summer 1993, pp. 22–49.

KAYE, G.D.; GRANT, D.A.; EDMUND, E.J., *Major Armed Conflict: A Compendium of Interstate and Intrastate Conflict, 1720 to 1985*, R95, Operational Research and Analysis Establishment, Ottawa, 1985.

KEEGAN, JOHN, *A History of Warfare*, Hutchinson, London, 1993; Pimlico, London, 1994.

NAVIAS, MARTIN, *Going Ballistic: The Build-Up of Missiles in the Middle East*, Brassey's, London, 1993.

SHUKMAN, DAVID, *The Sorcerer's Challenge: Fears and Hopes for the Weapons of the next Millennium*, Coronet, London, 1995.

SILVERLIGHT, JOHN, *The Victors' Dilemma. Allied Intervention in the Russian Civil War*, Barrie and Jenkins, London, 1970.

WYNN, HUMPHREY, *RAF Nuclear Deterrent Forces*, HMSO, London, 1994.

Index

absolute and limited war, 25–30
actors and factors, 42–3
Aden crisis (1966), 82–3
Afghanistan, displaced people from, 134
    Soviet incursion, 73, 76–7, 78, 217, 234
Aideed, General Farah, 101, 103
air power and bombing raids, 58–66
Akashi, Yasushi, 115
al-Jubayl, 141
Aleksandrov, Anatoliy, 63
Algerian extremism, 83
Ali Mahdi, 100, 101
American Civil War (1861–5), 20, 45
Amu Darya river, 137
Angell, Norman, 54, 133
    The Great Illusion, 53
Angola, UN operation in, 88
Arab-Israeli wars, 76, 77
    Armistice Agreements (1949), 85
    1967, 77, 138
    1973 (Yom Kippur), 77, 161
Aral Sea, 137
Armadiyah, 99
Armageddon, to the edge of, 44–69
Arthur, Vice-Admiral Stanley, 205
Aum Shinri Kyo cult, 131
Austen, Jane, 20
Austria, military support for environment, 147
    wars with Germany (1866 and 1870–1), 28
Aylwin-Foster, Lt Col. Nigel, 172

Bacon, Francis, 29
Baghdad in Gulf War, 120, 175, 184
Bahrain, attacked by Iraq with Scud missiles, 190
Baidoa, 101
Baledogle, 101
Bangladesh, 136, 145
Banja Luka, 119, 120, 175, 184
Baring's Bank collapse, 133
Beaufre, André, 55
Beirut, attack on US Marine base (1983), 83
Belgium, UN troops in Rwanda, 104, 105
Beria, Lavrentiy, 64
Berlin, 3, 176
    airlift (1948), 38
    demolition of Berlin Wall (1989), 24, 190
big wars since 1945, 75–7
    casualties, 75
Bihac, 114, 119

    named 'safe area' by UN (1993), 115, 169
Bikini Atoll test bomb (1946), 63
Bildt, Carl, 215
biological warfare, 236
Bletchley Park, 236
Bloch, Ivan, 52–3, 54
    Future War in its Technical, Economic and Political Relations, 52
Block, Robert, 169
Boer War, 49
Bombay, population by year 2000, 136
Borchgrevink, Lt Col. N., 95
Bosnia, post-war, 194–5, 207
    rebuilding, 215
Bosnia-Herzegovina, 111, 112
    displaced people, 134
    recognition as a nation state, 35, 112
    UNPROFOR 2 (UN command in), 112–13
Bosnian civil war, 1, 2, 5, 10–19, 21, 26, 27, 28, 68, 73, 83, 103, 111–23, 127, 143, 144, 146, 149–50, 151, 154–5, 156–7, 158, 160, 163–70, 182–3, 184, 185, 186, 188, 200, 201, 227, 228–9, 230, 231, 232
    cease-fire (1995), 111, 120, 121
    Dayton peace accord, 71, 111–12, 115, 120, 122
    'ethnic cleansing', 121–2
    Nato: air strikes on Bosnian Serbs, 68, 72, 94, 116–17, 118, 119–20, 123, 164, 174–7, 182, 184, 186, 231–2; peace operation, 6, 71, 113, 115, 121, 160
    UN arms embargo, 111
    UN intervention, 10, 12–18, 26, 28, 31, 32, 33, 68, 71, 86, 87, 88, 111–23, 153, 156–7, 160, 163–70, 182, 185, 188, 201, 227, 228–9, 230, 231, 232
Bosnian Muslims, 18, 34, 114, 122–3, 128, 149, 157, 166, 167, 174, 175, 208
    government army (BiH), 12–18, 112, 118; guerrilla war with Croat HVO, 114, 232
    massacre of civilians by Croats at Ahinici (1993), 114
    refugees, 122
    siege of Mostar enclave by Croats (1993), 112
    victims of Serb atrocities at Srebrenica, 118, 163
    see also Croat-Muslim Peace Federation
Bosnian Serbs
    Army of the Republic of Serb Krajina (ARSK) in Croatia, 112; defeats by Croats, 111, 114, 116, 118–19, 122–3, 130
    Bosnian Serb Army (VRS), 13–14, 18, 32, 68, 72, 112, 114, 127, 154, 155, 156, 157, 158, 164, 166–7, 168, 231, 233